THE
ATHENA
DOCTRINE

HOW WOMEN
(AND THE MEN WHO
THINK LIKE THEM)
WILL RULE THE FUTURE

John Gerzema

&

Michael D'Antonio

JOSSEY-BASS
A Wiley Imprint
www.josseybass.com

Published by Jossey-Bass
A Wiley Imprint
One Montgomery Street, Suite 1200 San Francisco, CA 94104—www.josseybass.com

Cover design by Chip Kidd
Peace Statue Image by J Marshall/Tribaleye Images/Alamy

Jossey-Bass books and products are available through most bookstores. To contact Jossey-
Bass directly call our Customer Care Department within the U.S.at 800-956-7739, outside
the U.S. at 317-572-3986, or fax 317-572-4002.

Wiley also publishes its books in a variety of electronic formats and by print-on-demand.
Not all content that is available in standard print versions of this book may appear or be
packaged in all book formats. If you have purchased a version of this book that did not
include media that is referenced by or accompanies a standard print version, you may
request this media by visiting http://booksupport.wiley.com. For more information about
Wiley products, visit us www.wiley.com.

Library of Congress Cataloging-in-Publication Data

Gerzema, John, 1961–
   The Athena doctrine : how women (and the men who think like them) will rule the
future / John Gerzema, Michael D'Antonio.—First edition.
        pages cm
   Includes bibliographical references and index.
   ISBN 978-1-118-45295-0 (cloth); ISBN 978-1-118-59620-3 (ebk); ISBN
978-1-118-59642-5 (ebk); ISBN 978-1-118-59649-4 (ebk)
1. Women executives—Psychology. 2. Business women—Psychology. 3. Leadership in
women. 4. Values. 5. Entrepreneurship. I. D'Antonio, Michael. II. Title.
   HD6054.3.G39 2013
   305.42—dc23

                                                              2012048455

Printed in the United States of America
FIRST EDITION
HB Printing 10 9 8 7 6 5 4 3

Throughout the development of this book, we came across the theme of loss and hardship. On a large scale, there was our time in Japan. On an individual level, several people we'd interviewed had recently lost partners, spouses, parents, and grandparents. And just as we headed to Brussels, Michael's mother passed away. We dedicate this book in her memory. Through this book we also pay tribute to the memory of Simon Sylvester, John's good friend and longtime colleague at Young & Rubicam, whose enormous intellect was matched by his humility and constant good cheer. Finally, this book was inspired by the battle John's mom continues to fight with breast cancer. Keep fighting, Jan.

Contents

Introduction

The Athena Doctrine

*"The world would be a better place if men
thought more like women."* (66% agree)

—Authors' proprietary global survey of
thirteen nations representing 65 percent of
global GDP

During the year after we described America's transition to a
"new normal" in our book *Spend Shift* (2010), we traveled the
country and heard from many people who agreed with the thesis
that a quiet revolution had taken place in "the way we buy, sell,
and live" and applauded how individuals, families, businesses, and
organizations were adapting to tougher economic conditions.[1]

We had stressed the theme of adaptation and not merely survival
because we saw that the effects of the Great Recession that began
in 2008 would not be reversed any time soon by a new bubble
or boom. And as policymakers in Washington and other capitals
struggled to resolve the crisis in various ways—low interest rates,
government spending, government cutbacks, bank bailouts—full
recovery seemed ever more elusive. Growth returned to the U.S.
economy, but its pace was anemic, and high unemployment kept

the squeeze on the middle class. Progress was even slower in the Eurozone and Britain, where recession returned at the start of 2012. Even China showed signs of trouble, which augured ill for our interconnected economies.

Considering the economic facts, it was clear that the crisis that started in 2008 would last longer than most analysts expected and could have an effect similar to the impact of the Great Depression of the 1930s. That earlier calamity shaped the social, political, and economic outlook of an entire generation. Some of these effects, such as an excess of caution and fear, were recognized as burdensome—but others proved beneficial. As historians William Strauss and Neil Howe have documented, people who came of age in the Depression tend to be practical rather than status oriented.[2] This so-called Silent Generation showed a creative ability to find happiness with or without wealth or an abundance of possessions. In our studies for *Spend Shift*, we discovered similar traits for this group and noted that today's young adults seem to admire the "silents" for their flexibility.

Although the immediate insights offered in *Spend Shift* were clear, we learned more as we presented them to audiences around the world, who began to notice something we had not fully appreciated. As many pointed out to us, most of the traits exhibited by the successful entrepreneurs, leaders, organizers, and creators we profiled seemed to come from aspects of human nature that are widely regarded as feminine. This isn't to say that these innovators were mainly women (they were not) or that we believe that any human quality belongs primarily to one gender or the other (we don't). It was simply that, time and again, we heard people say that the skills required to thrive in today's world—such as honesty, empathy, communication, and collaboration—come more naturally to women.

With what we heard in mind, we began looking for signs that some set of traditionally feminine values and traits might be ascendant among effective leaders in business, politics, government, or community organizations. This was, of course, easier said than done. One of the very first interviews for this book, conducted over breakfast at an east London café, was with Ann Danylkiw, who writes about economics, gender, and other issues. Ann, whose digital handle is "Ann Lytical," was a doctoral candidate at Goldsmiths College. We asked her opinion about the possibility that traditionally feminine traits and characteristics were gaining in value and respect.

As we sketched out our project, Ann squirmed and scrunched up her face like a professor listening to a student offer a terrible answer to an oral exam question. When we finished, she drew a deep breath and said, "I object to you calling these things feminine."[3]

It was not the best start. And in the tetchy conversation that ensued, we discovered that Ann didn't agree with us on anything that had to do with definitions of "masculine" or "feminine." When we spoke about traits that "many people traditionally associate with gender," she voiced strong doubts about our views of "traditions" and asked us to define the "people" we had in mind. By the time we were finished, we wondered if it was possible for two sincere but decidedly male and middle-aged men to meaningfully explore issues of masculinity and femininity. If this was the kind of response we got from someone who agreed to help us, what would our critics say?

Clearly, it was a nonstarter for us to decide in advance which approaches are "feminine" and which are "masculine." Instead, we needed to conduct research to discover how people in various parts of the world define traditionally masculine and feminine traits. Then we had to discover if the feminine qualities were more highly valued. If the answer turned out to be yes, then we could search for case studies to show the trend at work in the real world. Relying on our skills as researchers and storytellers, we began work in the summer of 2011.

•••

John manages the largest survey panel in the world, BrandAsset® Valuator, which has conducted studies on more than one-and-a-half million people and fifty-one thousand companies in fifty countries since 1993. We set upon the challenge of discovering if—due to the economy, technology, generational influences, globalization, or other factors—people in general might be placing more value on the feminine side of human nature. We constructed a special survey of sixty-four thousand people chosen to mirror the populations in thirteen countries that represent 65 percent of the world's gross domestic product. The countries we surveyed—Brazil, Canada, Chile, China, France, Germany, India, Indonesia, Japan, Mexico, South Korea, the United Kingdom, and the United States—reflect a wide range of cultural, geographical, political, religious, and economic diversity.

First, we wanted to understand how people gauge the times we live in. Were they optimistic or pessimistic, secure or vulnerable? The respondents to our survey talked as if they lived in an age of extended anxiety. Most rejected the idea that their children will have better lives than their own, and great majorities expressed worries about society's basic fairness. (See Figures I.1, I.2, I.3, and I.4.)

There is too much power in the hands of large institutions and corporations. **86% agree**

Figure I.1.

My country cares about its citizens more than it used to. **76% disagree**

Figure I.2.

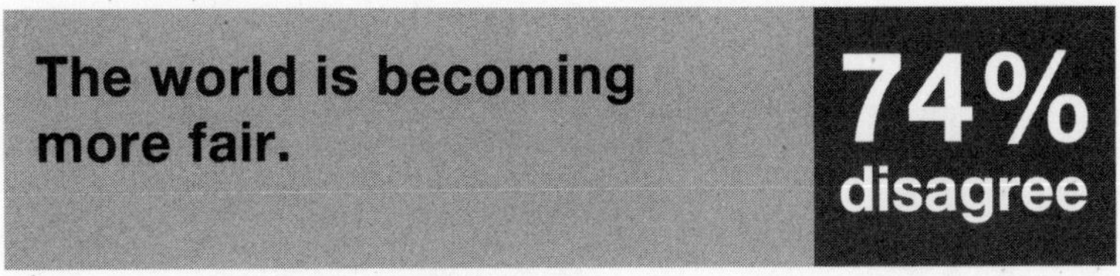

The world is becoming more fair. **74%** disagree

Figure I.3.

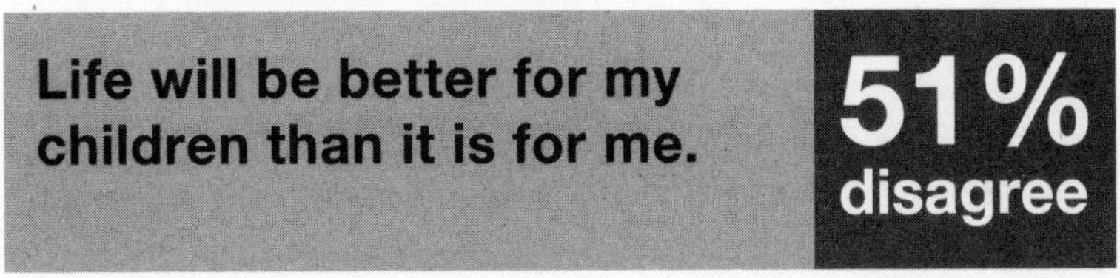

Life will be better for my children than it is for me. **51%** disagree

Figure I.4.

These big-picture anxieties seem consistent with the tenor of our times. In every country, press headlines remind us that we face big problems—job scarcity, economic stagnation, global warming, and so on—while our leaders and institutions seem continually mired in scandal and failure. Big banks that were once considered stable have collapsed. WikiLeaks exposes the skeletons closeted by national governments. Grand jury reports show clergymen to be serial abusers. Our survey revealed that since the financial crisis, people trust only one in four companies on average—a 50 percent drop from precrisis trust levels.

When we delved into the drivers of this turmoil, we found dissatisfaction not only with government and the economy but with the behavior of men in general (see Figure I.5).

A clear majority of people around the world are unhappy with the conduct of men, including 79 percent of people in Japan and South Korea and two-thirds of people in the United States, Indonesia, and Mexico—and the rate of dissatisfaction is nearly equal among men and women. Canadian men must be doing something right, but they are the anomaly in our data. Interestingly, Millennials have a fundamentally stronger appreciation of femininity and

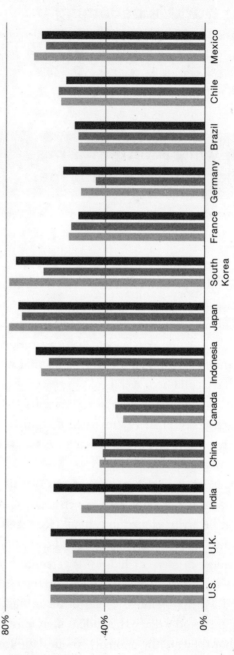

Figure I.5.

the role of women in their society. Three-quarters of Japanese and South Korean youth are critical of male behavior, and two-thirds of global Millennials. There is a double-digit generation gap between Millennials and men in Germany, South Korea, and India.

Universally, it seemed that people had grown frustrated by a world dominated by codes of what they saw as traditionally masculine thinking and behavior: codes of control, competition, aggression, and black-and-white thinking that have contributed to many of the problems we face today, from wars and income inequality to reckless risk-taking and scandal.

But as we pored through the data, one particular set of numbers caught our eye, as illustrated in Figure I.6. Nearly two-thirds of people around the world—including the majority of men—feel that the world would be a better place if men thought more like women. This includes 79 percent of Japanese men, 76 percent of people in France and Brazil, and 70 percent of people in Germany. This belief was shared regardless of age, income, or nation. Again, Millennials in highly masculine societies—China, Japan, South Korea, and India—agree even more than women. In *Spend Shift*, we found that these young adults were less focused on money and status and more interested in human connection and community. More adaptable and flexible, this generation places a premium on friendships, ethical behavior, and diversity. This orientation, we found, helps them live with hope and find happiness despite financial hardships.

Defining and Measuring Masculine and Feminine Traits

Next, we needed to define masculine and feminine traits in an understandable way and then measure the public's attitudes about these traits. We're talking here not about the most modern, politically sensitive definitions but rather about the beliefs people hold based on their subjective interpretations. To do this, we

The world would be a better place if men thought more like women.

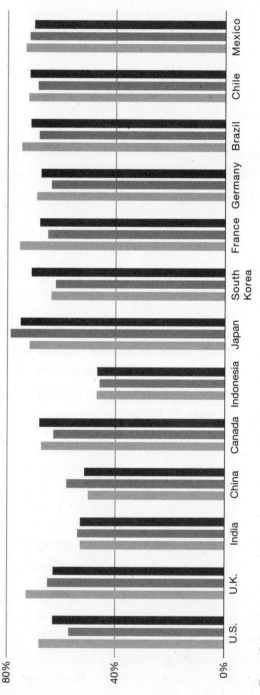

Figure I.6.

conducted two separate studies. In the first study, we asked half our global sample (thirty-two thousand people) to classify 125 different human behavioral traits as either masculine, feminine, or neither. (See Figure I.7.) We chose words like *selfless, trustworthy, curious,* and *kind* from previous empirical studies on behavioral psychology and gender-related research. Overall, there was strong consistency across countries in what was perceived as feminine, masculine, or neither.

MASCULINE		NEUTRAL
Rugged	Aggressive	Visionary
Dominant	Brave	Energetic
Strong	Daring	Simple
Arrogant	Competitive	Authentic
Rigid	Gutsy	Different
Leader	Stubborn	Agile
Natural Leader	Assertive	Carefree
Analytical	Driven	Collaborative
Proud	Direct	Intelligent
Decisive	Career Oriented	Cunning
Ambitious	Dynamic	Candid
Overbearing	Confident	Traditional
Hard Working	Straightforward	Fun
Logical	Selfish	
Consensus Builder	Independent	
Self-Reliant	Unapproachable	
Focused	Progressive	
Distinctive	Innovative	
Devoted	Restrained	
Resilient	Competent	

Figure I.7.

(*continued*)

FEMININE

Original	Good at Multitasking	Cooperative
Free Spirited	Kind 1	Involved
Charming	Supportive	Friendly
Trustworthy	Giving	Up to Date
Articulate	Good Listener	Selfless
Reliable	Loving	Perceptive
Dedicated	Sensuous	Socially Responsible
Dependable	Vulnerable	Kind 2
Reasonable	Gentle	Encouraging
Nimble	Stylish	Empathetic
Adaptable	Emotional	Expressive
Obliging	Down to Earth	Understanding
Healthy	Plans for the Future	Patient
Popular	Upper Class	Poised
Passive	Open to New Ideas	Trendy
Committed	Unique	Family Oriented
Community Oriented	Generous	Caring 2
Helpful	Team Player	Affectionate
Creative	Honest	Caring 1
Flexible	Imaginative	Sensitive
Intuitive	Humble	Nurturing
Social	Curious	Glamorous
Sincere	Loyal	
Passionate	Conscientious	

Figure I.7.   *(continued)*

Next, we presented that same list of words to the other half of our sample, only this time there was no attribution of gender to any of the words. We simply asked people to rate the importance of the traits to certain virtues: leadership, success, morality, and happiness—words that captured the essence of what human beings commonly mean when they talk about a good life for themselves and society.

By comparing the two samples, we could now statistically model how masculine and feminine traits relate to solving today's challenges. When all the data from the thirteen countries came back in, we could see that across age, gender, and culture, people around the world feel that feminine traits correlate more strongly with making the world a better place.

Examining the Impact of Feminine Traits

Leadership

As illustrated in Figure I.8, our data show that many of the qualities of an ideal modern leader are considered feminine. Most important, the responses show that we seek a more expressive style of leader, one who shares feelings and emotions more openly and honestly. In other words, across the globe, society wants those in power to connect more personally—an understandable response to the hidden agendas and tightly wound power circles often associated with men. Our survey responses indicate that people generally believe that patience is a more important virtue in leadership and that we seek a leader who can break gridlock through reason rather than ideology. People also feel that an ideal leader must be a long-term thinker who plans for the future to bring about sustainable solutions, rather than posturing for expediency. The qualities of being decisive and resilient (identified as more masculine) are both important, but our data highlights that the definition of "winning" is changing—it is becoming a more inclusive construct, rather than a zero-sum game. In a highly interconnected and interdependent economy, masculine traits like aggression and control (which are largely seen as "independent") are considered less effective than the feminine values of collaboration and sharing credit.

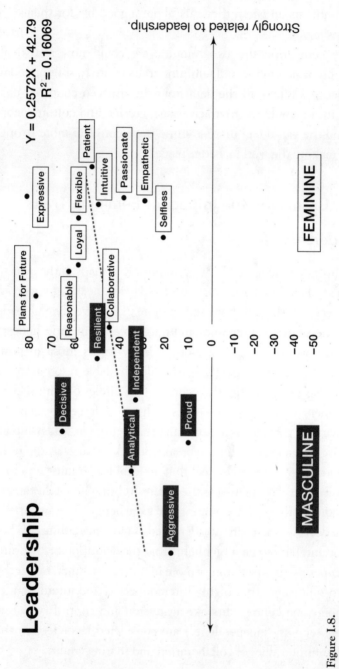

Figure I.8.

We also saw that being cause focused (rather than self-focused) is a more valued leadership trait. Perhaps this is why our sample indicated that being loyal (feminine) is more important than being proud (masculine). We want our leaders to be more intuitive, more understanding of others' feelings, and more able to assess various angles of a problem—or consequences of an action—before taking action. Finally, we found that being flexible is an essential modern skill: it permits people to listen, learn, and build consensus in order to get things done.

Success

Many of the survey questions we asked were intended to gauge how people imagined success. (See Figure I.9.) Over 80 percent of our respondents said that relationships and the respect of others count more toward success than money. Slightly more than 50 percent agreed that "nice people are more apt to thrive today than people who are aggressive and controlling." Among the other responses, we saw lots of people favoring collaboration, kindness, and empathy. With no previous studies to compare, we cannot say that the way people view success is changing. But we can say that a snapshot view taken in 2012 finds a solid majority, male and female, endorsing traditionally feminine traits as essential to the definition of a successful life.

Morality

When we explored the concept of morality, we expected to see many different pathways and definitions as defined by custom, religion, and culture. Yet our statistical correlations show that across the world, morality is strongly associated with loyalty, reason, empathy, and selflessness—all feminine traits. (See Figure I.10.) The value placed on these traits reflects society's outrage over the greed, corruption, and self-interest of our times. Societal structures

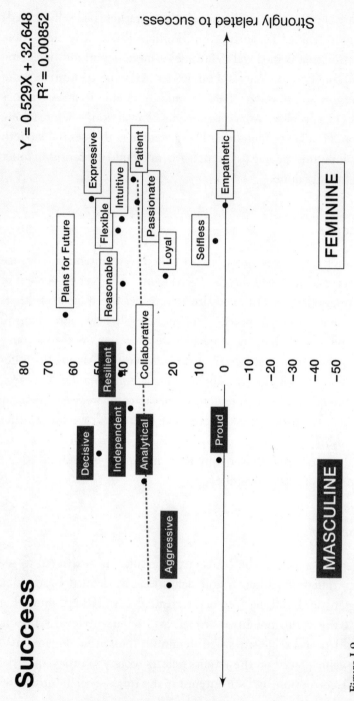

Figure I.9.

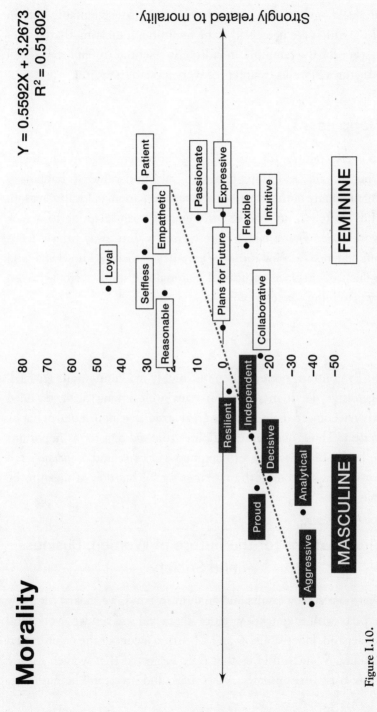

Figure I.10.

and economic markets alike depend on codes of morality and on trust, which are perceived to be feminine, indicating that greater respect for the feminine in culture is essential to improved social structures as well as market recovery around the world.

Happiness

In every country, the survey respondents were most in agreement when it came to linking feminine traits and values to happiness. Again, many of the same virtues, such as patience, loyalty, reason, and flexibility, underscored the emphasis on adapting to a new world. (See Figure I.11.) Here we see a shift away from a focus on affluence, as new forms of currency—such as knowledge and influence—replace traditional materialistic status symbols driven by masculine concepts of power and esteem.

• • •

By contrast, none of the most highly masculine traits (rugged, aggressive, dominant, brave, arrogant) were among the most valued when it comes to being either a great leader or a more moral or happy person. Those masculine attributes that *did* register as important to leadership, morality, or happiness—*decisive* and *confident*—fell toward the bottom of the rankings for "What does it mean to be masculine?"

Implications for the Future of Women, Business, and Society

With our survey results and analysis in hand, we looked for a few experts who might know more about values, gender, work, and leadership. Janet Walkow and Christine Jacobs of the organization Leading Women told us that they suspected that women inspire more trust (in consumers, coworkers, and investors) because they

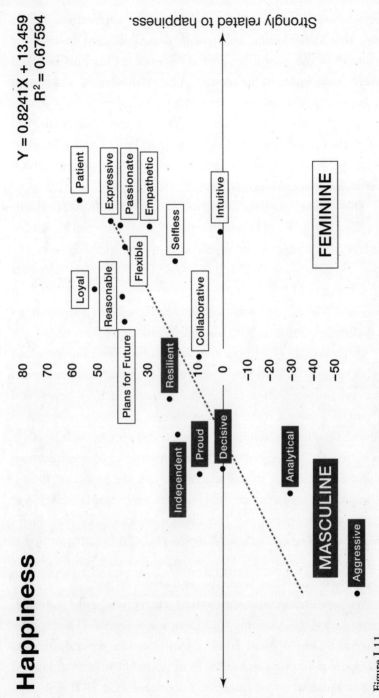

Figure I.11.

seem to listen more carefully and empathize with others. People with this ability, male and female, would succeed in times of crisis when the public has lost confidence in institutions. And given recent financial meltdowns, political upheavals, and natural disasters, confidence is in short supply.

"I guess you could say that things have to get really, really bad before they put women in charge," quipped Janet.[4] Said Christine, "I like to think that people know women, or men who can think like us, are wiser risk-takers."

There's much support for Christine's argument. In 2009, an outfit called Hedge Fund Research reported that funds run by women had for nine years straight significantly outperformed those run by men.[5] A 2012 study by Credit Suisse revealed that over a six-year period, shares of large companies (those with a market capitalization over $10 billion) with women board members outperformed comparable companies with all-male boards by 26 percent.[6]

Other statistics highlight the success of the feminine style and its importance for both women and men. In America, more women than men now enroll in college and graduate with bachelor's and advanced degrees. Even as women continue to fight the professional glass ceiling, four in ten wives out-earned their husbands in 2012, an increase of 50 percent from twenty years ago.[7] Meanwhile, men who see the decline in manufacturing jobs are becoming nurses, elementary school teachers, receptionists, and school counselors at significantly higher rates.[8] This change has coincided with men's greater involvement in housekeeping and child rearing at home. (One estimate from U.S. Census data shows that the number of stay-at-home dads has doubled over the past decade.[9])

We also heard about nonprofit enterprises with feminine-leaning ideals, blossoming in America and abroad. The Roberts Enterprise Development Fund of San Francisco reported that its investments in more than fifty local nonprofit organizations had created hundreds of jobs and generated more than $100 million in economic activity annually.[10] Seattle-based Pioneer Human Services has created more than a thousand jobs, and funds almost all of its $70 million budget with profits from its businesses.[11] In Spain, the Mondragon network of cooperative, worker-owned enterprises has grown to employ more than one hundred thousand people.[12] As reported in 2011 by the German journal *Analyse and Kritik*, 10 percent of the network's revenues must go to education, and 20 percent must be held in reserves.[13]

Considering the traits our survey respondents described as most feminine, we would say that much of the nonprofit sector is feminine in style and focus. More balanced in their pursuit of goals (profit is not the only measure of success), nonprofit leaders are typically responsive to human needs, inclusive in their decision making, and sensitive to the ripple effects of their actions. They are also becoming more creative and successful in the pursuit of growth and development. This view is supported by the *Stanford Social Innovation Review*, which reported a boom in the nonprofit sector in the first decade of the twenty-first century: "There was a proliferation of high-profile social entrepreneurs, an emergence of 'big bettor' philanthropists, and an increase in funding to the sector. Taken together, these trends fueled tremendous growth in the number and sheer size of nonprofits."[14]

Of course, nonprofit organizations also depend on lots of masculine energy to get things done, and it's easy to find feminine traits driving for-profit enterprises. Adelaide Lancaster, who advises female entrepreneurs in New York City, gave us many solid reasons why women can be great at managing business start-ups, and all of them had to do with attitudes and aptitudes that are traditionally linked to women. These strengths, including a more calculated approach to risk and superior multitasking abilities, seem perfect for the modern business environment. "What if gender difference made women even better business owners?" she asks. "It's not hard to make a compelling case."[15]

Beyond America, the rise of women into leadership positions appears to signal improvements in both social and economic development. When Brazil's president, Dilma Rousseff, opened the 2011 UN General Assembly, she argued that the "feminine voice" is also the voice of democracy and equality. Noting that her native Portuguese language considers the words for courage, sincerity, life, and hope to be feminine, Rousseff predicted a "century of women" that will bring peace and prosperity.[16] Indeed, many studies have found that as women gain in education, employment, and wealth, a nation's well-being rises too.

Decoding the Athena Values

The stories and data that point to feminine success give us just a partial view of a more complex world. Some of the growth in income for women comes from the fact that high-paying jobs for unskilled men are in decline. According to the U.S. Bureau of Labor Statistics, women are still paid an average of 80 percent of the salaries paid to men for the same job.[17] And even though the number of women with six-figure incomes is rising at twice the rate of men, they are still grossly underrepresented in executive suites. According to the think tank Catalyst, women held just 16.1 percent of board seats at Fortune 500 companies in 2011.[18] In politics, business, and even the arts, the top decision makers are still more likely to be male, just as all but three of the twenty richest people on the *Forbes* list of billionaires are men.[19]

Although women still haven't achieved parity, their steady progress points to the value of feminine traits in the modern economy. Patience, sensitivity, and the ability to understand others are extremely valuable traits in a fast-paced and interconnected world. In our surveys, 78 percent of people said that "today's times require we be more kind and empathetic"; another 79 percent affirmed that "a successful career today requires collaborating and sharing credit with others." These numbers affirm that "feminine" kindness and collaboration are essential values in the workplace as well as in the larger society.

Although this book is mainly concerned with leadership, we couldn't help but notice that feminine traits were essential in every corner of life. The vast majority of people agree that a good life is defined by a decent job, meaningful connections, and a modicum of security. Here again the traits most people associate with a good life are drawn mainly from the feminine side of the ledger. This is as true for men as it is for women.

• • •

Not only do the people we surveyed think that a mix of masculine and feminine are key to personal success, but 65 percent of people around the world believe that more female leadership in government would prompt a rise in trust and fairness and a decline in wars and scandal. The type of feminine leadership they described is not soft and squishy but wise and quietly strong. Boiled down to a manageable number, the keys to success, as our sixty-four thousand respondents saw it, were

Connectedness—an ability to form and maintain human networks

Humility—an approach to life that allows for listening, learning from others, and sharing credit

Candor—a willingness to speak openly and honestly

Patience—a recognition that some solutions emerge slowly

Empathy—a sensitivity to others that promotes understanding

Trustworthiness—a track record and strength of character that inspire confidence

Openness—being receptive to all people and concepts

Flexibility—the ability to change and adapt when circumstances require

Vulnerability—the courage to be human and make mistakes

Balance—a well-rounded sense of purpose

These traits all seem like timeless virtues to us. They reflect a strength of character that is both admirable and noble. Candor, flexibility, humility, and balance all require true integrity and confidence. To be both vulnerable and connected to others, you must be courageous.

Gathered together, the qualities most favored in our study resembled, in our minds, the character of the Greek goddess Athena. Venerated for her intelligence, skill, civilizing influence, and fairness, Athena was a goddess of industry, arts, and crafts. It is Athena who gave the Greeks the olive tree, which sustained their economy and culture. When conflicts arose, she responded with clever strategy and wise tactics, whereas her brother Ares acted in violence.

If Athena is the personification of the qualities that suit our times, then the ideals she represents can be considered a kind of doctrine, guiding us toward effective leadership and success in our work, our communities, and our personal lives. Mainly feminine in a traditional sense, the Athena model is nevertheless available and essential for men who hope to thrive in an era of constant change.

The negative assessment of males—62 percent are dissatisfied with their conduct—and the positive appraisal of feminine solutions to contemporary problems show that people understand, perhaps intuitively, that a change is already under way. Despite the many obstacles that women still face across the world, people—regardless of geography or gender—feel that girls today have an opportunity to thrive that's equal to if not greater than that of boys.

Considering the big gap between how people felt about the world in general (negative) and how they regarded their own prospects (positive), it seemed obvious that our survey respondents felt that they knew there were ways to find success, happiness, and hope for themselves. Social scientists report that when it comes to the economy, people typically feel best when society offers them a fair shot at financial success in a "sustainable" system that can function well over the long run. As we analyzed the answers to our questions about gender and success, it became clear that a strong majority of people already recognized, at least subconsciously, the importance of Athena virtues, believing that men and women needed to meet the challenges of life with a predominantly feminine sets of skills, traits, and attitudes. It was also clear that the people who were more optimistic and confident about the future were already embracing and deploying their feminine thinking.

We looked at the data once again to see if there was a difference in terms of economic development between countries whose citizens think in a feminine way and those whose citizens think in a more masculine way. We found that more developed and established countries are more neutral in their thinking, embracing more feminine values, whereas emerging economies are still more masculine in their orientation.

Moreover, the countries with higher levels of feminine thinking and behavior also have higher per capita GDP and higher reported quality of life. (See Figures I.12 and I.13.)

In our surveys, we found that people around the world who think in a more feminine way are nearly twice as happy and optimistic about the future as those who think in a more masculine way.

• • •

With people around the world telling us through their survey responses that they favored the Athena style (although they didn't use the term), we set out to document this shift toward feminine virtues. We visited the crowded neighborhoods of Lima, Peru, and the windswept landscape of Iceland. We've traversed mountain passes to reach the city of Medellin, Colombia, and white-knuckled our way to the Himalayan nation of Bhutan. In 150,000 miles of

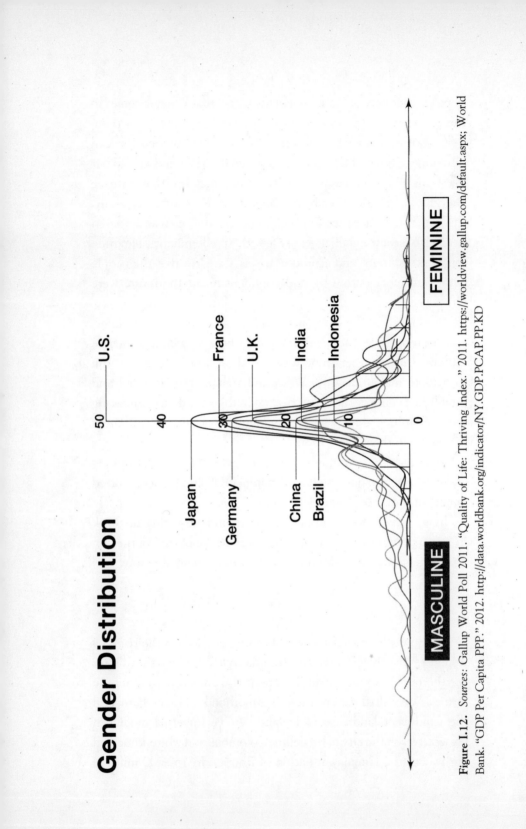

Figure I.12. *Sources:* Gallup World Poll 2011. "Quality of Life: Thriving Index." 2011. https://worldview.gallup.com/default.aspx; World Bank. "GDP Per Capita PPP." 2012. http://data.worldbank.org/indicator/NY.GDP.PCAP.PP.KD

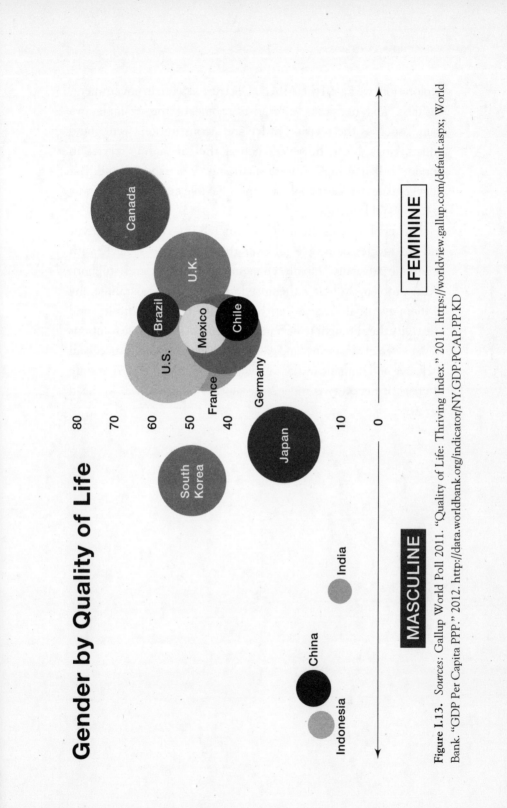

Gender by Quality of Life

MASCULINE

FEMININE

Canada

U.K.

Brazil

Mexico

Chile

U.S.

France

Germany

South Korea

Japan

India

China

Indonesia

80
70
60
50
40
10
0

Figure I.13. *Sources:* Gallup World Poll 2011. "Quality of Life: Thriving Index." 2011. https://worldview.gallup.com/default.aspx; World Bank. "GDP Per Capita PPP." 2012. http://data.worldbank.org/indicator/NY.GDP.PCAP.PP.KD

exploration, we found the Athena Doctrine at work in government, business, and nonprofit enterprises. Some of the examples we found, such as the revision of Iceland's constitution, were grand undertakings. Most, however, such as the car-sharing service in London called WhipCar, were small and even experimental. But in every case, we saw people seeking a flexible and sustainable way of living and leading.

This book reveals the insights garnered from our global survey and the stories of people all over the world who struggle with economic adversity, rapidly changing technology, and stubborn social problems. Their Athena-style values didn't guarantee any of them eventual success. But the sincerity, energy, curiosity, and creativity they brought to bear in the pursuit of sustainable solutions were extremely inspiring, and gave us reason to hope that successful inclusive and humane initiatives will emerge from the current state of crisis. If necessity is indeed the mother of invention, we need her now.

Chapter 1

Great Britain

"In a world with less money, close personal
relationships are more important."
(82.1% agree)

Fixed to trees and streetlights, the handmade posters were decorated with arrows and the words "Sea of Rage This Way." They pointed toward the student union building at the University of London. There, on the morning of November 9, 2011, a crowd grew larger by the minute beneath a sky of unbroken clouds. At noon, the scene resembled a street fair. An elderly man in an orange kilt danced a jig to music from a boom box that he had placed on the street. A few yards away, hip-hop beats poured out of a portable loudspeaker strapped to the back of a bicycle. These sounds echoed off the brick and stone walls of city buildings, mingling with chants of "No education cuts!"

At about 12:40 pm, more than two thousand men and women, a number equal to three brigades of the British Army, stepped off toward Trafalgar Square. They walked behind a banner—Occupy Everything, Take London—that stretched from sidewalk to side-walk. They were accompanied by hundreds of London police officers dressed in florescent yellow jackets and helmets with clear plastic face shields. Drummers pounded on instruments strapped around their necks. Overhead, a police helicopter pounded the air with its whirling blades and provided observers the best possible view of unfolding events.

Motivated by a sense that the economic system no longer works for them, the protesters vented their frustration with chants and by jeering at the helmeted riot police. Some covered their faces to avoid being identified by surveillance cameras. The scene illustrated the loss of trust between the younger generation and society's leaders, and it echoed similar protests occurring around the world. It seemed as if people everywhere were struggling to find hope and a sense of agency. In the personal realm, they sought new definitions of happiness and new ways to achieve it. As political actors, they voiced their dissatisfaction with gridlocked politics and stale policies. In 2011, no social development was more significant than the rise of this "Occupy" protest movement, which was a loosely organized effort that allowed people to express their thoughts and feelings in a time of great uncertainty.

Beginning with the "indignados" who marched in Spain, people in dozens of countries took to the streets to show their anger over banking scandals, unemployment, political stalemate, and the growing disparity between rich and poor. In America, the anger became focused on the wealthy and powerful—referred to as the "1 percent"—and on the plight of the "99 percent" who feared the decline of the middle class. Parks and city squares became encampments as thousands of people tried to show their distress by literally occupying public spaces. These demonstrations were the largest and most widespread since the antinuclear protests of the 1980s, but they targeted problems so complex that no simple No Nukes–type of slogan quite hit the target. Solving the global economic crisis couldn't be as simple as banning the bomb.

In London, the Occupy activists built tent cities in the districts of Islington and Hackney and at St. Paul's Cathedral. They intended to focus public attention on their opposition to bailouts for banks and cuts to government spending on education and social programs. This austerity agenda, adopted by Britain and the Euro-zone countries, differed from the American response to the Great Recession, which had included a large federal spending program to stimulate economic activity. In the United States, the mixed approach had been followed by improvements in employment and growth that were painfully slow but nevertheless real. In the United Kingdom and Europe, the pain of austerity had not brought con-sistent gain. Instead, unemployment bounced back up, and growth sputtered and then stalled.

With politicians failing to deliver progress, and austerity mak-ing daily life tougher, ordinary citizens became impatient and then angry. But while they forcefully declared the current system "unsus-tainable," the London protesters did not offer a considered second step toward reform or improvements in "the system." With no further outlet for the energy of the movement, it became mainly a matter of outcry, rather than action. Everyone in London knew what was upsetting the young occupiers—but structural solutions were no closer at hand.

However, at scattered locations around the city, inspired indi-viduals and groups were quietly working on their own alternatives. Although we happened to arrive just in time for the noisy protest, we had come to London to meet a number of revolutionaries who were both quieter and more deliberate. Here we would find women and men who were practicing business, community activism, and crafts with a true Athena spirit. In every case, they stressed the power of connection—to individual customers, colleagues, and communities—to multiply the effect of their efforts and produce innovative solutions to common problems.

• • •

A quarter mile from the route of the November 9 march, Vinay Gupta and Tom Wright sat in a small office and tapped away at computer keyboards. When they paused, the two young men heard the thwacking helicopter, but they felt no urge to go watch the scene on the street, let alone join it. Not that they weren't sympathetic. Young enough to fit right in with the protesters, they understood that millions of their countrymen felt aggrieved by the Great Recession and the austerity program their government had adopted in response. Traditional pathways to work and security were disappearing, and it was easy to feel unsteady. Unless you were blazing a new path.

As they worked their computers, Tom and Vinay were in fact acting as pioneers of the new economy, turning an idea into an asset. Their small company, WhipCar, allowed anyone with a safe and reliable automobile to rent it by the hour, day, or week to a neighbor who needed one. In a flash, their service could turn a ton of metal at rest by the curb into handy transport for the renter and a clutch of cash for the owner. The car, and the transaction, would be secured by WhipCar and its insurers. The service would take a small slice of the transaction, but charge no membership fees.

When we caught up with the founders of WhipCar, they were adding more than a hundred vehicles to their listings every day, and each week saw an uptick in the number of rentals they had facilitated. Soon to exceed fifteen thousand vehicles, the fleet of cars available through WhipCar was worth in excess of $20 million and would rank the service among the largest rental outfits in the market. This resource was marshaled not with a bank loan or stock offering but on the basis of a simple but courageous idea: people are essentially honest.

"The basic service we provide is building trust between the owners and the drivers," explained Vinay as he sipped tea in a quiet corner of the Hospital Club on Endell Street in Covent Garden.[1] (Occupying an old hospital building, the club caters to young entrepreneurs who use it as a social and business hub.) "We provide both the *insurance* for the car and the *assurance* that a driver has been vetted and the car is in good condition," said Vinay. "After that, the parties are in control of their own destiny."

A slimly built thirty-four year-old from New York, Vinay flashes a smile when he hears a question about the breakthrough thoughts that made WhipCar work. Perhaps the most important, he recalls, was the realization that most private cars spend far more time resting at curbside than they do working at transporting people. All this idle time—roughly twenty-three hours *every day*—represents lost value for owners who spend, on average, $10,000 per year per car on insurance, repairs, and lease or loan payments. "It's the second most expensive thing most people ever buy, after a home, and it just sits there, losing value. We thought that if we could help people turn that value into cash, they would take the chance."

Previous efforts at car-sharing projects had foundered because owners were wary of how renters might abuse their vehicles, and the services lacked the technology to quickly pair owners with renters. The spread of broadband Internet services and a well-engineered website solved the technology problems. WhipCar's site is so powerful that it can track thousands of vehicles and provide renters with instant maps showing the locations of many cars that fit their needs. (Most will be within a ten-minute walk of the renter's location.) The rules allow for drivers to bid for the car of their choice and require owners to accept or reject an offer within one hour.

With effective technology and rules in place, Vinay and Tom turned to the question of trust. According to one study, more than half the owners in the United Kingdom give names to their four-wheeled babies. How would they relate to perfect strangers arriving at their doorsteps and asking for the keys? More important, how would renters treat the vehicles they pick up on the street?

As it turned out, drivers who actually met the individuals who owned the cars they rented drove more carefully than Vinay or Tom expected. "We think that the human element actually reduced risk," noted Tom. With WhipCar, "you are in someone's car. It's not a faceless car owned by some corporation. Everyone is acutely aware that they have to bring the car back to someone who owns it. It's not like you say, 'I'm renting a car and driving to Scotland, and I don't care how I drive.' This is a human marketplace, and that human aspect brings out the best in people."[2]

Among car owners, the human aspect leads them to accept lower bids from frequent renters, who become like friends. Among renters, it leads to a sense of duty and even attachment. In almost two years of operation, WhipCar's founders had yet to see a serious dispute over the condition of a car that had been hired, and disputes over gasoline—drivers are expected to replace what they burn—could be counted on one hand. In the meantime, the service's most devoted car owners earned as much as $800 per month letting other people use their vehicles. Some actually consulted Vinay and Tom for advice before replacing their cars because they wanted to get one that renters preferred.

Beyond the benefits to WhipCar members, the founders count the financial and ecological payoffs that come with the more efficient use of thousands of cars. By various estimates, the manufacture of a single, medium-size car results in the production of more carbon dioxide that it will emit in a lifetime of operation. A WhipCar regular who chooses not to buy a car actually saves the planet the burden of roughly fifteen tons of manufacturing emissions. Driver payments to owners also convert the wealth frozen inside parked cars into cash that circulates in the economy. This resource is especially valuable, noted Tom, to "retirees who are on a fixed budget and hardly drive their cars at all[. They] really benefit from the extra income."

By keeping costs low, Vinay and Tom managed to steer WhipCar toward profitability at a faster pace than their business plan predicted. They are being helped by a change in the way people relate to cars as status symbols. In the United States, "the percentage of sixteen-year-olds with a license declined from 44 percent in 1988 to 30 percent in 2008," explained Vinay. "A similar thing is happening all over Europe. And owning a car just doesn't represent the same status that it once had." In fact, in recent years the United States has seen a decline in car ownership for the first time ever. This trend, and a drop in the number of miles logged by younger drivers, suggests that cars are losing their magic as a status symbol.

In a time of economic stress, owning a car when it's obviously cheaper to rent might be seen as a sign of bad judgment, if not a character flaw. Considering their peers—adults in their twenties and thirties—Tom and Vinay argue that flexibility, creativity, and independence are the new markers of a kind of success that is less ostentatious and more sustainable. "If you look at technology and the economy, you can see that we are going through a great disruption," added Vinay, who worked in telecommunications before becoming an entrepreneur. "I didn't own a mobile phone until I was twenty-two. Now five-year-olds carry them, and two-year-olds know how to use an iPad. It's completely understandable that people are upset by all the changes."

The shifts in employment and the popping of the real estate bubble have left many people with a sense of dislocation and anxiety, added Vinay. The antidote, he argues, can be found in new definitions of what makes a good life and in a creative response to the economy. He believes that the world holds endless possibilities for those who can improve a business or a service to give more people access to something of value.

"Houses are a good example," he said. "Home ownership used to be the definition of success. It doesn't mean the same thing anymore. Now we know that the housing boom was artificial and it's far more economical not to own a property. I don't own a house. I don't have a car. And I'm not sure I ever will. But I can buy access to a place to live and a car to use, and I have loads of experiences that make life richer."

A good example of this "access" approach to living is the Hospital Club, where we met. Set in a beautiful and expensive neighborhood, the club provides graceful spaces that many members could not otherwise afford to enjoy. Like WhipCar, the club allows those who need something expensive, but only on a short-term basis, to add it to their life. "Today, the thing people need is access to an experience, not necessarily ownership," observed Vinay. "And we can arrange that by relating to each other more personally."

• • •

The personal quality of the WhipCar formula prompts many people to add a little handwritten promise—"I'll be careful"—to the more formal commitment they make as they sign a rental agreement. The words are stronger than ink on paper because they help bind the buyer and seller in a relationship. In this, the WhipCar model stands out against the global trend toward an impersonal marketplace. Commerce conducted online and at scan-it-yourself checkout counters may be efficient, but it comes without the sense of security and connection we get when we can see, hear, and come to know the person on the other side of the transaction.

Much studied and much lamented, the alienation of modern life flows, at least in part, from the feeling that we don't know enough about how our world works. As technologies become more dazzling and our jobs become more specialized, we know less and less about how objects are imagined, designed, produced, and delivered. The feeling that we are isolated from the origins of things is relieved when we see a cook toss dough into the air at our local pizzeria or meet the owner of an orchard at the farmers market.

The basic human desire for connection inspired Katie Mowat to found a service that pairs consumers with knitters who make bespoke hats, scarves, and other winter woolens that they can design themselves online. The twist is that the knitters are actual grandmothers—and you get to pick your own granny! More than a dozen "grans" are featured on Katie's website, and customers are encouraged to communicate directly with the knitter they pick, working through preferences on shape, colors, and stitching. The finished goods are shipped with labels, stitched inside, that are addressed to the buyer and signed by the granny.

On the night we met her for dinner on the South Bank of the Thames, twenty-eight-year-old Katie arrived wearing a long fuchsia scarf, happy to report that a cold front was finally bringing a chill to the season. Autumn was arriving late to London, not good for a business that depends on people shivering when the wind cuts through their clothes. Grannies Inc. might be a playfully creative enterprise, Katie noted, but it is also a real business that provides income for knitters and needs revenues to keep humming.

"In my first year I made a mistake by pricing everything too low," recalls Katie. "I had to learn that for premium products you charge a premium price. Our knitters are really extraordinary, and the quality of what they make is so high you could wear it for years and years."[3]

The emotional premium in a Grannies Inc. purchase is delivered first as a buyer reads biographies of the grannies. "I didn't have grandparents on either side of my family when I was a child," recalled Katie. "The grannies we have are surrogates for me, and I think it works that way for a lot of people who use the site. But then you get invested in the design of the item and the collaboration. Finally, when you get that package with something in it that has been handmade specifically for you, it's a wonderful experience. A lot of people have never received a package like that in their lives."

Of course the thrill of receiving a granny-made hat, vest, or scarf would fade quickly if it were poorly made. Here, Katie's own experience as an avid knitter comes into play. As a college student studying in America during a knitting craze that began in 2001, Katie took up the craft and became extremely proficient. Knitting and the community of women who did it gave Katie both a creative outlet and a deep appreciation for social networks. Knitters, it turns out, are happy to share their secrets and encourage each other with great enthusiasm.

With Grannies Inc., Katie recreated her college knitting circle on a scale so grand that it reaches across the English countryside to include hundreds of highly skilled older women. The day after we met Katie, we hopped a Chiltern Railways train to the Oxfordshire town of Banbury. There, Holly, a tall, straight-backed woman with gray hair piled on her head, met us at the end of a long gravel driveway and walked us to the door of her house. Inside, she kicked off her shoes and led us to a cozy room warmed by a potbellied stove. A basket filled with wool and knitting needles rested beside the chair she sank into. The view from her window included a few dozen sheep grazing on a grassy hillside. In the distance, the sun met the horizon.

"I had a very, very good marriage, but when my husband died in 2006, I learned that the world isn't going to come up your drive and say, 'Please, can Holly come out to play,'" said Holly. "I realized that I had to make life work for myself."[4]

As she made her life, Holly pursued sailing and wound up in the Mediterranean, the Caribbean, and the choppy waters off the Orkney Islands. She became a devoted volunteer at the hospice center that helped her husband. This work reinforced her Buddhist sensibilities. "I appreciate how transient and fragile life is," she explained. In the quiet hours, needlework and knitting aid her in meditation and reflection.

"I learned to knit a long, long time ago," recalled Holly. With the rationing of World War II, skill with a needle made it possible for sweaters and hats to be repaired and remain in service. Knitting and sewing circles brought women together when their husbands were at war. The craft also made a young girl proud that she could do her part.

When Holly read a newspaper article about Grannies Inc., she emailed Katie to wish her well. Katie answered with a question: "Would you like to knit a sample beanie?" After Holly said yes, she received a package containing the yarn, needles, and pattern she was to use. The beanie was almost perfect, and Holly became an official Grannies Inc. knitter. A faster and more ambitious knitter than most, Holly has accepted big jobs, including an order for dozens of beanies placed by a European TV network. "I was really chuffed," she recalled, "when my children were watching TV and they called me because the commentators were wearing beanies I had knitted."

In a busy month, Holly might receive a check that will pay for an outing or two with her actual grandchildren or for some luxuries she might otherwise forgo. For other women who live on much more modest budgets, the payments make it possible for them to pay their monthly bills without the worry they once felt. The money and sense of accomplishment all flow from Katie Mowat's desire to make a small business and do something positive for others out of the craft she loves. A practical woman, Holly recognized the financial benefit she received by joining Grannies Inc., but harbored some skepticism about any social rewards that might come from Katie's idea.

In her lifetime, Holly had seen the coming together of the war years and then the loosening of social ties that occurred as women left the home to work, family size shrank, and the population shifted toward big cities. She appreciated the way Grannies Inc. established small connections between knitters and buyers, whose hearts were warmed by the notes she tucked into each item she completed and shipped. But she had trouble imagining how this little enterprise might do more for her—until she hit upon the notion of mixing the old and the new.

"Women have always done handicrafts in groups as a way of coming together and sharing," she told us. These gatherings allowed participants not only to share what they knew about technique but also, more important, to exchange information and ideas about anything and everything that mattered to them, from child rearing to the great public issues of the day. With Grannies Inc. providing projects to complete and a small profit motive, Holly began to recruit participants for a knitting circle that would engage village women for a few hours per week.

Reviving a tradition that pays dividends in so many ways clearly delighted the woman who was challenged to remake her life after her husband died. "We grannies are full of wisdom," she remarked.

Her wisdom is evident in her plan to expand on Katie's concept and make it pay more dividends to more people, echoing the community spirit of the England she knew as a girl.

● ● ●

The energy behind Grannies Inc. came from two basic human drives: creativity and the need for connection. In times of financial crisis, the value people attach to these pursuits seems to increase as people who are troubled by financial insecurity seek ways to feel happy and successful. Creative outlets, such as the production of handmade crafts, can be seen as opportunities for sharing oneself with the wider world. But what about people who lack a specific, in-demand skill or talent like the ability to turn a skein of wool into a cap? They can still connect by sharing their time through volunteer work.

It is a fact that volunteering increases with unemployment and recessions. Although some research suggests that people turn to help others because they have idle time on their hands, the volunteering impulse also arises in the hearts of busy people who simply want to pitch in. The trouble, for most of these folks, is to find a workable outlet for their volunteering desires.

Enter Anna Pearson and Spots of Time.

In her years of working as an advocate for charities in Britain and abroad, Pearson recognized a pattern: many people want to volunteer, but cannot find ways to do it. In some cases, organizations that claimed to need help attached onerous conditions to service, requiring people to make long-term commitments, undergo extensive training, or perform work that didn't suit them. In other cases, volunteers were thrown into big projects with mighty ambitions—feeding the hungry, ending violence in a neighborhood—that could never be achieved. Frustration would lead to disillusionment, and projects would be abandoned.

To bridge the gap between what volunteers can give and what people need, Anna reimagined volunteering—on a very small scale. As she explained to us over tea, "I thought, 'People need things as basic as a little happiness or joy in their day,' and I realized that with a humble idea, we could make that happen."[5]

The humble idea was a service—Spots of Time—that connects people with organizations that can use volunteers who can commit an hour or more to do something for someone else, and often at a moment's notice. Nursing homes (known as care homes in the United Kingdom) were among the first to sign up for the network, and soon Spots of Time was sending volunteers to spend time with the elderly and disabled residents of facilities in London and Essex. As Anna discovered, an hour or two was usually more than enough time for a volunteer to do some good, and his or her service could be something as small as reading aloud or accompanying someone on a walk.

The notion that someone might volunteer sporadically fits with what thirty-one-year-old Anna called the "freelance culture" of her generation. Accustomed to projects that last for a limited time, many young adults look for service opportunities "that are more like a gig than a job." In some cases, the volunteers are actual performers who are happy to find an audience, even if they offer a show for free.

Early feedback on her program, just months old when we met her, showed that volunteers are so sincere about doing something positive that they worry that a spot of time is not enough. "We have to convince people to just trust in the fact that doing something good, even though it's really small, is worth it." She counsels volunteers to stop worrying and just go and sit for tea with someone who would appreciate the company. Anna offers similar counsel to leaders of organizations who are accustomed to old ways of accepting help, which too often meant they received no help at all.

"I understand if people are worried that we are all fur coat and no knickers," said Anna, using a British expression for someone who is all flash and no substance. "I'm keenly aware of what we haven't done yet, but I also know there's a big resource here and a big need, and I think it should be possible to break down the barriers that keep them apart."

• • •

The obstacles that separate the financial center called the City of London and the nearby neighborhood of Hackney are scaled, every day, by the honeybees that occupy a hive atop the Nomura Bank building. The bees produce honey for a small outfit called Golden Company, which partners with the young people of Hackney to teach bankers and other high-flying Londoners about the environment, sustainability, and the delicate balance of nature.

Vital to food supplies, the work that bees accomplish as pollinators of British crops is estimated to be worth more than $700 million per year, according to the United Kingdom's National Ecosystem Assessment.[6] Bees help produce one out of three mouthfuls of food in the British diet.[7] However, in the United Kingdom, as elsewhere, bee populations began to decline in the 1990s.[8] As the bee problem became evident, the British government funded several investigations into solutions. In the meantime, bee enthusiasts across the country went about the practical business of starting new hives. In 2007, a pair of entrepreneurs started Golden Company to raise bees, produce honey, employ local youth, and bring attention to the crisis in the garden. They located it in the poor neighborhood of Hackney, where staff at a community center called Hackney City Farm help manage the work.

Golden Company is a distinctly British type of organization—called a social enterprise—that blends business with a social agenda to accomplish several goals. The bees that live in the many hives it maintains pollinate plants and produce honey that sells briskly at public markets. At the Nomura building, Golden's young employees outfit their elders in bee-proof gear and then teach them to work with the hives unafraid. In this role, the youth discover confidence and competence. The professionals at Nomura Bank learn about bees and the capabilities of young people they would otherwise never encounter.

The connection between bankers and Hackney youth is the most important product of Golden Company. "The young people we work with are most at risk of being excluded from the economic system and from society," explains Zoe Palmer, one of the founders of the honey company.[9] Born and raised in Hackney, Zoe attended University College London with the idea that she would return to her community to do something to make it better. "I studied human ecology, and it teaches you to balance the head, the heart, and the hands," she recalled for us. "I started thinking about a business that would use all three in a self-sustaining way."

Zoe obtained seed money for the business, acquired bees from Shropshire, and found sites for the hives with corporate partners at places like Nomura Bank, the London Stock Exchange, and at the big Chancery Lane law firm Lewis Silkin, LLP, where a queen bee named Lucy arrived in September 2011. Young beekeepers (called guardians by Golden) assumed responsibility at each hive and became mentors for employees of their host corporations. Other hives were installed in various parks and at Hackney City Farm. There, enterprise manager Gustavo Montes de Oca saw Golden as a perfect way to establish ties with the professionals in the city's banking sector and get local youth involved. "Beekeeping has everything that might attract kids," he said. "Honey, danger, funny outfits."[10]

Moreover, as Gustavo explained to us when we visited him at Hackney Farms, London's powerful financial district "has always been on our doorstep, but we never had a way to connect with the people there—it was like there were two different worlds that never connected, and both were losing out because of it."

Indeed, as the income gap between the wealthy of the City and places like Hackney grew, people in both communities began to worry about the effects of their mutual isolation. Gustavo imagined that Hackney City Farm could be a place where that isolation might be broken and mutual empathy might be encouraged.

Golden Company's values, posted on its website, include discipline, self-reliance, and a commitment to learning—and all of its activities revolve around building respect for nature and humanity's role in the environment. As founder Zoe Palmer envisioned, the bees teach their keepers something about the "wildness of nature." In a radio documentary about the program, a bee guardian named Devente said, "Once you understand the bee, once you know what it's doing, your perspective changes from swatting to staying still."[11] Another beekeeper named King marveled at the industry of the insects. With a kind of awe in his voice, he explained, "They love work."[12]

Experience with bees helped King and Devente develop patience and recognize the parts of an extremely complex system. In the bee colonies, they saw finely tuned teams without leaders survive and thrive on the basis of communication, cooperation, responsibility, and selflessness. These talents and traits, which people in our global surveys consider traditionally feminine, can be applied directly to school, work, and family life. They also match many of the values promoted at Hackney City Farm. Set on a former industrial property where manufacturers have made everything from beer to buttons, the farm was established by Hackney residents who used public and private funds to renovate buildings and clear land. The property now supports a demonstration farm, small businesses, social programs, and hybrids like Golden.

On the morning when we visited Hackney City Farm, half a dozen people lingered over breakfast in the farm's Frizzante (Italian for "fizzy") Café while workers at an outbuilding devoted to a shop called Bike Yard East took wrenches to a lineup of bicycles left for repair. At about ten, women began arriving for a yoga class taught inside a building made of straw bales where the floor had been cleared to make space available for mats. Referred by the Red Cross and other agencies, the women were all refugees and asylum seekers. Besides the practice of yoga, participants share a meal and receive English language instruction.

All the activity we saw at Hackney City Farm was sustained by a combination of grants and earned income designed to generate enough cash flow to meet its social service goals. Golden's workers are educated in business management as well as beekeeping, and they have been responsible for managing payroll and inventory as well as for developing new products. Required to present detailed proposals to support their ideas, the young workers are often surprised to discover that questions raised by their colleagues force them to improve their concepts. The most successful ancillary product to come out of this process, a honey-based lip balm, was so well formulated and marketed that it sells out whenever it is offered.

The creativity and persistence of the people who participate in Hackney programs match the kind of effort that might be seen at an exciting business start-up. When the farm opened a public garden in a nearby park, Gustavo was startled to discover that the only people who violated the rules of the garden were the ones who sought to install extra trees and plants.

One evening, Gustavo was startled to see a man using a screwdriver to loosen hard-packed earth and create a hole for a seedling of an apricot tree that his daughter had sprouted on a windowsill. The man returned to tend the tree and also pitched in to care for trees that others had planted.

"We had no expert horticulturalist, and as far as I know, this fellow, who was an immigrant, taught himself everything he tried," Gustavo told us. The trees grew to bear fruit, which is shared by the entire community.

For Gustavo, the fruit tree experience revealed that much expertise and wisdom lie hidden in the community. He has learned a great deal from talking with locals who lived through the hard times of World War II and its aftermath, when rationing and a tough employment market forced great numbers of people to economize. "People would find many uses for something as basic as a jam jar, which became a sugar bowl or a container for pence. They remembered selling rags to be recycled and growing their own vegetables and herbs for cooking."

The example set by the older generation inspired Hackney managers to open resale markets for children's clothing and toys and to maximize use of the space at the farm by renting it to groups and corporations that are planning events. Farm officials are also working on a large-scale program to collect, separate, and sell waste and cast-off items that retain significant value. Each week, area homes and businesses produce tons of recyclables, from used cooking oils to paper, which could yield more than $600,000 per year in revenues. Gustavo describes this activity as "harvesting the city" and imagines it growing to employ dozens of locals in an activity that is profitable, self-sustaining, and good for the environment.

In harvesting the city, Gustavo intends to advance a complex mix of ideals: masculine and feminine, profit driven and socially aware, generous and conservationist. He explores the issues his generation faces in a new and changing world on a blog titled "GoldenGus," where he admonishes his fellow "greens" with a warning—"thou shalt not moralise"—but also considers Britain's chief rabbi's call for "remoralising" the world with new organizations to push for happier communities and a healthier planet. He quotes Rabbi Jonathan Sacks recalling how people in the United States and the United Kingdom organized themselves to confront the disruption of the Industrial Revolution of the nineteenth century: "People did not leave it to government or the market. They did it themselves in communities, congregations, groups of every shape and size. They understood the connection between morality and morale."[13]

In the midst of the current technological and economic revolution, when workers are displaced and insecurity seems rampant, solutions may come from modern formulations of nineteenth-century associations like the YMCA, temperance unions, orphans societies, guilds, and community trusts. The new versions will undoubtedly be based, at least in part, in the online world. But in localities, they may also look much like Hackney City Farm and Golden Company, where hard work and imagination support innovation on a human-to-human (or human-to-bee) scale.

● ● ●

The local efforts made by Gustavo, Zoe, and others yield results that Londoners can see and even taste, but their efforts also motivate others to pursue solutions that can be seen nationally and even internationally. Because it deals in products that are readily transferred over the Internet, finance is an attractive corner of the economy for those seeking modern versions of mutual aid. Operating out of a second-floor suite of offices in a Victorian commercial building on Newman Street, Giles Andrews offers this kind of help to borrowers and lenders with a start-up finance company called Zopa, named for the concept known as Zone of Possible Agreement.

Zopa pulls together information on large numbers of individuals who want personal loans on better terms than they would get from a traditional lender. Together, these borrowers present less risk than a single applicant; protected by the strength in the collective credit history of the borrowers, investors provide the cash that Zopa lends. For all its trouble, the firm takes fees from lenders and borrowers that amount to less than 2.5 percent of a loan.

The modest fees are explained in plain English on the Zopa website, where both sides of the lending business can also learn the basics of its peer-to-peer process. As the site explains, Zopa evaluates borrowers and assigns them to groups labeled A*, A, B, C, or "Young Market." The best borrowing rates are available to the A* borrowers. The highest return for lenders comes when they offer money to the lower-grade pools, such as C and Young Market. They are protected from big losses by a system that restricts the amount any one investor can commit to any one borrower to roughly $15. A default by someone who has taken $15 from a hundred lenders causes much less pain than a default by a borrower who fails to repay $1,500 put up by a single person.

"The idea is to treat everyone fairly—lenders and borrowers—and be very open about how we do business," Andrews told us on the day we arrived at Zopa's offices just off the Goode Street tube.[14] The big, open, white-walled space was quiet, save for the clicking of people working at computers and muffled phone conversations taking place on the other side of the room. Before Zopa, Giles was a consultant for big companies like the Tesco supermarkets and Internet start-ups. He and a partner named Richard Duvall began Zopa in 2005 with about $10 million from venture capitalists who agreed that banks served consumers poorly, leaving a huge opening for a start-up alternative.

Richard, who had founded one of the first and most successful online banks—Egg.com—hosted the brainstorming for Zopa at the barn on his country estate, where some of the best ideas emerged at the Ping-Pong table. Regarded by Microsoft founder Bill Gates as "one of the most dynamic people I have ever met,"[15] Duvall preached the value of businesses based on trusting relationships with a growing population of consumers who feel comfortable with online transactions. He dubbed these potential customers "freeformers" and estimated that more than six million British citizens fit into the category. Sadly, Duvall was diagnosed with pancreatic cancer and died the year after Zopa's launch. He wasn't around for the start of the global bank crisis in 2007. Zopa, however, was poised to profit.

Because nations support banks with guarantees, the collapse of banks around the world, including Britain's Northern Rock Bank, saddled taxpayers with the responsibility to make depositors whole. But even as they rescued these huge financial institutions, everyday citizens found that banks would no longer lend to them, and interest rates paid for savings dropped well below the rate of inflation. "The public got this feeling that whenever they were dealing with these big institutions, the bankers were telling them, 'We're going to get you in the end,'" recalled Giles. Zopa presented an alternative "that says, 'We're going to talk to you respectfully, and you are going to know exactly how we do business. There will be no surprises in the end.'"

With other lenders turning off the flow of loans, Zopa's portfolio exploded. The raw numbers—from $10 million to more than $250 million—are small when compared with banks that carry billions of dollars in outstanding loans. However, by the end of 2011, more than half a million people had signed up as investors or borrowers.

The average return paid to investors was just over 7 percent, and defaults across Zopa's range of loans were less than 2 percent. Meanwhile, the rates charged to borrowers averaged 20 percent below the average for banks.

Playing off the Zopa model, peer-to-peer lenders have cropped up around the world. All operate as information managers, using the data about their pool of borrowers to estimate risk and assign rates. The numbers are made public, which reduces the mystery around lending and gives peer-to-peer finance a trustworthy image. Members, who know that traditional banks are regulated and backstopped by the government, prefer the higher returns they earn to the security of state-issued guarantees. Similar to old-fashioned credit unions, Zopa and its imitators "are a way for people participate in building their own institutions," said Giles.

Zopa itself is a new kind of financial center where an extremely lean staff of twenty-three manage an ever-growing army of lenders and borrowers. The pace is hectic, but employees work with the intensity of people on a mission. Determined that the company serve its employees as well as it serves its customers, Giles experiments with ways to track how his team is faring. On the day we visited, he had set out a bin full of colored balls and two wastebaskets labeled Good and Bad. Staffers were advised to toss a ball into the basket that indicated how they felt about things in the office. In a testament to the spirit of trust that is the hallmark of Zopa's business model, the bins were almost at the same level.

• • •

By aggregating borrowers and lenders, Zopa creates efficiencies in the Zone of Possible Agreement. The operators of Made.com exploit a similar process, using the power of community to disrupt the furniture business.

Two entrepreneurs in their thirties, Ning Li and Julien Callede, targeted the furniture business after studying the cost of retail space and warehousing built into the price of every sofa or ottoman sold the old-fashioned way. Even giant companies like IKEA, which revolutionized the business with build-it-yourself kits, spend enormous amounts of money constructing, maintaining, and running facilities that are mainly way stations between the manufacturer and your living room. The real value in the product rests in great design and solid construction, Ning and Julien reasoned. Why not find a way to deliver that value without all the markups required to pay for all that storage?

Breaking the business down to its essence, Julien and Ning looked for ways to connect consumers who needed furnishings to the source. They settled on a system that allows people to "vote" with orders for a small number of designs that are offered on Made.com's website every Thursday. When the number of orders reaches a point where an item can be manufactured efficiently and shipped at a reasonable cost, the design "wins," and a factory swings into production. "It's the opposite of the very masculine way, which is to buy a lot of stuff, put it on display, and say take it or leave it," explained Julien when we met him. "We take the relationship with customers seriously, ask them what they want, and respond in real time."[16]

On the day that Made.com debuted, the site offered one table and two chairs. The company's first big hit was a playful desk by Stuart Padwick, one of London's most successful designers. At roughly $500, the sleek desk was sold by Made.com at roughly one-third the price it would fetch in a shop window. As visitors voted for more items, the offerings swelled to include plush chairs, sofa beds, and leather club chairs for the same price. A dozen more designers were gradually added to the team, and the site was upgraded to give customers daily reports on the path their purchases followed from door to delivery, including maps that chart the progress of ships loaded with Made.com's wares.

Ning, who travels to China to scout suppliers, delights in the shared interests of every participant in the Made.com equation.

"The factories are looking for new export markets and to use their excess capacity. The consumers are happy because they get a $1,500 item from High Street for $500, and the designers are happy because instead of selling one item per month, they may sell hundreds."[17] They also get the reward of knowing that their work is finding its way into the lives of thousands of people.

At the Made.com office in Notting Hill Gate, a few dozen people can manage thousands of relationships that produce millions of dollars' worth of sales each quarter. Remarkably, none of the workers are employed as salespeople. Instead they work as listeners who try to tune in to the desires of their community of customers. "How do you sell?" asked Julien, rhetorically. "You sell by listening to people. If you listen, they will tell you exactly what they want. If you listen, you can change the system and do it better."

•••

Most of the innovators we met in Britain had established new business models that engaged consumers and citizens directly and made things better, one person at a time. Borrowers who turned to Zopa were able to buy cars or renovate kitchens (the two most common reasons for people to apply), and Golden Company bee guardians earned paychecks as they acquired skills. But these kinds of direct efforts were not the only signs of innovation we discovered. Though no longer the seat of an empire, London remains a place where people with a broad vision for changing the world cultivate new ideas.

A few blocks from Regent's Park, in the center of London, we met two of the directors of Social Finance, an organization that has found a way to tap private wealth to solve public problems. Turning an old paradigm on its head, the firm is working on deals with different levels of government, promising social programs that produce measurably better results than existing agencies. Investors are being courted to supply the up-front cash, while government is being asked to repay them, with interest, and give them a return if the projects are deemed a success after a certain period of years.

Called social impact bonds, the experimental funding scheme is being used in the small city of Peterborough, which is east of Birmingham, to pay for services to help inmates make the transition from prison to life in society. Investors who front the money for mentoring, housing support, mental health interventions, and more stand to make a profit of as much as 13 percent. Their net will be determined by the rate at which former inmates reoffend and return to the criminal justice system. The risk for those who put up the money is that the project might fall short of the goal of a 7.5 percent reduction in recidivism. For the government, it's a no-lose proposition because the premium it might pay will come from the savings realized as fewer men return to lockup.

"The idea is to use money as an incentive for creativity and improved outcomes," explained Emily Bolton, a director at Social Finance. "Money tends to make people focus."[18]

By adding investors to the process of delivering social services to prisoners, Emily and her colleagues are establishing a new layer of accountability. The outcome of the efforts made by advisers, community members, counselors, and others who work with clients will be monitored by people who want the program to succeed because they want their money back, plus interest.

In the United Kingdom, where transition services were all but nonexistent, 60 percent of those released are convicted of an offense within a year. The new program, which includes counselors who literally greet prisoners at the gate when they are released, will be offered to three thousand men over six years. These counselors serve as a point of contact for every kind of help a released prisoner might need. This early intervention and streamlined access to services are expected to produce the reduction in recidivism that would meet the 7.5 percent threshold. Early reports from Peterborough police suggested that they had seen a positive change in the behavior of well-known local offenders, but as of 2011, the project was still too new to assess.

The social impact bond scheme has been supported by all the major political parties in Britain and has received wide publicity, which does put a bit of pressure on the directors at Social Finance. "We are hoping for a good outcome and that the investors will get their return," said Emily. The first wave of funders came from the ranks of people who see their investment as both a play for profit and a way to do some good in the world. But if the idea works, said Emily, mainstream investors could conceivably make social impact bonds just another component of their portfolios. "The concept isn't a silver bullet for solving social problems," she concluded, "but it can be one answer among many." Next on the investment agenda, if the prison project works, will be bonds to fund services for the homeless, the unemployed, and drug and alcohol rehabilitation centers.

•••

Emily Bolton was optimistic about the future of what she called "impact investment" and sees it as a way for people of all political stripes to work together for the common good. She also regarded the nascent field of social finance as the ultimate expression of the Athena Doctrine. In her work, she can use all her masculine and feminine values as well as the skills that she acquired working at both KPMG (one of the world's "big four" auditing companies) and a settlement camp for Tibetan refugees. "We're at the early stages," she says of the effort to combine hardheaded business practices with compassion, "but I can see a world where these things all connect."

Cherie Blair can imagine a future like the one Emily Bolton pursues, but in her effort to promote women entrepreneurs in the less-developed world, she has learned to beware the persistence of prejudice and the obstacles women still face. We met her at the Cherie Blair Foundation, which is less than a block from the famous Marble Arch of Hyde Park. Outside, the street bustled with tourists and shoppers. Inside, a small team of staffers quietly tended to the work of overseeing roughly $1.5 million in annual investments in small businesses led by women around the world. The foundation had just issued its annual report for 2011, which highlighted enterprise development projects in India, Lebanon, Israel, the Palestinian territories, and several African nations.

"To survive and thrive, everyone needs the wherewithal to be productive," says Cherie, a barrister and part-time judge who is also married to former prime minister Tony Blair. "You need the feeling of belonging and of being entitled to support."[19] Cherie began the foundation to provide women in developing and emerging markets support and a sense of belonging by training them in business practices and financing start-ups. In Kenya and Malawi, for example, the foundation helps entrepreneurs sell solar lighting products. In India, it teaches craftswomen how to turn their goods into profits.

In visiting projects around the world, Cherie has seen that "both the economic and social spheres have been dislocated" by the financial crisis. "People are struggling to find the work and family balance in their lives." She has felt personally challenged in this regard, first when she was a younger working mother and later, after she left 10 Downing Street for private life. "I was in the position many women find themselves in at key moments of their lives," she recalled. "I had to find my way again, find the right balance. It isn't a women's issue; it's a human issue, but women are in the lead."

Cherie said that she has found, in women entrepreneurs, affirmation of the strength and values she saw in her own mother and grandmother, reflective of a traditionally feminine style of leadership. "Mothers think long term," she noted to us. "That kind of thinking is a very good balance for the risk-taking and assertiveness" that is required to make a new enterprise succeed.

Remarkably, Cherie noted, some corners of the developing world are friendlier to strong women than certain precincts of the West. "Look at boards of directors at major corporations," she explained. "It's disheartening that there's been so little progress in bringing women on to them." The presence of more women, she speculated, "might have led to more cautious risk assessments" at the big banks that faltered in the past decade. "Look at those boards that are all male and ask yourself, 'Who's providing the countervailing views to keep things balanced?'"

Chapter 2

Iceland

"My government should do a better job of
listening to the needs of its people." (92% agree)

E ven Cherie Blair wouldn't say that with a few more women in key spots, Iceland could have avoided its spectacular economic collapse. Still, it's hard to find anyone in Reykjavik who thinks that it was merely a coincidence that the guys who wrecked Iceland's economy were all, well, *guys*.

Halla Tomasdottir remembered well the moment she realized that her country's financial leaders were heading for trouble. She had encouraged a couple of them to sit down and talk before their massive leverage would cause serious issues. Although she was director of the national chamber of commerce at the time and definitely on their side, she couldn't persuade them that this was their common problem. They refused to cooperate, in part because of personal issues, each one of them thinking that he was doing things right but that the others were not. Egos were inflamed, and most people were in denial of the systemic risk. She recalled, "It wasn't just that they were all men. They also all went to the same schools at about the same time and came out with the same ideas.

When they got rich, they bought the same kinds of cars and houses and clothes. They weren't bad people, but they became victims of what I call the great-big-penis syndrome. You know what I mean? They were caught up in the relentless pursuit of more, and they couldn't stop competing."[1]

The smile that Halla flashed as she finished her story was both ironic and wistful. Three years after Iceland's superhot financial sector collapsed in a pile of bad debt, she was widely recognized for having been right when everyone else was wrong. Audur Capital, the small investment firm she founded with partner Kristin Petursdottir, had weathered the crisis well. (Named after the Icelandic Viking woman, Audur means wealth, happiness, and clear space. The company emphasizes profit with principles and long-term thinking in its investment approach.) Halla refused to celebrate its success, however. "We've still got a lot of cleaning up to do," she said.

We visited Iceland in early 2012 to see what happens when an entire country must respond to a profound economic crisis caused by a serious lapse in social values. The crisis, precipitated by excessive financial risk-taking, shocked everyday Icelanders and led to criminal investigations. As we arrived, several former government officials and executives of the country's three failed banks—Landsbanki, Kaupthing, and Glitnir—faced trial on various charges brought by a special prosecutor tasked with investigating the boom and bust in the financial sector. Many of the granular details had yet to emerge and would ultimately prove too esoteric for common understanding. But the basic outlines of the crisis were clear.

Long captive to a small group known collectively as the Octopus, Iceland's economy had been opened to competitive forces beginning in the 1970s. Around the year 2000, the three formerly state-owned banks began borrowing heavily abroad, promising high returns to both investors and ordinary depositors. Major European

banks lent to the Icelanders, confident that the national government in Reykjavik would backstop the deals. In the meantime, the
Icelanders placed ads in European newspapers attracting deposits
from more than four hundred thousand individuals (mostly from
Great Britain and Denmark) as well as from government agencies
and municipalities. With rates as high as 11.6 percent, Icelandic
certificates of deposit even found their way into accounts at conservative American mutual funds.

As the money poured in, Landsbanki, Kaupthing, and Glitnir
functioned like a magic machine, pulling money in from foreign
sources and handing it to the managers of local investment firms,
who believed they were the equals of hedge fund operators in
London and New York. They bought up companies all over the
world, often paying prices that others deemed exorbitant. Somewhere in the back of their minds, they understood that the loans
that fueled all this activity would have to be paid off, but that
reality lived in the unseen future. In the meantime, the local stock
exchange boomed, and real estate prices soared. As private jets
began to crowd the tarmac at Keflavik airport, the country became
the richest per capita on Earth.

For a while it seemed as though everyone believed in the Iceland
miracle. The United Nations ranked Iceland first in its human
development index (a measure of social well-being),[2] and the Cato
Institute, a fiercely conservative Washington think tank, urged
other nations to "learn from Iceland's success" with tax cutting and
deregulation.[3] The Wall Street Journal praised the government's
policies,[4] and the Honorable Ólafur Ragnar Grímsson, president
of Iceland, traveled the world to announce new international
business ventures. At the University of Iceland, demand for classes
in finance became so great that the engineering department began
offering courses in constructing deals.

Inevitably, the financial mania reached the man on Laugavegur
(the main shopping street in Reykjavik). The city set records for
sales of Range Rovers, Bang & Olufsen electronics, and Kobe

beef. Expensive kitchen renovations and shopping trips to London became de rigueur for the professional class, while the super-rich dined on risotto spiced with flakes of gold. Among the less wealthy, flat-screen televisions and new cars became affordable luxuries as credit made it possible for consumers to increase their spending by almost 30 percent while their incomes rose only half as much.

Although some skeptics questioned the notion that Iceland could thrive as a financial center, they didn't get much of a hearing. Something deep in Icelandic culture—the power of social agreements—made their doubts seem rude and unacceptable, explained Halla. "We were raised to agree and to discourage dissent. The nail that sticks up will be hammered down."

This groupthink allowed people to dismiss Danish economist Carsten Valgreen, who visited in 2006 and warned that a crash was imminent.[5] Given the historically painful relationship between the two nations—Denmark ruled Iceland as a colony until 1944—reaction to the report was what you might expect: angry, defensive, and dismissive. The country's biggest daily, *Frettabladid* (the Newspaper), mocked Valgreen in a grotesque cartoon, and Landsbanki's senior economist called his report "almost amusing."[6] Icelanders who had cheered their corporate raiders as they bought up foreign assets, including Denmark's iconic Magasin du Nord department store, generally agreed with their prime minister, who called Valgreen's work "absurd."[7] They also took comfort in high ratings from Standard and Poor's and Moody's, whom investors trusted for unbiased evaluations.

One stray Danish economist may have been easy to dismiss, but the echoes that later came from analysts for the investment banks Merrill Lynch and Barclay's rattled nerves. Outsiders who once snapped up Iceland's bonds began to doubt that an isolated island country of three hundred thousand people who traditionally made cod the basis for their wealth could serve as a global leader in finance. When reports surfaced showing that the banks had amassed debts worth more than eight times the entire country's gross domestic product, the outsiders who had supported Iceland's boom stopped sending cash. Banking and government leaders held their breath as the magic machine stalled.[8]

Finally, when the American bank Lehman Brothers went bankrupt in fall 2008, the krona (Iceland's currency) dropped like an anvil in a Road Runner cartoon. Banks in other countries ceased lending to their counterparts in Iceland and stopped accepting the Icelandic currency. Reykjavik's stock market shut down, and trading partners suspended deals. Icelanders abroad suddenly found that their cash was worthless and their credit cards no longer worked. At home, they found it impossible to repay loans they had taken in foreign currencies. Iceland became a very good place to find a deal on a used Range Rover. It also became a very good place to develop new ideas about how a country should be run.

"The universe is magnificent," observed Halla, whose favorite childhood game was "office." By this she meant that time inevitably brings balance to politics, bank accounts, and our lives. In the wake of Iceland's economic collapse, "everyone is talking about the need for transparency in all things and for careful decision making," she said cheerfully. "I always believed that the way to make progress was to support principles, and principled people. And to get everyone involved. Now, everyone is involved."

Örn Bárður Jónsson tried to get involved at the moment when he first began to fear that his country had lost its way. The government had just approved the sale of the nation's complete genetic profile—the people in Iceland are almost as purebred as their famous ponies—to a corporation that would make it available to researchers for drug companies. A Lutheran minister by profession and a writer by passion, Örn thought about his countrymen's sudden obsession with money and sat down to write a fable called "exPORT Mountains Inc."[9]

Published in a supplement to the Reykjavik daily *Morgunbladid*, "exPORT Mountains Inc." told the story of an entrepreneur named Peter Glacierson who "advised investors and spoke at meetings of the Icelandic Chamber of Commerce and the Confederation of Icelandic Employers where he inspired Icelandic entrepreneurs to think big."

Peter's biggest idea, to sell Iceland's iconic Mt. Esja, began as a joke. Visible from Reykjavik, the mountain defines the national landscape and is so important to the Icelandic psyche that parents name their children after it. Selling it would be anathema. But then a government study deemed it feasible to separate the mountain from the bedrock and tow it to mainland Europe, where it could fill in lowland areas prone to floods. Faced with an intriguing challenge, wrote Örn, Icelanders became "berserkers" who were determined to "assault the task before them and finish it off." They founded a giant company called exPORT Mountains Inc. and adorned it with the slogan, "Go, sell 'em all the mountains." Örn wrote,

> All available engineering firms got involved and still there was need for more. Equipment and tools were imported; consultants and specialists flowed in. There was drilling and sawing around the clock. The government had ear plugs issued to every man, woman and child...
>
> Slowly, very slowly, Mt. Esja budged from its bedrock. Front Street and Ocean Drive and the streets of the Shadow District were jam-packed with the crowd observing technology's divine omnipotence. What a sight, what a genius!—Peter is definitely our man, said an awed municipal worker of some seniority, standing in the crowd at the intersection of Water Path and Fountain Street. People all around him joined in a chorus of enthusiastic admiration.—Imagine all the jobs that were created by this project alone, all the euros for this one mountain, someone added.

In the fable, the most powerful ships ever to ply the North Atlantic pulled Mt. Esja into a nearby fjord and out to sea. Disaster struck somewhere south of the Faroe Islands, where the mountain capsized and sank. The check "in billions of euros" written to pay for the mountain was cancelled. Peter Glacierson went to foreign investors, hoping to save exPORT Mountains Inc., but they turned him down. "Who is crazy enough to invest in the nonsense of a nonsensical nation?" wrote Örn. In the end, the place where Esja had stood became a monument to "soulless people who sold beauty for bread and lentils ... Remembering her made people numb."

Although Peter Glacierson and his allies were fictional char-acters, they resembled real people, and, because Iceland is such a small and interconnected place, everyone knew, or thought they knew, the targets of Örn's satire. Iceland's prime minister com-plained to the head bishop of the Church of Iceland, and Örn suddenly found himself relieved of his position at the national office. Örn was shaken by this reaction, but after he found work at a small church called Neskirkja on the west side of the city, he regained his voice and continued writing.

"I wrote about the fact that our mistakes are not out there, but in here," said Örn, pointing to his own heart. "It's in here, and we have to struggle with ourselves and our nature if we are going to have a balanced way of life."[10]

A tall, white-haired man with bright blue eyes, Örn was born on November 23, 1949, in the town of Isafyordur. Nestled beside a fjord at the Arctic Circle, the place is so far north that direct sunlight doesn't reach the ground there from mid-November until the end of January. "The sun didn't shine on me until I was two months old," explained Örn when we met. "In a place like that you learn to have hope, and faith, even if it's just for the fact that summer will come."

We spoke with Örn in the sanctuary at his parish, which was a modern, open space of light-colored woods, red upholstered chairs, and a high peaked ceiling. Warmly colored light streamed in through stained glass windows that were positioned to take best advantage of the precious few sunbeams that fall on Reykjavik in

January. Like the active volcanoes that fill the sky with smoke and the earthquakes that make the ground shake, the sun's advance and retreat confronts Icelanders with forces beyond their control. For a time, the country lost touch with the humility that unrelenting nature teaches, said Örn. "We went a little crazy."

The craziness culminated with the collapse of the banks in October 2008. As the government authorities took them over, the krona became worthless abroad, and prices for imports—and almost everything except for fish must be imported—skyrocketed. Inflation zoomed into the double digits. People with high car payments bought classified ads offering cash payments to anyone willing to take their vehicles and pay their loans. The prime minister announced the end of the banking "fairy tale" and called for a return to an economy based on tangible goods, including fish pulled from the sea and aluminum produced at three smelters that had been built to take advantage of low-cost hydro and geothermal energy.

Although the fairy tale ended abruptly, the nightmare that followed was long and gruesome. A bailout from the International Monetary Fund forced cuts in government spending and increases in taxes. Interest rates charged for mortgages and other loans indexed to foreign currencies skyrocketed to more than 20 percent, forcing many people to make payments in excess of their take-home pay. Worse still, the amount they owed on their homes actually increased because lenders were permitted to adjust principal amounts monthly, to accommodate for inflation.

Public outrage over these events began on a Saturday when a single man, Hördur Torfason, set a microphone and loudspeaker on the pavement of the Austurvöllur—the central square in Reykjavik—and invited people to speak their minds. "So we're in ruins now," he said at the time. "Let's stick together and rebuild the country on different terms."[11]

Torfason's call for unity and change struck a nerve. Every Saturday, ever-larger crowds joined him until thousands took to the streets, banging pots and pans and chanting demands for

change. The homemade signs people carried included pictures of
pigs decorated with dollar signs and slogans such as "Off with Their
Heads." Banners with the names of the collapsed banks were set
on fire, and bonfires blazed. Crowds swelled to more than eight
thousand despite cold temperatures. Fists were raised in anger, and
masked men scaled buildings to drape them with banners.

One of the first to address the protesters, a young human rights
lawyer named Katrin Oddsdottir, took to the microphone and
said that the rallies would continue, and grow larger, until those in
power gave it up. "If you don't leave," she said loudly, "we will carry
on."[12] Katrin couldn't help but connect the rallies she attended
with an earlier time when Iceland's women organized their own
political party and demanded equal pay and other rights. In 1975, as
the United Nations declared the Year of the Woman, 90 percent of
Iceland's women took part in a one-day strike. On October 24, the
women refused to report to their jobs or attended to housekeeping
or child-care duties. Twenty-five thousand of them gathered for an
outdoor rally in Reykjavik. Many of the women put on their best
clothes for the day. Others wore uniforms from their jobs. Then, as
now, women blamed male excess for the problems of society. "Men
have governed the world since time immemorial, and what has
the world been like?" asked Adalheidur Bjarnfredsdottir, who then
observed the world to be a place of war, pollution, and corruption.[13]

The 1975 women's strike was followed by victories for many
female candidates, including Adalheidur, in the subsequent parliamentary elections. Admitted to the world of politics, the women
of Iceland didn't assert themselves again with the same vigor until
Katrin's generation confronted the economic crisis of 2008. She
explained this to us over a lunch of traditional Icelandic stew
thick with chunks of cod and tiny coldwater shrimp. A blue-eyed
thirty-five-year-old with wavy blonde hair, she wore a bulky red
plaid shirt with a bright blue collar and cuffs.

"Before the crash, we weren't shouting from every street corner
saying 'What the heck is going on?' but we could tell the whole

culture had gone awry. Every TV program was about investments or redoing apartments, and while a few people actually got rich, everyone else said, 'I'm going to *behave like* I'm rich.' Icelanders are like that. Everyone wants to be equal to everyone else. That's why one Christmas, when the big thing was foot massagers, every grandmother in Iceland got one."

As the side effects of the banking collapse afflicted ordinary households, people quickly returned to old-fashioned interests like gardening, knitting, and family, said Katrin. "And a lot of the energy that once went into shopping was put into protesting."

True to Iceland's character, the protests remained peaceful for the most part, but stones were hurled at government buildings, and the police did use pepper spray and tear gas to disperse crowds that threatened public buildings. Called the Pots-and-Pans Revolution, the protests grew to the point where the government finally resigned. It was replaced by a new coalition, including the country's first female prime minister, Johanna Sigurdardottir. As she was elected, her spokesperson noted that "men, especially young men, made a mess of things."[14] Johanna promised to act with "prudence and responsibility."

The new prime minister was joined in government by a surge of women parliamentarians, who took more than 40 percent of the seats. Johanna appointed a majority female cabinet, and women were picked to fill the chief executive spots at the nationalized banks. A woman was even selected to head the most masculine company in Iceland, the big aluminum producer Rio Tinto Alcan. All of this was done with the support of men who cast their votes for women with almost the same enthusiasm as their mothers, wives, sisters, and daughters.

Iceland's new government dealt with the financial crisis with swift measures that were the opposite of the austerity impulse that swept Europe. Spending on social programs was increased to ease the suffering of families, and the krona was devalued. The devaluation made imports so expensive that the local people focused their spending on domestically produced goods. It also made Iceland's fish available to the world at bargain basement prices, which led to increased production and employment. Icelanders who lost money in the collapse of the banking sector were made whole by the deposit guarantee system, but foreigners were told to wait. Although this move angered officials in Great Britain and Denmark, it was widely favored at home. And by saving only the domestic elements of the banking system, the government spared taxpayers from a huge obligation that would have made their lives even more difficult.

As Iceland's new leaders moved to deal with the immediate crisis, they also looked for ways to revive the balanced values that had made the country stable in the past. "I think we were looking for a way to go back to the time when there was more gender balance," noted Katrin. "In the old days, the men were away at sea for long periods of time, and women took care of things. Women didn't take risks. They took care of things."

The vehicle for restoring the country would be a new constitution that would replace one inherited from Denmark. In a remarkable display of egalitarianism, the government sent invitations, at random, to 1,000 citizens, who were asked to join a constitutional forum. About 950 invitees gathered at a sports arena; they donned name tags—first names only—and took places at tables seating eight.

Streamed continuously on the Internet, the forum settled on eight themes, ranging from democracy to transparency and the separation of powers, that should dominate the new constitution. Nature was given a high value, and the forum said that the country's resources should be used to benefit all. Iceland's distinctive culture, including its language, arts, and history, was identified as a kind of common wealth to be shared and protected. Other key values embraced by the forum included equality, human rights, harmony, security, and the pursuit of happiness for current and future generations.

With a framework of national values set, a call went out for those who wanted to serve on the elected assembly that would write a new national constitution. Örn Bárður Jónsson leaped at the chance. He added his name to a list of more than five hundred candidates and discovered, after the polling, that he was elected. The assembly went to work, not behind closes doors, but in public view and with real-time reports to the public on YouTube, Facebook, Twitter, and Flickr. Citizens offered instant feedback via the Internet, and their comments fed the deliberations.

•••

Although it was "crowdsourced" with the help of the Internet, the drafting of the constitution also required lots of old-fashioned labor. The members of the assembly picked Salvör Nordal, director of the Center for Ethics at the University of Iceland, to serve as chairwoman. Nordal came at Iceland's problems from a perspective that was probably unique. Although she was trained in the abstractions of philosophy and ethics, her father was governor of the central bank of Iceland, and she grew up listening to animated discussions of practical financial matters. As a result of these two influences, she developed a healthy regard for the power of human nature and its desires, and respect for the role of money and business in the life of a society.

"I am skeptical by nature," Salvör recalled when we met at her university office.[15] Her son's brightly colored drawings—waxy crayon on white paper—decorated the walls inside. Freezing rain fell on the campus walkways outside. "When there was so much money being thrown around here, I kept saying there was a sort of recklessness taking over," she recalled for us. "I mean, greed is a natural force, and it had gotten out of control. The country gave in to a mania."

The problem, as Salvör saw it, was an imbalance in values. "Money was seen as something that's unquestionably good, but

everything else, including the welfare of the society, was ignored."
With cash and other signs of wealth becoming the main measures
of status and success, Icelanders competed ferociously. "Nothing
was ever big enough or expensive enough. The pressure just kept
building."

The financial crash "took the pressure off," recalled Salvör,
allowing people to feel good about living modestly. However, it
also created an immediate "trust shock," which was expressed in
the Saturday protests, and stirred many to reconsider the country's
character. Icelanders are sometimes seen competing with the larger
countries around the world. This attitude, which found Iceland in
the position of either "winner" or "loser" in some eternal competition, was classically masculine, observed Salvör. The response to
the crisis was classically feminine.

Indeed, tight money required that many individual Icelanders
give up their foreign shopping trips, practice conservation, and
find satisfaction in relationships. On a broader scale, the country
was challenged to move past "the anger and the craving for what
was lost" to establish a more stable economy and society. The
constitutional assembly, informed by the values approved at the
forum, formed committees and working groups to draft sections of
the constitution.

Discussion in these groups was sometimes heated, but it never
became angry or stalemated. Parts of the constitution that related
to nature drew many of the comments via the Internet. Drafters
who wanted to declare nature to be sacred, in an almost religious
way, backed off this position when criticism mounted. Instead they
would declare nature to be "basis for life in the country," and they
called on all citizens to "respect and protect it."[16] After a great deal
of debate over the country's abundant fisheries, mineral deposits,
and hydropower and thermal energy reserves, they agreed that these
would be "the joint and perpetual property of the nation," which
should be safeguarded for sustainable development. The right to

exploit these resources would be granted "on an equal-opportunity basis" and for limited periods of time.

"We worked by consensus," recalled Salvör as she described the drafting process. "We also felt a lot of pressure to reach a good result."

The final document included rights for children, whose well-being would be guaranteed by the larger society. It gave ownership of natural resources to "the people of Iceland," and it clarified the powers of the legislative, judicial, and executive branches of government. The new constitution enshrined property rights and the right of free association and assembly; it prohibited inhumane treatment of both people and animals.

These quite general provisions were joined with very specific ones that reflected the widespread belief that the powerful should be more responsive to ordinary citizens, who were given the power to undo government actions or propose new legislation via petition. Not surprisingly, the assembly made it hard for the legislature to change regulations governing business and finance, requiring a supermajority of two-thirds. They also empowered individuals and the media with free speech and access to information about the government. The constitution also held the media responsible by requiring "transparency of ownership."

The last item considered by the assembly was the preamble, which Örn Bárður Jónsson undertook at the request of the assembly. Although he consulted with others, including some well-known writers, the actual words were his alone. He began with the phrase "We, the people," which echoed the U.S. Constitution, and he endeavored to make the passage as brief as he could.

> We, the people who inhabit Iceland, wish to create a just society where every person has equal opportunity. Our diverse origin enriches our society and together we are responsible for the heritage of generations, our country and its history, nature, language and culture. Iceland

is a free and sovereign state with freedom, equality, democracy and human rights as its cornerstones. The government shall endeavour to strengthen the welfare of the country's inhabitants, encourage their culture and respect the diversity of the life of the people, the country and its biosphere. We wish to promote harmony, security and happiness amongst us and coming generations. We are determined to work towards peace with other nations and respect for the earth and all mankind. In light thereof we set a new Constitution, the supreme law of the land that all must observe.[17]

Considered in the context of our global survey, the ambitions of the constitution, including harmony, security, and happiness for today's citizens and future generations, are traditionally feminine. In Örn's view, they are also classically Icelandic, because they tie together the practical and the spiritual while honoring both humanity and the power of nature. Just three generations ago, most Icelanders depended on the land and the sea for their survival. "We lived because the Earth gave up something for us," he said. "A sheep or a fish gives its life so we can survive. Nature is the basis. Dust to dust, ashes to ashes."

The completed constitution was posted on the Internet and submitted to Icelanders, who would debate it and consider it in a future referendum election. With their job done, the framers returned to their regular lives as businesspeople, professionals, parents, partners, and citizens. In a country of three hundred thousand, the idea that one might serve the nation in some dramatic and historic way and then return to an ordinary life is widely accepted. Iceland is a place that needs more from everyone, which means that a farmer can also be a government minister, and a pastor can be a social critic who then writes the preamble to the nation's foundational document.

• • •

Of course, the demands Iceland places on citizens who are willing to accept responsibility are matched by opportunities. In a place so small, where competition is limited, pioneers and creative people can quietly nurture their ideas with less concern about imitators and naysayers. This advantage was magnified in Iceland's time of crisis. For a while, people were willing to consider almost any alternative, even a mock political movement called the Best Party, which declared that "we've come to the clean-out hour."[18]

Led by actor-comedian Jón Gnarr Kristinsson, the "Bests" adopted Tina Turner's "Simply the Best" as its theme song, but altered the lyrics to call for a city that's "cuddly and cool" with "fountains, wild animals, and electric trains." In their Reykjavik city election campaign, the Best Party called the country's previous leaders "squatters" and "blathering loons" and promised to break all of its own promises. Its platform called for construction of a new Disney resort and bringing a polar bear to the national zoo. To economize, the city would cut back to one ceremonial Santa every winter.

True to its name and claims, the Best Party won the most votes in the 2010 city elections, Jón became mayor of Reykjavik, and none of his outlandish campaign promises came to fruition. However, the new mayor did encourage cheerfulness by declaring September 1 "Hello Day," and had the city seal tattooed on his arm. He also set about reforming the municipal budget and made an entirely serious bid to bring the people of Reykjavik into the work of running their city through the Internet. Based on a concept called "electronic democracy," the scheme invites people to propose and vote for projects and priorities on a website called Better Reykjavik. It emerged from a wildfire of postcollapse initiatives that included a website called Shadow Parliament, which put every action in the parliament online, and Shadow City, which subjected the government of Reykjavik to the same scrutiny.

The shadow projects depended on computer programs that were cobbled together by a community of self-proclaimed democracy geeks who consider free access to information the lifeblood of good politics. It evolved into a permanent endeavor, the Citizens Foundation, which operates Better Reykjavik for the city but also licenses its democracy software—called Your Priorities—free of cost to communities and governments around the world. The program has advanced more than a dozen projects locally, from facilities for artists to fields trips for schoolchildren. Following Reykjavik's lead, the national government hired the Citizens Foundation to run its own citizen site called Better Iceland, where everything from health care to tourism—Should a water park be developed?—is up for discussion.

Around the world, Your Priorities technology has involved people in debate over the future of the Brazilian rainforest, the best agenda for the United Nations, and the prospects of the European economy. Online support for all this sharing and communication is managed from a hulking white industrial building on a gritty street called Skipholt. Once a commercial bakery, the high-ceilinged structure looks a little like an aircraft hangar from the 1930s. It houses artists' studios and a sprawling office-play space where Gunnar Grímsson and Robert Vidar Bjarnason believe they are "upgrading democracy for the twenty-first century."[19]

We arrived at the Citizens Foundation as the sun was setting. It was a little after three. Thick ice coated the sloped parking area in front of the building, which made shuffling to the door a dangerously slippery endeavor. Inside, the hot-water heat, which pours out of the Earth for free, made the space surprisingly warm. Gunnar and Robert met us with cups of herbal tea and led us to a big open area furnished like a dorm room—strings of Christmas lights, a foosball table, a piano, a bar strewn with empty cups and beer bottles. They plopped down on a dilapidated sofa and explained how crisis led to creativity.

"It came from being freaked out," recalled Gunnar. "People were angry. They wanted the government to fall, and they wanted reforms, but after they did resign, no one knew what to do. People were worried about basic things like 'Will there be food at the grocery store?' and 'Am I going to lose my home?'"

A stocky fellow with thinning brown hair and a scraggly goatee, Gunnar was raised by a father who worked as an iron smith and a mother who ran a children's clothing shop. "They saw the country go from poor to rich," he said. "They raised me to have a conscience and to care about what is going on around me." Gunnar's parents were hardly radicals. In fact, his first foray into politics, at age fourteen, brought him into a youth group of the Conservative Party. "It was a while before I declared myself some sort of anarchist," he said with a smile.

On this day, Gunnar is dressed in an orange, zippered cardigan and matching orange trousers. A regular at the annual Burning Man festival of radical self-expression in the Nevada desert, he seems at first to be cast in the slacker-anarchist mold of Nordic punks. In fact, he is a serious techie who helped start up Iceland's first Internet provider—Centrum.Is—and has taught programming and Web design for more than fifteen years. In that time, he had dabbled in protest politics, but never made it his central focus. His priorities changed when he joined the Pots-and-Pans Revolution.

"I realized that I could participate on a different level by using the Web to help organize, rather than stand in the protests myself," recalled Gunnar. Glued to a computer screen, he spent much of the fall and winter of 2008–2009 helping create online links for protest organizers and developing the Shadow Parliament and Shadow City projects.

The depth of the public outrage that arose after the country's economic crash caught Gunnar by surprise. Like most Icelanders, he was shocked when demonstrations turned violent. Police used pepper spray and tear gas, and pushed into crowds with their plastic shields thrust forward. Protesters responded with pushing, shoving, and rock throwing. At the worst moment, when even television viewers could see fear in the eyes of some young policemen, a few protesters stepped out of the crowd to protect them. Word spread that in the future, peacekeepers should wear orange to signal their solidarity with the protests and their commitment to nonviolence. Gunnar started wearing orange often.

Gunnar agreed with many many Icelanders who were weary of traditional politics. He found hope in the Internet. "The free flow of information and transparency are basic to the Web," he noted. "It helps us to actually see each other."

At Better Reykjavik and Better Iceland, people can see that they have more in common than they might have expected. Gunnar's partner, Robert, sees traditional Icelandic values coming to the fore. "When people are allowed to express themselves and they trust that the forum is open and safe, they do find consensus."[20] The broad consensus he sees emerging has to do with shared sacrifice and responsibility. "Until about ten years ago, you had the feeling that everyone in Iceland thought the society was moving forward together. That changed for a while when everyone began to think they should get more and more from themselves and if they couldn't earn it, they would just take out huge loans so they could get it."

Like many young Icelanders, Robert had left home to seek fortune and accomplishment, first in California and then in London. He had done so well as an entrepreneur that when the crisis arrived, he was able to return to Iceland and work at the non-profit foundation without too much concern about income. The move brought him full circle in his friendship with Gunnar. The two had met in 1984. Robert was a twelve-year-old who prowled electronics shops to find parts for his homemade computers. A bit older, Gunnar worked in one of those stores and helped Robert find the bits and pieces he needed. They worked together in the local computer industry before Robert went abroad. Together again, they find themselves motivated by much more than a shared interest in technology.

"It's a good feeling, giving people access to information, and it balances out some of the power that big business and big government can have over people," said Robert. Gunnar said, "You get better democracy by connecting the representatives to the people. And based on the way the politicians are responding, they actually seem to want to do a good job. That's not something I would have expected."

• • •

After the fall, people across Iceland looked for ways to feel good about themselves and their country while they nursed both anger and a feeling of innocence lost. "We thought we were special, the least corrupt, the most honest, and the most ethical," said Snorri Valsoon, the manager of the Hotel Holt in downtown Reykjavik.[21] "I guess everyone thinks they are exceptional, whether they are in London or New York, or Iceland. Now we're learning that we're just like everyone else. I mean, there was a guy running one of these banks who shifted his retirement accounts to foreign stocks six weeks before the collapse. Another demanded $1 million to keep working a month before his bank went under. It was really shocking."

From a business perspective, Snorri considered the hotels built during the boom times and others that underwent expensive renovations and said he was grateful that the owners of the Holt had paid off their mortgage long ago and resisted taking on debt. "We have some zombie hotels now," he said, referring to some that are open but losing money every month. "We've cut back on staff, but we're going to be okay."

"Okay" is not what it once was, in Iceland. Snorri and his wife just had a baby, but the paid maternity leave once covered by the state has been reduced. The loan on their apartment, which they bought as the crisis began, has gone up so steeply that he thinks "it will take me until I'm seventy years old to pay it off." Nevertheless, he feels fortunate to be old enough, at age thirty-one, that he was established in his job when the crisis arrived. "It's the young ones that have the most to worry about."

If Sandra Hrafnildur is right, young Icelanders will cope with the uncertainty in the country with perseverance and long-term thinking. Like many college graduates, Sandra has been unable to find work in her field, which is social work. We found her behind the counter at a gift shop called Woolcano, where a giant stuffed polar bear greets customers at the door. She admits she feels "a little bit angry" at the executives and politicians who knocked Iceland off its slow but gentle path toward prosperity and made prospects so tough for her generation.[22] However, she sees the end of the hypermasculine era as "an opportunity for us women to do things better."

Taking the challenge personally, Sandra started crafting inexpensive jewelry, including wire and crystal pendants that she sells at Woolcano and via the Internet. In the first three months, she netted a profit of 93,500 krona or roughly $725. She gave the money to a local charity that provides food and clothing to the homeless. Until the recent death of a homeless man, which had shocked Reykjavik, many locals had been unaware of the dozens of men and women who depended on the city's shelter. After his death, the needs of the homeless became a leading topic on the Better Reykjavik website.

"All of this doesn't have to end badly," said Sandra, surveying the emotional, political, and economic landscape her generation will inherit. "Most of our problems come from not understanding who we are and what we are doing. Now more voices are being heard, and I think more people are being understood. We're becoming ourselves again."

Chapter 3

Israel

"Power is about influence rather than control."
(74% agree)

The young soldier stood at a small roundabout on a deserted beachfront road north of the Israeli city of Netanya. Behind him, a sandy beach stretched to the blue Mediterranean. In front of him, arid parkland sprouted with sage and spiny shrubs. A duffle bag and overstuffed rucksack—both the same olive drab as his uniform—squatted at his feet. As we approached in our little rented car, he raised one hand to shield his squinting eyes from the bright sun and used the other to flag us down.

Inspired by the spirit of the country, we pulled over. In Hebrew and then in English, he begged a ride to the Yanai Interchange on Highway 2, where he was supposed to meet some fellows from his unit in the Israeli Defense Forces (IDF). They would travel together to Tel Aviv.

The soldier and his belongings were so heavy that our Fiat 500 sagged under the weight, and we needed to rev the tiny engine just to get it rolling. Once we were under way, he quizzed us about the United States and criticized the way universal military service binds Israelis to the cause of their country. At Yanai he said good-bye and *shalom* and shook our hands. We felt as though we had done our good deed for the day. We had not.

• • •

"Where did you pick him up?"[1]

Two minutes into our meeting at IDF headquarters with Brigadier General Rachel Weisel, our little anecdote about the hitchhiking soldier ceased to be a charming icebreaker and instead became a smile-smothering point of contention. We described the road up north and said something about how everyone in Israel seemed so generous and friendly that it seemed almost a duty to offer a ride. We didn't know the soldier's name, and, given our overall ignorance of all things military, we couldn't describe any of the insignia he wore or even note his rank.

"Well, you were wrong, but you didn't know better. He was wrong, and he did know better—and he's in trouble."

As it turned out, the IDF has a long institutional memory that includes the case of a hitchhiking sergeant who was picked up by Palestinian fighters and then killed, along with one of his rescuers, when commandoes tried to free him. The military was about to begin a big campaign to stop soldiers from thumbing altogether.

With sigh and a look that said, "How stupid can you guys be?" the general promised an investigation and then dropped the subject. We hadn't endured the background checks and security screenings required to access IDF headquarters for a lesson in travel safety. We had come to discuss masculinity, femininity, and Israel. Of course, Weisel's reaction to our poor judgment demonstrated the value of more than one traditionally feminine trait. Perceptive and keenly attuned to right and wrong, she noted our ignorance and the soldier's carelessness without actually humiliating us. Her words persuaded us never to stop for another hitchhiker in Israel, or anywhere else, for the rest of our lives. Her tone, which was light on military bark and bite and heavy on instruction, preserved the harmony in the room and let us proceed with the business at hand.

The general's blunt response to our stupid choice demonstrated perfectly the Athena trait we hoped to find in Israel: candor. As our survey results showed, people place a high value on feminine qualities related to candor, including the open expression of feelings (77 percent favor this). We suspected that honest and clear communication would be most important in a country where people live every day on the edge of conflict. It's hard to imagine a place where miscommunication would have more serious consequences than this country, where sworn enemies live side-by-side and provocateurs are constantly trying to stir up trouble.

Isolated in a region where many of its neighbors are avowed enemies and recent battlefield opponents, Israel faces more external threats than any small country on Earth. It must also cope with the constant possibility of terror attacks, including suicide bombing within its borders, and Israeli citizens facing the danger of terrorism when they travel abroad.

With a population of roughly eight million, Israel can't afford to exclude anyone from the work of building and preserving the nation. Like Israeli men, Israeli women have always been subject to conscription—today, even combat roles are open to them. Those who possess such traditionally feminine qualities as patience and empathy can prove invaluable in danger spots like the checkpoints where traffic flows in and out of Palestinian territories.

"It's a different point of view," Weisel told us as she considered a female soldier at a checkpoint. At checkpoints, people waiting to be screened often resent the inconvenience and the feeling of being treated with suspicion. The wrong word or touch can incite loud protests and even physical confrontation. A woman who can approach a tense situation with empathy will recognize that showing people respect and kindness can save lives. These qualities also make the army itself function in a more informed, disciplined, and deliberate way.

"The old idea" was that the IDF was a macho boys' club where the most aggressive risk-takers rose to the top. Israeli men made lifelong friendships as they conducted everyday duties and more dangerous missions—and this experience gave them bragging rights for a lifetime. Today's commanders encourage a more thoughtful approach that depends on observation, data collection, and analysis. Weisel describes this as "a wider view," influenced by the perspective of women officers. "You know that if a woman participates in a [difficult] decision like going to war," she added, "all of the implications are going to be considered."

Weisel served under the IDF's only female major general, a formidable woman named Orna Barbivai, who commands the Personnel Directorate from a corner office in the Matkal building, which is Israel's Pentagon. On the day we met her, Barbivai had spent much of her day in meetings devoted to research and development of military technology. Drones, satellites, and other advances give soldiers lethal options that were once the stuff of science fiction. This power makes careful, informed decision making all the more essential. Officers especially "have to have a broader perspective than what you see looking through a gun sight," Barbivai said.[2]

With an intense and focused stare, Barbivai has the look of a woman who has peered through a few gun sights in her time. Dressed in military-issue green trousers and a black cardigan with epaulets, she still resembles the young woman in a framed photo she keeps on her windowsill. It's a picture of her on the day she enlisted in 1981, at age eighteen. She also keeps a framed copy of "The Spirit of the IDF"—the IDF's ethical code—on her wall, and she refers to it often. "All humans are to be valued, regardless of race, creed, nationality, gender, status or role," it states.[3]

Barbivai told us that there are those who believe that upholding the IDF's code may come more naturally to women, who, she believes, excel at negotiating to avert conflict. For this reason, she often stations female soldiers at the front lines—including her two daughters. (Her younger daughter served in the IDF border police in the Judea and Samaria region, and her older daughter is currently a major serving as a senior personnel officer in the Navy.) Barbivai believes that they more readily use respectful communication and negotiation to avert violence.

•••

The kind of moral course promoted by General Barbivai (and informed by historic Jewish experience with injustice) informs innovators across Israeli society, although some are reluctant to say that a feminine energy could be powering their efforts. At age fifty, Yadin Kaufmann was one of Israel's most aggressive investors, and his firm, Veritas Venture Partners, sported an enviable track record in high-tech start-ups and initial public offerings. Kaufmann had helped lead Israel's sprint into the software and medical technology industries. This strategy, which depends on a highly educated and skilled workforce, boosted Israel to number thirty in the U.S. government's ranking of gross domestic product per capita. Israel stands ahead of Italy, Spain, and many other older societies, and grew briskly while the Great Recession hobbled most other nations.

We met Kaufmann in the bustling little city of Ra'anana (population roughly ninety thousand), where Veritas occupies the third floor of a shiny new office building. We saw signs of Israel's robust technology sector all over Ra'anana. Microsoft, Hewlett-Packard, SAP, and many other big names in technology operate nearby. More significant are the homegrown technology firms that hum inside big new buildings that have risen near farms on the north side of the city. Here, where industrial parks bump up against newly planted fields, the landscape could be mistaken for the edge of Silicon Valley.

A taut and tanned man with an angular face and a runner's build, Kaufmann spoke in the firm and measured manner of a person who targets objectives with precision and pursues them with passion. Through Veritas he and his partners have provided or coordinated funding for dozens of technology firms; many have since been sold to larger concerns or gone public through stock offerings.

Focusing on communications, software, and health care, Kaufmann raised money from investors all over the world and backed dozens of start-ups. Many of these firms grew into substantial companies with global reputations. But as he piled one success on another, Kaufmann recognized that professional and financial successes weren't enough. He longed for a way to address the needs of other people and, more broadly, Israeli society. Always interested in job creation and finding solutions to social problems, he became fascinated by the Hebrew word *tmura*, which means both "metamorphosis" and "gift of transcendent value." Kaufmann then considered what he knew about start-up businesses and devised a plan to get the entrepreneurs he met into service projects with a long-range horizon.

Chronically overworked and generally short on cash, Israel's ambitious entrepreneurs rarely had time or money to give, even though most longed for some way outside their work to make the world a better place. However, as they started their companies, all these go-getters held substantial equity in their own firms—equity worth very little in the beginning but possessing high growth potential. Kaufmann began pitching them the idea of contributing stock and stock options to an organization he called Tmura (a Hebrew word meaning both "metamorphosis" and "value for money"). Labeled a "public service venture fund," Tmura would be free to sell its donated shares when the donor firm went public or a buyer came along, and then distribute the proceeds to worthy applicants. Kaufmann would favor projects benefiting children and poor neighborhoods, but the final decisions would be made by an independent board.

Kaufmann began pitching the concept in 2002 and discovered that many of the engineers, scientists, and businesspeople in Israel's burgeoning tech sector were extremely receptive to a way to connect with the community outside their air-conditioned offices. "There is a real perception, and sometimes it's a reality, that the high-tech sector exists in some sort of bubble," he explained to us.[4] "If you are inside the bubble, you know you are isolated, and if you are at all sensitive to what's going on in the world, you want to do something about it."

Kaufmann's sales pitch was aided by the fact that he was someone entrepreneurs knew and trusted. He recruited Baruch Lipner, a Canadian immigrant, to run the organization, and in roughly a decade, they and their colleagues built up a sponsor list of more than 250 companies that gave stock and stock options to Tmura. As firms succeeded (or failed), the portfolio grew to more than $6 million, and Tmura gave grants to a host of public ventures, including Big Brothers and Big Sisters of Israel, a network of youth centers called Kadima, the Tel Aviv Rape Crisis Center, and a group called Technoda, which brings science and technology education to children in poorer families.

Today, with many donor companies becoming stable and profitable, Tmura is on track to becoming self-sustaining. Yadin spoke proudly of his creation, but as he talked, he used his thumb to rhythmically click the mechanism of a ballpoint pen. Working the pen at a rate of more than eighty clicks per minute, he changed the topic to discuss a profit-making initiative with regional implications.

For years, Kaufmann had thought about finding a way to use some of the experience, networks, and knowledge that had been developed in the Israeli high-tech and venture sectors, to help establish entrepreneurship elsewhere in the Middle East. "In 2006, I began getting to know Palestinians involved in the nascent tech sector in Ramallah," he recalled. "Some of them had begun doing outsourced software development work for California-based Cisco Systems, through Cisco's office in Netanya, Israel—and Cisco was getting great results. What I found in Ramallah reminded me in many ways of what we had seen in Israel in the 1980s." Some of Kaufmann's early Palestinian contacts introduced him to Saed Nashef, who had recently returned to the region after many years in the United States with Microsoft and a couple of start-ups and who was now back trying to help build a technology sector. Educated in computer science at California State University, Long Beach, Nashef had started an outsourcing company called Equiom Mena. Energetic, ambitious, and talented, he was a familiar kind of person, very much like the entrepreneurs Kaufmann funded in Herzliya, and the two immediately clicked.

Kaufmann, who had seen the impact of a technology sector in Israel, believed that helping in the development of a similar industry in the Palestinian Territories could both represent a significant and untapped business opportunity and also have major "social" implications for Palestinians and, by extension, their Israeli neighbors. Together, Kaufmann and Nashef decided to try to raise a fund that would invest in Internet and mobile technology companies originating in the West Bank's small but developing community of technology entrepreneurs. The U.S.-based firm, called Sadara Ventures, would be the first fund dedicated to information technology start-ups in the Palestinian Territories. Not a charity, the fund was established with the goal of providing "financial returns for its investors" while aiding in "the development of a vibrant and sustainable knowledge-based economy in Palestine."

With Kaufmann and Nashef shuttling potential investors in and out of the West Bank and putting their own credibility on the line, Sadara built a $30 million war chest with checks from a number of global institutions and individuals who admired the twin goals of the enterprise. On the day we met, the company had screened the first round of applicants and signed a term sheet to provide money to its first start-up.

Referring to the Palestinian regions as "green fields" awaiting development, Kaufmann spoke with the excitement of a man whose long-running interest in nurturing peace had finally found an outlet. When we asked if his empathy for Nashef and his commitment to cooperation weren't "a little bit" feminine, he squirmed in his chair and clicked his pen. "You're not going to get me to say that," he said. "But I will say that it has been a matter of listening, showing respect, and being sensitive to the needs of the other side. Call it what you want. I just think it's what needs to be done right now."

• • •

Yadin Kaufmann squirmed when we asked him about the "feminine" side of his ambitions because he was a man who possessed a strong competitive drive and lived in a country that many consider masculine to its core. According to the Israeli cliché, raw power elicits respect, and anything softer invites defeat. But a counternarrative, one that elevates community, cooperation, emotion, and creativity, has always been a part of the national story too. When older, native-born "sabras" (also the name of a local cactus) talk about the nation's founding and early decades, they invariably speak of the shared sacrifice and cooperation that were essential to survival. These traditionally feminine responses to a profound challenge are as much a part of the Israeli character as physical courage and mental toughness.

Born in Israel to a Polish father and an Israeli mother, Hana Hertsman comes from the pioneer stock that created the nation of Israel. She grew up on a farm on the Plain of Sharon, where her father was known as a local politician and the man who invented an advanced type of irrigation system and a cure for a disease that afflicted local olive groves. She recalled an idyllic childhood as the "spoiled daughter" of the entire rural community. The idyll was shattered when she was sixteen and her parents were involved in a high-speed car wreck. Her father was killed. Her mother suffered massive injuries.

As the eldest child, a teenage Hertsman became the head of the family and threw herself into the job. She cared for her mother through a long and difficult rehabilitation, and when she reached the age for military service, she enlisted to fulfill her duty. In the army, Hertsman performed so well that she was promoted to the officer corps. During her four years in the IDF, Hertsman saw the positive effects of strong leadership and ingenuity and the negative effects of excessive ego. Soon after she left the service and began working in personnel management, she saw that many of her male colleagues displayed the strength and ego from their IDF days—but had lost their ingenuity and passion.

Hired to work with the municipal manager in the city of Holon, Hertsman found a moribund bureaucracy filled with people pushing paper, and a community in decline. Unlike its immediate neighbor, Tel Aviv, Holon was losing businesses and population. Real estate values declined, and public facilities—parks, schools, streets, and sidewalks—deteriorated. When a new mayor, Moti Sasson, was elected in 1993, he gave Hertsman the chance to move into the city manager's post and plan Holon's recovery. Mindful of reelection, Sasson told her he needed both immediate improvements and a long-term vision.

We met Hertsman on an evening when rush hour on the streets of Holon was subsiding and most of the offices in City Hall were dark. She bustled around an office jammed full of souvenirs and gifts collected during her twenty years of service to the city. A no-nonsense woman, she wore her dark hair cropped short and conservative hoop earrings. Behind her, a poster she acquired in South America showed a strong woman flexing a bicep and smiling confidently. As Hertsman told us how she and the mayor had led the transformation of Holon, we began to think of her as the biceped woman in the poster.

Back in 1993, Hertsman saw Holon's crisis in a holistic way, believing it needed not just development but an identity. Noting that Tel Aviv was a cultural center and a magnet for young single adults, she saw an opening for Holon to serve families and, more specifically, children. At a conference for municipal leaders, she scrawled "Holon—City of Children" on a chalkboard and solicited ideas for making the slogan a reality. The group agreed that Holon would offer safe neighborhoods, superior education, and better recreation opportunities. They also recognized that these goals would have to be reached without extra money or city workers.

Although she was committed to the ambition, Hertsman joined it with a modesty that insisted that no one make a claim to improvement, or excellence, until it had been achieved. Hertsman motivated more than a thousand city workers with enthusiastic talks about the long-term effects of early childhood. She taught them about the vital nature of early education—that it sets the template for life—and persuaded them that a community could make itself into a nurturing, child-focused place. And beyond doing "good" for future generations, the City of Children project could make the city livable for all and reverse the decline in real estate.

City employees who wanted to keep their jobs were required to buy in to the plan. To shake them out of their complacency, Hertsman shifted her key managers to new departments. The head of the city's building office became education chief. The director of youth programs took over recycling, where absenteeism was high and morale low. Excited by the challenge, the new director inspired the sanitation workers to take pride in creating a city devoted to children. Absenteeism went down. Performance rose.

Drawing on the experience of other cities, Holon's team turned one shuttered school into a national children's museum and another into an art center with an emphasis on hands-on experiences. The arts became a central element of the city's rebirth, as music, literary, and dance programs were created to serve every age group. Much of this creative work was done at little or no cost because Hertsman had the chutzpah to ask. Artists filled a "story garden" with sculptures of characters from famous children's books, and illustrators donated their work to a cartoon museum. More works of art were planted in highway medians and in ordinary parks.

Of course, pleas for help could only go so far. When plans to rebuild schools and other facilities required funding, Hertsman slashed the bureaucracy, cutting hundreds of jobs. These moves set off an intense battle with municipal workers. Hundreds went on strike. Death threats were telephoned to Hertsman's home. Her car was set on fire. For three months she didn't go anywhere without a bodyguard. But as citizens and municipal workers began to see that Holon could function well with a leaner bureaucracy, the conflict cooled.

Once the spirit of renewal took hold in the city, neighborhoods began to clamor for improvements. New parks, including Israel's largest water park, were spotted around the city, bringing the total of green spaces to more than three hundred acres. As the look and feel of the community changed, families stopped fleeing for the suburbs. Three years ago, the trend was reversed as Holon began to gain population. New residential construction projects were approved for sites that would be connected by sections of sand dunes that would be preserved in perpetuity.

The dunes echo with meaning in the minds and hearts of Holon's residents. The word *holon* means "dunes" in Hebrew, and when the region was settled in 1924, the pioneers found nothing but the yellow dunes and the occasional sycamore tree. Battles raged in the dunes during Israel's war of independence. In times of peace, the dunes offered a place for children to play and a glimpse of what was once the natural landscape.

Holon's turnaround is a testament to long-term planning, collaboration, and a shared commitment to nurturing the young. Hertsman brought local businesses and industry into the effort with an office dedicated to their needs, and she has lured investment dollars to the city by showing off Holon's quality of life to people looking for a places to build new offices and factories. This was all done with an almost maternal focus on future generations. Considering how this approach will reverberate through the years, Hertsman predicted that children nurtured in the shelter of Holon will want to raise their own families in the same way and the same place.

The City of Children that Hana Hertsman imagined in 1993 became so real that by 2010, Holon was recognized worldwide. A survey of residents found that more than 80 percent of the people were satisfied with their lives, and more than three-quarters would urge their out-of-town friends to move to Holon. The city's popularity with young families spurred the construction of new schools and kindergartens. Today, officials are working on ways to contain Holon's growth to allow it to remain a boutique city of about 250,000 where families can be comfortable.

●●●

Rated a miniature Bilbao by travel writers, Holon is one of two Israeli cities that have gained international acclaim in the past decade through innovative leadership. The other, greater Tel Aviv, was saved from the brink of bankruptcy by a former high school principal named Ron Huldai, who became mayor in 1998. Upon taking office, Huldai focused on quality of life in the city, creating what he called "human ecosystems" in various neighborhoods to attract smart, ambitious young people. Fifteen years later, Tel Aviv was home to dozens of new theaters and museums, nearly two thousand bars and nightclubs, and a booming high-tech industry.

Construction cranes filled the sky as developers built new apartment towers and shopping centers. New construction and major renovations were done at the Tel Aviv Museum of Art, Habima National Theatre, and Tel Aviv Cinémathèque. Tourism boomed as more than 2.7 million people flocked to enjoy the city's Mediterranean beaches and sophisticated nightlife.

We caught up with the mayor at the reception marking the start of ArtWeekend 2012, which brought hundreds of people to a renovated waterfront warehouse at an abandoned railway station called HaTachana. The redevelopment project, which produced a restaurant and retail complex, is one of Huldai's most visible. It draws thousands of visitors nightly. At the art opening, several hundred packed into a brick-and-timber space and gazed at paintings that were mainly modern and impressionistic in style. Huldai enjoyed the spectacle, but didn't take much credit for the energy behind the city's boom.

"I am a very commonsense man," he said, noting that his method of leadership calls for small developments, such as bike paths, that offer incremental improvements in the quality of life.[5] "The point is not to find the big solution for anything," he said over the din of the party. "The goal is to simply do better, even if it's just a little better." This task has been made easier by dramatic reductions in attacks on Israel by Palestinians and their supporters in the last decade. Though highly controversial, construction of a security wall was followed by a dramatic drop in bombings. The relative peace and quiet is credited by many to have prompted an increased sense of confidence in Tel Aviv. (However, dissenters say that the public has disengaged from important political issues that still wait to be addressed.)

After fourteen years on the job, sixty-eight-year-old Huldai moved and talked as though he were born into the role of big-city mayor. He has visited his counterparts in Europe, America, and even Vietnam, where he discovered that the mayor of Hanoi has the same goal: to create a livable, working city where people can live happy, contented lives. In Tel Aviv, he is certain that this agenda requires respect for diversity. The city was rated one of the best for gay tourists by *Time Out* magazine, but it is also home to a strong religious community. "Contradictions and pluralism are a fact here, and for that reason you have to be tolerant."

Tolerance depends on constant communication, and for this Huldai relies on new media like Facebook and Twitter. These Internet channels cut out the middlemen of the mainstream media, allowing Huldai to speak directly to his constituents. "It's perfect for me. I can correct what the newspaper and television say about me," he says with a smile. It also allows citizens to bring their concerns to him in an equally direct way. What he hears about, on a regular basis, is the high cost of living, the terrible state of mass transit, and the frustrations of the young.

"I listen," said Huldai. It's one of the skills he acquired from his parents, who lived much of their lives on a farm collective, called a kibbutz. "I heard from my mother, every day, that we are all human beings and deserve the same respect. What I know is that very often, one guy is 'right' but the other guy is 'right,' too. This is the nature of life. We are not looking for the one solution. We are looking to get along and improve, just a little."

As we later learned, however, this ability to get along and improve is not without significant challenges and setbacks.

• • •

On July 7, 2011, Daphni Leef pitched a tent in Habima Square, where four major streets converge, and major theaters mark the cultural center of the city. With this dramatic gesture, she asked that her neighbors consider the challenge that Tel Aviv's young are facing as they try to make it in the big city. Despite "making my world as small and inexpensive as possible," Leef had been priced out of the housing market in the city and was running out of options to avoid homelessness. Worse, she felt that the Israeli "we're all in this together" spirit was being lost.[6] With a post on Facebook headlined "Take a Tent Take a Stand," she invited others to join her living on the sidewalk to protest.

Even before the uprising of the Arab Spring and by Occupy Wall Street, young Israelis from across the country flocked to join Daphni for the "tent-in." Within one month, four hundred tents crowded the streets, and the protesters had organized themselves into a functioning community complete with food and sanitation services, communications, entertainment, and educational programs. Peaceful and relatively quiet, the gathering never seemed to pose a threat to the local community; it actually led to increased business for cafés and shops in the area.

Along with the crowd, the subject of the protests grew to take in a host of complaints about inequality in the economy, much like the Occupy protest in America that followed. The main difference was that the Israeli version accomplished some of its purpose: the Israeli cabinet approved a plan to build two hundred thousand apartments for low- and middle-income renters, to raise taxes on wealthy individuals and corporations, and to provide expanded and free kindergartens for all children ages three to five. A twenty-five-year-old woman with a Facebook account and a hunger for community had moved a nation.

We met Daphni at a Tel Aviv café, where the conversation was fueled by espresso and ice cream drizzled with honey. Much in demand due to her startling success as an organizer, she arrived a bit late and a bit disheveled, her black cardigan falling off one shoulder and her bright orange scarf askew, carrying a tablet computer and smartphone in hand. Born in Jerusalem, she is the daughter of a prominent composer and descended from some of the earliest Zionist settlers.

Before she became an activist, Daphni worked as a freelance film editor and struggled to support herself. In her short adult life, the competition for work had grown more intense, and rents had tripled. The last straw came when her landlord gave her three weeks to move out because he planned to convert the building to luxury apartments that could be priced much higher. Her protest idea was born in a moment she called "an emergency," and she sparked a cascade of responses when she mistakenly clicked "invite all" to send a Facebook posting she intended for a few friends. Among her twelve hundred contacts were hundreds of people who also worked in media. They forwarded the invitation to thousands of people, and thus a movement was born.

The Tel Aviv protesters recognized that their government would ultimately facilitate the solutions to their problems—the point of their protest was to get the government to listen. Day by day, Daphni told us, she and her fellow protesters tried to communicate with the prime minister and the government, with the intent of making the government people uncomfortable until they did something. As the Tel Aviv gatherings swelled to fill several city blocks, smaller protests occurred across Israel, even in Arab and Druze villages. The result was that "people who had never really met each other came together around needs that they had in common." In Daphni's view, the policy shifts that came in response to the outpouring of public demands reflected a level of empathy inherent in human nature. Although deemed to be traditionally feminine, this sensitivity to the distress shown by others is also vital to any politician, male or female, who might want to win election or reelection.

Daphni's success brought her worldwide attention. Two weeks after we met, she was in America as a guest of the Clinton Global Initiative, explaining to an auditorium that her movement was not spun out of desire to take over the world, but simply to have a decent life.

Yet months later, in June 2012, Daphni attempted to revive the social protests on Tel Aviv's Rothschild Boulevard—but this time the police confronted the activists, preventing the crowd from pitching tents and setting up camp. Chaos ensued, resulting in the arrest of Daphni and eleven others. As protesters chanted "Democracy" in the background, officers deposited her into a police van and drove her away to a police station. According to Daphni, her requests for medical treatment while in police custody went unanswered for seven hours. The following night, people gathered in downtown Tel Aviv to voice their opposition to the police. Again, police turned out in force, arresting eighty-five.

The arrests marked a role reversal for Mayor Huldai, who had been conciliatory toward the 2011 protests. They also showed that although Athena values are gaining ground in Israeli society, progress is not linear, and setbacks are frequent.

For her part, Daphni goes undeterred, using courage and communication—two primary elements in the Athena paradigm—to advocate change in Israeli society. It was a "from the guts" appeal to common humanity, she said, that brought Israel together to address serious problems. This same combination has been used by those pressing for solutions to even tougher, larger-scale problems.

• • •

We literally ran into Shai Reshef in the lobby of a Tel Aviv hotel as he was returning from the United States, where he spends roughly half his time working out of an office in Pasadena, California. Like Daphni Leef, Shai is trying to organize and inspire people to band together for a higher purpose. The big difference is that he is targeting the entire world. His vehicle is a shockingly simple yet ambitious Web-based enterprise called University of the People, which offers free online courses from some of the best college professors in the world, to any student in the world.

A few months short of fifty-seven, Shai exuded the energy of a much younger man. In fact, he said, he was energized by the reception his project has received from governments and universities who might have resisted his overtures a decade ago. "People recognize that education is the thing that will make the difference everywhere in the world," he said. "And there is more goodwill out there than you can even imagine."[7]

Goodwill is the main source of energy behind University of the People, which Shai began in 2009 with $1 million from the fortune he acquired developing and selling Israel's first test preparation service to Kaplan, an American education firm. Since then, he has formed alliances with professors at schools around the world, who make their online courses available and volunteer to mentor students. Students must pay a $10 to $50 fee to apply for admission (it's based on the gross domestic product of their home country), and they must pass a test to show they are proficient in English and familiar with computers. Instruction is provided free of charge. Students do much of the learning together in online "classrooms" of twenty to thirty men and women. These groups are monitored and led by the professors, who answer questions and provide direction.

In theory and in practice, University of the People mixes education with social interaction in a way that opens minds and hearts. "Survivors of genocide in Rwanda have study buddies at Harvard, and every time a Palestinian kid takes a class, he is almost certain to encounter an Israeli," explained Shai. "What they both discover is that as supposed enemies they are much closer, in cultural terms, than they ever imagined. This is especially true of young people. Everywhere it seems that young people believe that they can accomplish really great things only by working together. Heroes today are the people who have a lot of 'likes' on Facebook, not the people who go it alone and act like they don't need anyone else."

Of the more than one million "likes" accumulated by University of the People on Facebook, two-thirds have been posted by people in the Muslim world, which Shai takes as a sign that people everywhere appreciate the value of education. The lessons offered in the school's most popular courses, business management and computer science, can be applied anywhere in the world, regardless of local language and customs. They are delivered in a form that doesn't require high-speed Internet service, which is essential, as roughly half the students who have signed up for University of the People access the curriculum at Internet cafés with less than optimum service. Roughly one hundred students attend via satellite Internet service powered by generators at two student centers opened with partners in Haiti.

Since 2009, enrollment in the university has grown to thirteen hundred students in 130 countries. Shai's supporters include the director of the Indian Institute of Technology, the vice chancellor of the University of Oxford, and the president of New York University. Last year, NYU announced that it would open enrollment to University of the People students at its new campus in Abu Dhabi and grant credit for courses completed with the online university. The very first student accepted flew in an airplane for the first time when he went to attend an orientation program in the United Arab Emirates. His success is the product of low- and no-cost technology, his own drive, and the selfless commitment of volunteer educators from around the world.

"This is an idea that gives people who have a lot, like me and all the others who volunteer, a chance to give back and do something on behalf of the world," said Shai. "It started with the thought that, you know, we really should try peace for a change. We should try helping people to develop themselves no matter where in the world they might be." Considering freedom movements around the globe, including the Arab Spring uprisings in the Arab world, Shai noted that they were as much about the desire for opportunity as they were about politics. The impulse to share and teach represented by a free online university can give hope to those who would lead communities and countries into a more peaceful age. "We're only beginning to see the benefit of what goes on between people in settings like this that bring learning across borders," he said excitedly. "I can imagine this being a model for all kinds of projects that will change the world."

●●●

The subject of courage arises time and again when activist Israelis talk about confronting their own society with difficult questions. In a country of sharp elbows, it takes a special blend of toughness and commitment—to one's home, one's neighbors, and one's ideals—to speak truth to power. As a host of a TV news show called *Uvda* (Truth), Ilana Dayan may be the most outspoken journalist in her country's mainstream media. A military veteran with a law degree, Dayan has endured repeated lawsuits for her reports on corruption and crime.

A short fireplug of a women with neat blond hair and a tough exterior, Dayan met us at her TV studio, where we talked in an office that was almost all business, except for her son's drawing of the cartoon character SpongeBob. One of the most feared investigative reporters in the Middle East, Dayan told us that she had recently begun to approach her subjects with more empathy and patience. And it is working.

"I recently had a special experience," she explained.[8] "I met this woman whose brother, a lawyer, allegedly murdered his parents because of gambling debts (hoping, presumably, to put his hands on their money). I went to see her with a research assistant named Yaara. As the meeting started, I told the sister, 'There's no good reason for you to do an interview with us unless you think telling the story of yourself and your family will make you feel good, will say something about your family and about who your parents were.' I left the choice completely up to her, and I didn't pressure her at that point."

Dayan said she left the meeting not knowing what her subject would decide. "Later Yaara asked me, 'Was that a tactic, or did you really mean it?' I told her, 'It's both. I put myself in her position and realized that she knows what's good for her, not me. She must come to the decision.'"

In the end, Dayan got her interview, and the experience taught her something she couldn't have known as an assertive cub reporter. (In the old days, she was so aggressive that she once ripped a telephone line out of a wall to prevent another reporter from filing a story.) By acknowledging the feelings and needs of the people she interviews, she wins their trust and cooperation. In the end, the product of her work is improved by the person-to-person bonds she forms with even the most challenging people. The method has worked with a range of subjects, including an orthodox rabbi accused of sexually molesting minors, and mothers of soldiers killed in combat. Dayan sees her growth into this way of working as an example of change in the larger society. She sees Israel as becoming a kinder place, more cooperative and receptive to different styles of work and leadership.

"This society is changing very rapidly," said Dayan, as she packed a backpack for an upcoming trip to Pakistan. "One of the most important changes is the ascent of women to real power. Right now women are the leaders of three Israeli political parties." Besides these three, Dayan counts women in finance, the military, and business as major influences, leavening the old, macho military way. But this doesn't mean that women leaders, and men who can think like them, are pushovers.

"One of my friends has a daughter who is a commander in an infantry unit," she noted. "She was having this problem with soldiers who wouldn't get up in the morning on time. I was so flattered when she told me that she thought to herself, 'What would Ilana do?' And then she imitated my voice as she yelled, 'You get up now!' It worked."

•••

The change represented by Ilana Dayan is probably as broad and deep as she reported. And as women have risen in all sectors of Israeli society, their leadership has been recognized and embraced by many men. The most visible among them was an eighty-nine-year-old man who was born into the ultra-Orthodox Jewish community, served with the fighters who created the state of Israel, and long stood as a hawk on defense issues. By 2012, however, Shimon Peres, president of Israel, was an ardent peace advocate who had staffed his office mainly with women and used his position to argue for communication, compassion, and leadership based on Jewish morality.

Many Israelis know that Peres had brought a new way of working to the office of the president, and it seemed essential that we visit the presidential palace and see it for ourselves. Efrat Duvdevani, Peres's director general, welcomed us on a sunny afternoon when tourists filled the streets of old Jerusalem and military officials prepared a swearing-in ceremony for new soldiers at the historic Western Wall of the Temple Mount. Duvdevani has worked with Peres for over seventeen years, since the assassination of former prime minister Yitzhak Rabin, and brings with her a belief in the power of female management and the importance of placing women in senior roles:

"All the leading positions here at the Office of the President are held by women, most of them mothers," Duvdevani told us.[9] "Women have to combine many aspects of their lives into one life—and if the work place facilitates this, then everyone gains. The modern world can provide solutions for working mothers—with technology you can work at any hour and through the night—it's how the modern economy should be.

"Today you have to have happy employees; they have to feel taken care of, and it's more than money," she said.

In her office, we found about a dozen crowded around a low table set with pots of tea and cold water—Duvdevani wants everyone involved in the conversation, so everyone gets a seat. The women who joined us, and they were all women, held top positions as aides and advisers, and the main point they wanted to make was that collaboration, not ego, made the place work.

"The world is so complicated that you must have different people with different expertise putting their heads together to solve problems," said Duvdevani. "Here it's a matter of teamwork, teamwork, teamwork. And once again, teamwork."

Women, she believes, are exemplary of teamwork and are well rounded in the workplace, adept at understanding multiple perspectives. Speaking of her staff, she noted, "My legal adviser knows very well how the media works. The person responsible for the budget knows what's happening on the legal side and understands public opinion. In the past, the focus was on one-dimensional professionalism, with employees encouraged to be experts in their own field only."

She added, "Today the workforce requires excellence and an ability to combine different fields, to work together and to put ego aside. My approach to management is based upon cooperation, brainstorming together, and getting everybody's input; it is an approach built for the complex environment in which we operate. The traits needed for this approach to work shine through with women."

For his part, President Peres had just recently returned from a trip to America, where he met with President Obama and visited the main offices of Google, Facebook, and IBM, serving as an authoritative voice not only of Israel but also of the larger international community. At every turn, he reminded his hosts of the cause of peace. Noting how Facebook brought the world together online, he told chief operating office Sheryl Sandberg, "What you are doing is convincing people they don't have reason to hate."

In a meeting with President Obama, Peres spoke about the Arab Spring revolutions and the role that women could play in resolving the hostilities that have marked Israel's relations with the Muslim world. "He knows that women think about the consequences of what they do," explained Duvdevani. When we asked her to elaborate on the president's point, she smiled and then turned to a colleague for a brief consultation in Hebrew. Then she turned back and suggested we ask him ourselves. Minutes later, we were ushered past security guards and into the office where the president worked, surrounded by books and mementoes of his long political life.

Though still recovering from the rigors of travel abroad, Peres sprang out of the chair he occupied at a big desk and beamed as he welcomed us for a discussion around what he considers one of society's most profound issues: the critical importance of women in creating a more peaceful, harmonious society. He immediately recalled that when he had visited the White House, "President Obama asked me, 'What's holding back democracy and peace in the Middle East?' I answered him by saying, 'The husbands.'"[10] As Peres elaborated, it became clear that he was referring to men who jealously excluded others from power and governed through aggression. Too many husbands and fathers inhibit the region's progress toward peace by failing to educate their children, he said, and by discouraging their wives and daughters from getting involved in larger society. If they could conduct the dialogue, Arab women and Jewish women would create peace in short order, he said. "But right now too many husbands won't let their wives participate."

Peres said that the world has reached a moment of transformation that made him feel optimistic and excited. First, technology, in the form of Facebook, Twitter, and other forms of unbridled communications, allows for people to discover the truth about their leaders, to build mass movements for change, and to rally people to action. "Zuckerberg," he said, referring to Facebook founder Mark Zuckerberg, "is creating a greater revolution than Marx or Lenin." At the same time, the globalization of trade, which requires that companies work effectively across borders and cultures, is creating new avenues for communication and cooperation.

Second, Peres noted that there are no longer any national economies—only one global economy. As a result, global corporations "are unintentionally in the position of being asked to fulfill a moral role," he said. "A global company cannot afford to be racist because you cannot sell your products all over the world without goodwill. They must be multicultural and multinational. Globalization opens eyes." When eyes are opened, "it's hard to behave like a dictator because dictators can only operate in darkness."

The president spoke enthusiastically of his late-life conversion to what he called a "more feminine" leadership style that emphasizes flexibility, humility, diversity of opinion, and service. "We are in a new world with many old minds, and the task is to adapt yourself," he said. "Don't exaggerate. You are not so great. You are not so wise." A modern leader "is there to serve. Nothing gives me greater pleasure than to serve. If I go to sleep at night and I can think 'I served today,' then I feel good."

Once a hawk, now a dove, Shimon Peres showed by example how both a man and a country can evolve. Israel cannot afford to leave the strengths of women on the sidelines as it develops into a mature country, and, Peres insisted, the world cannot thrive by neglecting the feminine half of human nature. He credits women, who give birth to future generations, with "the real acts of creation" and a perspective that respects the future and promotes peace. Late in life, he has come to live and lead by this perspective as an old lion of the Zionist cause. "Men will not stop warring," he said. "Women will not stop pacifying. They know that wars are unhealthy."

Chapter 4

Japan

*"Real change will only come about if we are
patient and able to plan for the future."*
(71% agree)

One scientist who measured of the force of the 2011 Sendai
earthquake reported that it was so strong that it literally made
the Earth move—the day was shortened by a fraction of a second
as the planet spun faster on it axis. The U.S. Geological Survey
estimated that the quake, which occurred eighty miles from shore,
shifted the position of the entire island of Honshu eight feet to the
west. The tsunami caused as the quake buckled the seabed reached
a height of thirty feet and raced toward the main island of the
Japanese archipelago with the speed of a jet airplane.

On shore, the terrible waves swept over coastal cities and
towns, where the quake had already knocked down buildings and
severed gas lines, causing hundreds of fires at industrial facilities,
commercial buildings, and residences. Arriving less than an hour
after the temblor, the tsunami swept away cars, buses, trains, and
oceangoing ships. In some places, gas-fed fires continued to burn
as buildings were surrounded by the sea. They looked like oil wells
on the ocean, flaring off natural gas.

The zone of devastation stretched for more than 150 miles along Honshu's coastline. Houses, schools, bridges, and public buildings disappeared, and entire communities were reduced to rubble. The death toll, which began in the double digits, grew by the minute. By dawn, tens of thousands were among the homeless, and ten million were without electric power. Soon their discomfort would be replaced by fear as the press revealed that radiation was leaking from nuclear power reactors at Fukushima. Three reactors had melted down, and hydrogen explosions had blown holes in containment buildings. The worst nuclear disaster since Chernobyl had begun.

The count of the dead and the missing in the triple disaster that devastated Japan would eventually exceed nineteen thousand, and the estimated economic losses—destroyed property, business disruption, lost wages—would surpass $200 billion.[1] The profound effects of the events that began on March 11, 2011, moved people in ways that were similar to the terror attacks on America that occurred on September 11, 2001. Just as people in the United States came to speak of 9/11 as a point of historical demarcation, the Japanese adopted the shorthand 3/11 to reference the month that changed so much about their country.

The grief suffered by individuals and the nation as a whole filled the world press, but was quickly joined by images of outrage, empathy, and action. These responses came as the Japanese people realized that their government was failing to provide the aid required by hundreds of thousands of victims. Frustration grew as power plant operators dumped ten thousand tons of contaminated water into the ocean and people were ordered to abandon areas previously declared safe from radiation.

Public sentiment was evidenced in mass rallies where thousands of citizens vented their frustration over the slow pace of aid and official censorship, which kept secret the true extent of the trouble at Fukushima. More people took to the streets in more places than at any time since the 1970s. And in the spirit of those brought together by organizers, some of whom called themselves *Shiroto No Ran* (Amateur Revolt), the marchers were notably peaceful and even playful. They dressed like cows and drums of toxic waste and waved fans decorated with drawings of two-headed bunnies.

Remarkable as they were, the protests paled in comparison with the spontaneous efforts made by Japanese citizens who noted their government's failure and acted on their own. This was the phenomenon we visited Japan to explore. To us, the citizens who sprang into action represented the Athena value of personal responsibility. In our survey, large majorities said that big organizations wield too much power and that problems are better solved close to home. In 2011, the Japanese people responded to their disasters by taking the initiative in many decisive ways.

Moments after the quake, individuals began using social media to overcome information blackouts and communicate what they knew about conditions across the country. Within a week of the earthquake, a Keio University sophomore named Kohei Fukuzaki had launched the website Roomdonor.jp to match displaced individuals and families with those who volunteered vacant houses, apartments, and rooms. In two weeks, Fukuzaki recruited two thousand spaces and placed hundreds of homeless in free accommodations.

We met Fukuzaki at a technology incubator called Lightning Spot, in the bustling business and entertainment district of Shibuya. The famously crowded neighborhood is known for its busy train station, where a statue honors the loyal dog Hachiko, who came there looking for his owner, every afternoon, for nine years after the man died. Lightning Spot offers low-cost space, Internet access, and community to entrepreneurs who arrive with laptops in hand to work on Web-based ventures. Similar work spaces serve business developers in most of the world's major cities and act as magnets for visiting digital dignitaries. While we were talking with Kohei, one of the Finnish creators of the famous Angry Birds game emerged from the elevator looking for an Aeron chair and a WiFi connection. Outfitted in a T-shirt that featured a big red angry bird, Peter Vesterbacka attracted a few greetings but quickly settled in at his keyboard—just another pioneer in a room full of them.

Between sips from a bottle of cold green tea, Kohei recalled that he was four years old when Japan was struck by the Kobe earthquake, but he learned about the tragedy and the slow government response to it when he went to school. "The government held a tight rein, controlling everything and putting people in places where the walls were very thin and no pets were allowed."[2] In the aftermath of 3/11, he went to a convention center in Yokohama to find a friend who had been evacuated and was struck by the enormity of the demand for housing.

"More than five thousand people were at the convention center, and they were each getting just one bottle of tea and two tangerines to eat for a meal," he told us. At home, Kohei saw that people were trying to find help on the Internet, but having trouble. He spoke with some friends who were skilled at Web design, and they settled on a concept inspired by the website called Airbnb.com, which matches people with empty homes with travelers who need accommodations.

"A lot of people were posting tweets [messages on Twitter] offering places to stay, so we knew that there was a desire to help," said Kohei. Within three days, Roomdonor.jp was available online, including a version for smartphones. Designed to be searchable, the site enabled users to find matches for any number of people and in any region of the country outside the disaster zone. They could even determine which donors accepted pets and which would not.

With the website constructed, the big challenge became getting out the word at a time when the mass media were swamped by news related to the multiple disasters. Kohei got a little attention when he sent out press releases announcing that the site was in service and that it had been constructed by college students. But Roomdonor.jp didn't gain a wide following until Daisuke Tsuda, a prominent young journalist, began posting reports about it. When U.S. ambassador to Japan John Roos added his support, traffic spiked further, and hundreds of homeless people found shelter.

With the website abuzz with activity and the media clamoring for interviews, Kohei didn't get the chance to meet any of the Roomdonor participants until March 30, almost two weeks after the earthquake. "The lady requested a room for herself and her daughter on March 25 and received a match on March 26," reported Kohei. "They went to an apartment in Tokyo that was empty." When the refugees arrived, neighbors helped furnish the apartment and got them food and other household supplies. The process was repeated thousands of times, as people bypassed the government's emergency response system, which was overwhelmed, to make compassionate connections on their own. Everyday citizens like Kohei became leaders who took moral responsibility for dealing with the crisis.

Just twenty-one years old in 3/11, Kohei didn't look like the kind of person who might be embraced as a moral leader. Indeed, with his slim frame and his long hair cut at an angle, he looks more like a singer in a Japanese boy band than a source of wisdom and strength. But online, no one knows how old you are, and workable ideas can find support. Kohei believes that his effort also reflected the sensibility of a generation that is eager to use technology to make positive human connections. "The younger generations feel the possibilities in technology," he told us. "We are always looking for ways to connect."

When we pressed Kohei to consider the cultural and historical import of his effort, he said he saw it in the context of Japan's continuing adjustment to an era of limited economic opportunity and overstressed government services. "Japanese people had become very quick to criticize," he observed, noting the impatience people expressed over the faltering official response to the disasters. The lesson he took away from 3/11 points to a revival of individual responsibility and a one-to-one, personal response to serious social problems.

In Kohei's view, massive corporations and government agencies came to dominate society during Japan's great boom period. While they provided financial security that was practically cradle to grave, "neighborliness disappeared." The generation born and raised in the so-called Lost Decades—Kohei's generation—didn't know this time of plenty mixed with dependency. (The Lost Decades refer to Japan's long period of low or no economic growth, beginning in 1991.) When 3/11 came, they responded with "an old Japanese spirit people used to show whenever there was a fire or some other emergency. They helped each other directly. I think social media triggered a memory of the old, traditional Japanese personality," said Kohei with a smile. "We returned to a persona that is truly Japanese."

• • •

No example of people helping people in the wake of 3/11 could be more dramatic than the case of Kinoya-Ishinomaki Suisan Company and its cans of mackerel. The fish is a traditional, middle-class favorite and a key product of the Kinoya cannery. When the Tokyo community of Kyodo discovered that the cannery had been wrecked by the tsunami, its citizens rushed north to help.

When they arrived in the city of Ishinomaki, home of Kinoya, they saw that the cannery had been destroyed and that its landmark—a thirty-foot-tall fish-oil tank painted to look like a can of whale—lay battered on the ground three hundred feet away. Amid the rubble, covered with sand, were thousands upon thousands of unlabeled cans of fish. Still shiny and new, most of the cans seemed unaffected. A few test openings determined that the fish inside was good. But without labels, the products couldn't be readily identified, and authorities wouldn't allow it to be sold through regular channels.

Undaunted, the folks from Kyodo decided to salvage hundreds of cases of fish, bring them back to Tokyo, and sell them informally at shops around the neighborhood.

We went to Kyodo by subway and then walked down streets lined by antique shops and record stores to find the Kinoya Café, where the usual fare of drinks and snacks was served amid towers of shiny cans. Salvagers had decorated what they called "cans of hope" with images of cartoon characters, animals, landscapes, and the Japanese flag. Some greeted shoppers with phrases such as "Help each other, Japan" and "We will survive and thrive."

Inside in the café, Nagato Kimura sat at a table where a dozen tins had been stacked, and marveled at the variety of the artwork and the generosity the cans represented. "They [the rescuers of Kyodo] came right away," said Kimura, whose family owns the cannery business.[3] "While the government plodded along, they came to help. I was very surprised. For a small family-owned company like ours that doesn't have the advantages of a big producer with many factories, it was almost a miracle."

The Kimura family opened the cannery in 1957. For more than half a century, the company bought whatever fishermen brought in from the sea, from tiny young lancefish to enormous whales, and canned it in a variety of sauces. When the rest of the industry turned to using frozen fish, which was less expensive because if could be imported from anywhere, Kinoya chose to continue processing only the fresh, local catch. Consumers who favor the brand say they can taste the difference.

Over the years, the Kimuras turned away larger companies that came with buyout proposals, choosing instead to maintain its modest presence in Ishinomaki, where it employed about eighty local workers. Many of them lived in apartments that the cannery owned. Their children attended the neighborhood school. (A photo from 2006 shows workers gathered in front of the giant facsimile can, which had been painted with a celebratory slogan that, translated roughly, reads, "Celebrating fifty years of having the whale!")

On the day of the disaster, the quake shook the cannery at about 2:45 pm. Working in an office on an upper floor, Kimura felt the trembling of the Earth and immediately anticipated a tsunami.

"I think it will be a smaller one," he recalled, but to be safe, he evacuated workers from the factory floor. The tsunami struck at 3:52 with a force he could not have imagined. It flooded the cannery and poured about two feet of water into the second-floor office. Kimura survived the wave and scrambled to safety. But outside, as the water receded, he saw that his factory, warehouse, and the entire waterfront district of Ishinomaki had been devastated. Small ships, including fishing vessels, had been thrown up on the shore. Commercial buildings were washed away. Hundreds of homes were reduced to rubble.

Ishinomaki bore the brunt of the tsunami. More than three thousand residents were killed, including seventy-four children and ten teachers at an elementary school near the cannery. More than ten thousand people were rendered homeless. In the immediate aftermath of the tragedy, locals and emergency workers from outside focused on rescuing survivors and supporting them in a region lacking such basics as shelter, electricity, water, and fuel. Living in a state of shock, Kimura didn't think much about the future of his company. Then, as roads were opened, the "cans of hope" volunteers arrived at the cannery site. Armed with shovels and rubber gloves, they dug up thousands of cans that had been buried under sand and debris, washed them, and piled them in crates. Before the earthquake, "they were normal customers," said Kimura. "After the earthquake, they were part of a healing."

The volunteers, who numbered as many as fifty, worked for days on end. They camped overnight, sharing with disaster survivors the food and water they brought. They urged Kimura to rebuild and help the seafood industry power the recovery of the community. When we saw him, government officials hadn't yet decided on the future of the city and other shoreline communities affected by the disasters. Some argued that population centers be moved to safer, higher ground. Others insisted that the people who inhabited these long-established communities be supported in reconstructing wherever they chose.

Months after the destruction, the cleanup continued, and the debate around reconstruction was not close to being settled—but the help that customers gave to the cannery had made Nagato Kimura believe in the human spirit and feel as though the future held opportunity. "The Japanese fishing industry has a lot of problems, and this gives us a chance to think about them and deal with them in a fresh way," he said, considering the blank slate left by the tsunami. Local and global fisheries needed to be managed more sustainably, he said, and the oceans needed to be protected from pollution. "Things have to change," he said soberly. "Maybe we can lead the way."

•••

Kimura could hope for a brighter day because he had seen the unity and selflessness of people involved in the disaster recovery effort. Japanese people who lived away from the earthquake and tsunami zones didn't witness the struggle firsthand. Instead they experienced power outages caused by the damage and meltdowns at the Daiichi nuclear complex, and followed the government's stumbling response with ever-growing frustration. Over time, as people learned that key facts were obscured and officials failed to act decisively, dissatisfaction with both government and corporate leaders grew. The Tokyo Electric Power Company and the national government both came in for heated criticism, and rallies held to protest their actions, and inaction, drew thousands of people who felt betrayed by the major power brokers in the country.

This feeling is not new. At the University of Tokyo, professor Kaori Hayashi has tracked Japanese attitudes, especially as they are expressed through the media, for decades. Over this period, she had noted increasing wariness of major institutions. The 3/11 crisis crystallized this feeling, she told us. "It made people truly recognize that what the government says is not trustworthy."[4] After the quake and tsunami, mainstream media sources offered so little information that "it opened opportunities for social media" on the Internet. Reports from individuals living in the disaster zone replaced official sources, "and their information helped people take action."

We met professor Hayashi in her office at Fukutake Hall, a gleaming glass-and-concrete building on the university's main campus. The walls of her small space were lined with floor-to-ceiling bookshelves, which were filled with thousands of volumes. A journalist in the 1980s, she became an academic in the 1990s and has taught at the university for well over a decade. In all this time, she has followed generational shifts in social attitudes, and she sees trends in Japan that mirror the industrialized West.

"The Cold War has ended, and the big clash of cultures has ended," said Hayashi. "Politics and power don't mean what they did in the past. My father's generation considered devotion to the country and the state as a direct expression of nationalism. Young people like Japan, but they worry about the state and government having too much power. And it has been said that what is more important to them than class, or other issues, is hope. They don't classify society based on wealth but on whether there is hope."

Hope is especially important to young adults who find themselves in an economy that offers limited employment opportunities and less security than their parents knew. "This is why one of the favorite movies today is *Always*, which is about a poor Japanese family at the time of the 1960 Tokyo Olympics," explained the professor. "They were poor. The whole country was relatively poor. But they had hope."

In Japan circa 1960, the world of work and its rewards were considered masculine; domestic life and its comforts were deemed to be feminine. Today, young adults seek to blend the two, hoping to maximize their chances for happiness with a well-rounded life. Critics of this more androgynous view of life have warned that men risk becoming passive "herbivores" who lack the aggressive energy needed for success. Professor Hayashi sees in this trend a more positive regard for diversity and self-determination.

The herbivores "are radical and questioning," she said, adding with a smile, "but maybe they are not radical enough."

•••

In a country where strength in the face of adversity remains a high social ideal, perhaps no one is more radical than a young man who admits he suffers from depression and goes public with his struggle in order to help others. Yasuhiro Toudou has taken both these steps with an enterprise he calls U2Plus, which links people in need with psychologists offering a practically oriented treatment called cognitive-behavioral therapy (CBT).

Yasuhiro's personal struggle began when he was working as an Internet specialist for a cell phone company. The manager of his work group handled people so poorly that projects fell behind schedule, and punishing overtime was required to complete ordinary tasks. Everyone on the team felt discouraged, and the group fell apart. Disillusioned, Yasuhiro left the company and quickly fell into despair. Stricken with all the classic symptoms of depression—fatigue, sleeplessness, lack of motivation—he moved back to his parents' home; as his symptoms worsened, he felt drained of energy and unable to leave the house. He lost interest in everything that once pleased him—hobbies, friends, even food—and considered suicide. Things started getting better when he finally talked about what he was feeling.

"None of this was acceptable in Japanese society," Yasuhiro told us when we met him in Shibuya. "Japanese people tend to be shy, and there's an element of shame in depression that is an impediment to getting help. People don't communicate about how they are feeling, and they don't share what they are going through."[5]

With encouragement from family and friends, Yasuhiro went to an informational meeting at a mental health center, where CBT was presented as one option for people hoping to deal with their pain. Intrigued by the logic of this discipline, he found a CBT specialist, and in the first few sessions felt the stirrings of recovery. "As small as these things sound, it was important that I was able to get up and make something to eat. I could go outside and see the sky and the trees and get to the train on time."

CBT challenges patients to reconsider the way they think about themselves, using logic against the negative assumptions that can make someone who's depressed feel even worse. As Yasuhiro recalled, "Something bad happened; I felt bad; those feelings led to more pessimistic thoughts and then worse feelings." CBT tested Yasuhiro's feelings of hopelessness and doom against the fact that he had supportive family and friends and many skills and talents that would help him cope with the world. As he began to recognize that his perspective was unrealistically dark, the treatment began to work.

As Yasuhiro's energy and creativity returned, he examined the broader problem of depression in Japan and realized that he was far from alone. Millions of Japanese people suffered symptoms of depression each year—on average, thirty thousand commit suicide—but only a small percentage received help. As he read up on mental health problems in Japan, he came upon work done by a professor at Chiba University named Osamu Koburi.

Osamu has written extensively on common mental health disorders, including perfectionism, obsessive compulsive disorder, and phobias. He has paid special attention to the issues affecting young adults in Japan. In some cases, he discovers that an apparent problem masks unexpected benefits. For example, he has discovered that negative thinking can shield one from disappointment and that perfectionists can realize remarkable achievements as they continually raise their standards.

After meeting to discuss the great gap between the incidence of depression in Japan and the low rates of treatment, Osamu and Yasuhiro agreed they would try to do something about it by developing a website to provide information and referrals for people with depression. Together they wrote content for the website they called

U2Plus.jp, which gave users reliable and accurate information on the rate of depression in Japan, treatment possibilities ranging from exercise to medication and hospitalization, and even practical tips, including "Communicate with family, contact lovers, friends, acquaintances, etc." and "Enjoy music and video."

In addition to the basic information on depression and the home remedies, the site offers videos from seminars and slide shows on mental health issues. Yasuhiro and Osamu also recruited about a dozen CBT therapists who were willing to participate by answering questions posted by visitors and by accepting some for treatment. These same therapists also contribute to online discussions, which can be carried out over the course of weeks and even months. The effect is comparable to what one might experience as a member of a large group therapy meeting.

"Someone will post about a problem—say, that they don't feel as motivated as they want to be—and the only thing that crosses their mind as they think about it is negativity," explained Yasuhiro. "They will talk about this and even say, 'I'm just running away from my problem,' but other people will point out that they are talking about it and confronting it. You must think about these small accomplishments and nurture those thoughts."

As he described the CBT methods promoted by U2Plus, Yasuhiro acknowledged that he could have been speaking about himself. He overcame his own depression by focusing on the positive elements of his life and on small signs of success. In his research for the website, he also discovered that his depression arose in the context of a society plagued with uncertainty and insecurity. For generations, Japanese have embraced the "salaryman" model of work, which called for men (and, later, women) to devote themselves to a corporation that would, in turn, provide long-term employment. According to the lore and legend, the salaryman worked extremely hard and also played hard after-hours in Tokyo nightclubs and bars. Like workers everywhere, he drew status as well as a sense of purpose and identity from his job. Losing it was all but unthinkable.

Born into the Lost Decades of low growth with fewer secure positions available in big corporations, a vast cohort of young adults must now reconsider the salaryman ideal and invent other ways to establish themselves. "I am twenty-nine, and my entire life has been spent in a bad economy," Yasuhiro told us. "But I am not alone. I am one of many people who are defining happiness for themselves." For millions of younger Japanese, their online and offline social networks offer pathways to happiness and fulfillment through relationships and service to others. This option "doesn't move you into a position of power, but it is powerful," added Yasuhiro. "I'm not sure how much it's a shift of values, but it feels free."

• • •

The freedom young people like Yasuhiro feel comes with discovering empathy and caring in the hearts of others. In our search for Athena values in Japan, we found many examples of this kind of compassion in action practiced by people who were looking for ways to feel connected, of service to others, and successful. Often these efforts were led by young people, and an outsider might consider this to be a sign of the times and conclude that something new is emerging. Westerners in particular tend to imagine a traditional Japanese culture that values quiet, personal strength and seeks to deny suffering. This assumption resided in press accounts of events following the Sendai quake, which were filled with words like "stoic" and "resilient." A typical article in the Los Angeles Times stated that "Japanese restraint is steeped in a culture of tested resilience."[6]

The phenomenon noted by the Times and others is known generally as gaman, which is a term used in Zen Buddhism to describe grace in the face of enormous suffering. Gaman is real, and it is intrinsic to Japanese culture in the same way, perhaps, that a "stiff upper lip" is intrinsic to the British outlook on life. However, no single quality defines a nation's character, and it would be a mistake to assume that Japanese people always, and in every circumstance, favor stoicism or silence. Yasuhiro said that his parents and grandparents supported his open attitude about depression, and he believes that the mutual aid that participants offer in the Internet community of U2Plus is as much a part of Japanese culture as gaman.

As young mothers, Maco Yoshioka and Chisato Kitazawa experienced something common to new moms all over the world. With a baby's arrival, friends and family celebrate and fawn over mother and child. But at some point, the visitors depart, the household grows quiet, and a young mother is left alone to care for a tiny human being who can make enormous demands. And although babies receive regular medical attention as they reach certain milestones in their young lives, mothers are left on their own. For those without close ties to more experienced mothers who could offer advice and support, the first weeks and months of taking primary responsibility for a baby can be filled with doubts, fears, loneliness, and exhaustion.

"Ten percent of mothers are actually diagnosed with postnatal depression," Maco told us when we met her. "I know from my own experience that there was no place for support and that I would have felt a lot better if I had been able to take care of myself at the same time that I was taking care of my son."[7]

In her own desire for something better, Maco developed the idea of a service for mothers with new babies that would bring them together to exchange ideas, lift one another's spirits, and get a bit of exercise. "It takes a year to recover physically from being pregnant and having a baby," noted Maco. "I know that if I had been physically healthier, I would have been a lot happier."

Beginning in her own neighborhood, Maco created a self-help group called Madre Bonita (Spanish for "beautiful mother") that offered regular meetings where mothers could talk about their challenges, support each other, and participate in exercise classes. The gentle workouts were built around aerobics and the use of inflated exercise balls, which help users improve balance and abdominal strength. Over time, Maco welcomed a participating mother, Chisato Kitazawa, as a partner in Madre Bonita. They added informational sessions on subjects ranging from nutrition to child development and even domestic violence. Madre Bonita became a holistic program, offering something for every aspect of a mother's life. But Maco and Chisato came to see that the friendship and intellectual interactions women found at Madre Bonita meetings had the greatest value.

"Mothers who are at home alone all the time tend to lose even their vocabularies,"[8] recalled Chisato, referring to a syndrome Americans call "mommy brain." Chisato said that the stimulation of adult conversation was one of the greatest benefits of Madre Bonita. In other settings where mothers get together, they are generally asked to bring along their babies, and the children become the focus. In fact, mothers are often asked to write their child's name on their own name tags, identifying themselves not as individuals but as a baby's mother. This practice is so common that newcomers to Madre Bonita do it reflexively. They are quickly reminded that it's *their* identity that matters most—the moms, not the babies, are the priority in these sessions.

When she first attended Madre Bonita, Chisato was so shy about focusing on her own needs that she didn't tell her husband, Daisuke, what she was doing. When she eventually told him about the meetings, he was supportive, but they had a second conversation when she decided to go to work with Maco to expand the project. "He had a belief that mothers stayed home, and it was difficult for him to change," she told us. "His parents were typical Japanese from the past generation." However, at his job for an international software company called Red Hat, Daisuke met many working women. He soon came around to the idea that

Chisato would be a happier and more fulfilled person if she added working for Madre Bonita to her life. As a side benefit, Chisato reported, Daisuke learned to enjoy being a more engaged father. "Now he takes my daughter to kindergarten, and they both like it."

Madre Bonita was so popular with mothers that demand quickly outpaced what two mothers could offer on their own. To meet the need, Maco and Chisato trained more than twenty leaders, who conduct more than fifty group sessions per week, attended by about six hundred women in nine prefectures. For those who attend weekly, annual fees total about $125 per person, which covers payroll and operating costs. Chisato and Maco enjoy modest incomes from their effort, but Madre Bonita is a nonprofit organization with a higher purpose. Their measures of success include service to mothers and raising public awareness of their needs. One sign of progress may be seen in a recent suggestion made by fathers eager for support. They would like to see a spin-off of Madre Bonita called Madre Danshi—Mother Men.

• • •

Madre Danshi are still a rare breed, but it is not hard to find Japanese men who embrace the Athena Doctrine in pursuit of success and a rewarding life. Not quite the passive "herbivore men" who are the subject of Japanese social critics, these men practice collaboration, generosity, and modesty while also achieving as entrepreneurs and social innovators. We met several. Kentaro Ohara's Colish.net helps people with shared interests—musicians, Web entrepreneurs, programmers, and even first-time parents—share housing and build communities. His goal is to help those who share interests online move closer in the physical world. Ryo Nakagawa's service, called Share0, helps self-employed entrepreneurs and consultants find office space in companies with empty suites. Ryo believes that the future belongs not to big organizations but to individuals with skills who come together for collaboration. Juto Ohki has exploited his skill with sign language, and the fame he gained as an interpreter on television, to create a service that provides instant communication help on smartphones and on the Internet to deaf people across Japan. The service makes it possible for them to perform simple transactions in a variety of settings—from banks to shops to government agencies. More important, it breaks the isolation that limits life.

Among the men we met in Japan, Yosh Kanematsu stood out as the most ambitious and free spirited. Yosh operates several businesses built around a Web-based magazine called *Greenz*, which focuses on sustainable development ideas and environmental news. (He also runs a beverage company called Green Drinks, and the Green School, which conducts seminars.) The young people who work in these businesses draw small cash salaries but also consider the social mission of the enterprise a kind of reward. As entrepreneurs, they also own a stake in the little Green empire, which means that they with benefit financially if they find success.

Children of the Lost Decades, who are just now becoming adults, know Japan's long period of economic boom (1960 to 1990) only as something of a legend. Their parents may talk of days when real estate prices and the stock market soared, but the bubble that burst in the early 1990s was never reinflated. Today, fewer jobs pay well enough to allow a working man to support a family. More women have entered the workforce, and the old masculine identity, based on work and achievement, is giving way to new ideals.

"A good life is both *chikara*, which means 'power,' and *ai*, which means 'love,'" says Yosh. "The masculine side likes to deliver on its promises and push forward, with tunnel vision. The feminine side is more inclusive and comprehensive in its view. It is strong, but it is also perceptive and considerate."[9]

The blend of masculine and feminine that Yosh brings to his life would seem unremarkable in some cultures, but he describes it as a radical departure from the traditional norm for Japanese working men. His father has worked for the same electric utility for his entire life. His older brother took a position with a government transportation agency when he graduated from college, and plans to stay until retirement. "It is *rice work*," Yosh says, using a slang term for labor that provides long-term security. With fewer opportunities for such predictable work, his generation "wants *life work* instead. This is work with a purpose, something that gives meaning to your life."

Life work, as Yosh defines it, brings people together in the pursuit of a series of goals that include profit and employment but also new relationships, improved communities, and, if possible, a better world. *Greenz* readers use the online community to share and promote ideas that meet these goals. One recent product of this collaboration was a smartphone application that measures and reports the energy use of any single appliance. "Many different companies are open to developing these ideas," said Yosh. "We help people through the whole process, from [refining] their idea to spreading the word that their project is ready."

● ● ●

As an Internet-based innovator, Yosh is an effective advocate, but his main role is as a sort of middleman. His information network helps others deliver goods and services. For an example of a successful, top-to-bottom Athena enterprise, you have to visit the famous Ginza shopping district. A few blocks away from the bustling train station, a red sign announces the location of the Motherhouse store.

On the day we visited, a vendor who operated a wood-fired stove on the back of a tiny truck sold just-cooked sweet potatoes to pedestrians. Like pretzel sellers in Manhattan, sweet potato men are staples of autumn in Tokyo, and the street was filled with a pleasant, smoky-sweet scent. Inside Motherhouse, we discovered a collection of handbags and other accessories in colors consistent with the season, including umber, rust, yellow, and deep red.

Company founder and chief designer Eriko Yamaguchi greeted us with cups of warm green tea. A slightly built woman who wore a buttoned-up, cream-colored cardigan, she hardly looked the part of a power player in the fashion business, but that is just what she is. In 2004, as Yamaguchi finished an internship at the Inter-American Development Bank in Washington, she looked for an opportunity to learn more about economic development in poor countries. The bank, and many other organizations, annually send hundreds of billions of dollars in grants and loans to developing countries, but progress in the fight against poverty is grindingly slow. Curious to learn why, and desiring to add to her education, Yamaguchi decided to enroll in a graduate degree program in Bangladesh. The decision turned the usual academic practice, which sees students leave poor countries for school in rich ones, on its head. It also opened a path to discovery.

"I went on Yahoo.com on the computer and asked, 'What's the poorest country in Asia?'" she recalled for us. "I saw the photos of Bangladesh and thought, 'Oh my God.' The next thing I thought was, 'I should go there.'"[10]

Eriko felt a personal connection to those who struggle against great odds. As a girl, she was first bullied in elementary school, and somehow her peers got the idea that they should pick on her throughout her childhood. She describes herself as a "teenage juvenile delinquent" who studied judo to defend herself and adopted a tough exterior. Fortunately, she got her bearings before finishing high school, which allowed her to attend university at Brac University in Dahka, Bangladesh. When she wasn't studying, she scouted the local economy looking for clues to the nation's problems and for opportunities. Always interested in fashion, she was drawn to the areas where people worked at sewing machines in small shops and factories, turning out low-end textile products.

For two years, Yamaguchi explored and pondered, watching local people endure strikes, floods, epidemics, and economic crises. She wrote everything in her diary, along with notes about her own dreams and ambitions, which revolved around starting a business. Inspired by a coffee bag made of coarse jute fabric, she settled on the notion of designing and making handbags in Bangladesh to sell in Tokyo. The concept would exploit her own interest in fashion and the big women's fashion market in Tokyo while providing work for people in Dahka. It was a great idea, but at first she had trouble finding anyone in Bangladesh who believed that local workers were up to the task. Although she wouldn't tell us how, she said she was "misled, lied to, and betrayed" many times before she began a partnership with a shop where workers turned coarse jute fabric into sacks for grain and potatoes.

"They were making these sacks that cost one dollar each, and we had to get them to sew fashion bags worth a hundred dollars and more," she recalled. "To make things more difficult, I was a young woman in an Islamic country who had to be the boss." Months of effort were required before Yamaguchi could get workers to start stitching some samples based on her designs, and even then she discarded two dozen attempts before she got one bag that was good enough to show retailers in Japan. But gradually she coaxed workers to improve their skills, and she built a stock of 160 pieces.

Yamaguchi's fashion sense was evident in the designs she brought to department store buyers, who were also intrigued by the story she told of her enterprise, which she named Motherhouse in tribute to the famous Catholic nun Mother Teresa. In her first round of sales visits, Yamaguchi won orders to place bags in thirteen stores. "Everyone in Bangladesh thought that when I left to go to Tokyo I would never come back. When I returned with orders, they realized this was a real opportunity," said Yamaguchi.

In order to seize the opportunity, Yamaguchi had to overcome a series of practical and cultural obstacles. Workers had to be convinced that she really considered them partners and that when she asked, "What do you think?" they were supposed to offer genuine replies. "No boss had ever asked them questions like this, and no one was used to being part of a team." To build a sense of team, Yamaguchi issued photo identification cards to employees. Many workers had never possessed a photo of themselves, and they prized the cards. She opened a lunchroom and served free meals to her workers. She also raised their pay above the going rate, in order to acknowledge the superior skills required to make quality leather goods.

Those skills were slow to come, and Yamaguchi had to acquire better equipment in order to improve productivity. But gradually the shop started making more "keepers" than "rejects," and word came from Japan that the bags were popular. Consumers liked the price, which fell below the prices set for goods made elsewhere, and they liked the idea of buying from a business established by a Japanese woman to make both a profit and a difference in the lives of people in one of the world's poorest countries.

"The quality of the bags surprised people who think that when you get something from a poor country, it's going to be low quality and low price. We went for high quality at a middle price, and it worked." It worked so well that additional retailers placed orders, and Motherhouse was able to open eight retail shops in Japan and four in Taiwan. The factory in Bangladesh has outgrown its quarters and moved three times, and wages have increased to double the rate paid by other manufacturing companies. Most important, says Yamaguchi, more than half her customers know nothing of her social mission and make their purchase based entirely on the fashion she offers, and the workmanship.

Of course, the mission beyond profit remains a source of intense satisfaction for Yamaguchi. By investing in workers whom she respected and in a place others ignored, she had overcome many of the obstacles that thwarted more formal development schemes. Instead of receiving subsistence wages, her employees earn salaries that support them as working-class citizens, and they feel a self-regard that is even more valuable. Yamaguchi reaped similar rewards as she saw her Athena-style model for business succeed.

"How do you define success and happiness?" she asked, looking around a brightly lit shop with dozens of bags on offer. "In the past, it was possible to belong to a big organization and believe that you were guaranteed some success and happiness by just staying there. Today I think it's about contributing something more. What you do, even in creating a business, can be about partnership, collaboration, trust, and making other people happy too. There's a new business ecosystem, and it requires better thinking," she said. "Sure, you have to compete, but that doesn't always mean paying the lowest wages. Sometimes it means understanding things better and being more creative. It can work."

• • •

Japan may indeed be a window into the future of many developed markets: aging population, slow growth, new pathways to happiness. The young people of Japan—without any context for the excess and materialism of the 1980s—are building business models based on valuing values. They care less about affluence and more about influence.

Chapter 5

Colombia and Peru

"Today's times require we be more kind and empathetic to others." (80% agree)

The road from the José María Córdova Airport to the city center of Medellin climbs steeply into the central range of the Andes—the Cordillera Central—where switchbacks and blind curves will make a speeding taxicab sway and buck like the cars on a roller coaster. It is night, and the lush trees of the forest drip with recent rainfall, but no one on the road is slowed by the slippery conditions. Everyone races toward the city at breakneck speed as if it's the El Dorado of Spanish myth.

At mile sixteen, on a road aptly named Via Santa (Way of the Saints), a first glimpse of the city reveals white lights twinkling on mountainsides, like thousands of sparks flashing on black velvet. A little further and through breaks in the trees, you can see tall apartment buildings and low-slung neighborhoods. Then the car reaches the final crest and descends into the Aburra Valley.

Creeping up mountainsides and anchored by compact business districts, Medellin looks a bit like Rio de Janeiro without the ocean, or San Francisco without the Golden Gate Bridge. Roll down the window, and the cab fills with cool, blossom-scented air. Breathe deeply, gaze at the city, and you understand immediately why the people of Medellin have fought so hard to save their city. It may not be the mythical city of gold, but it is a mile-high gift of nature with an almost perfect climate. It looks the kind of place where peace and happiness might be taken for granted.

This is, of course, a city long renowned for violence of every sort. Street gangs, drug lords, and even revolutionaries carried out so many killings that the name Medellin became synonymous with danger. From the late 1970s into the early 1990s, the Medellin drug cartel, ruled by the notorious Carlos Escobar, used murder and intimidation to control a cocaine trade that did millions of dollars in business per day. The criminal cultivation of coca leaves became the mainstay of the rural Colombian economy, and the drug became the nation's leading export, exceeding even coffee in its value.

At the peak of the drug trade, in the early 1990s, Medellin's murder rate reached more than twenty per day in a city of less than two million souls.[1] Most of the shootings, car bombings, and other attacks targeted criminals or police, but innocent bystanders also fell. As 350 police officers were killed in the space of thirteen months, some citizens who were not in the drug trade became so frightened and enraged by the lawlessness that they formed their own militias. With names like Robocop and the Friendly Group of Medellin, these groups carried out killings, which they called "cleansings," that targeted drug addicts and street people.

The pall cast over Medellin began to lift in 1993 as the Catholic Church joined with civic leaders to promote a "Climate for Peace." Local parishes sponsored regular meetings that drew hundreds to talk about ending the violence. In May, more than four hundred thousand people attended a public rally for peace, and authorities expanded programs that helped gang members leave criminal lives and establish themselves as law-abiding citizens. The big turning point came when Colombian troops, aided by Americans, found Escobar and killed him as he tried to escape his hiding place in the city.

Escobar's death heralded a steep decline for the cartel and an opening for the people of Medellin to remake their city. Beginning with a cease-fire agreement signed by gang leaders, amnesties were offered to allow former criminals to reenter society, and plans were drawn up to make striking architecture a key principle of urban redevelopment projects. A succession of city, state, and national government initiatives produced major improvements in schools, parks, museums, and libraries. Already a university city, and home of the widely acclaimed artist Fernando Botero, Medellin had always been a cultural and commercial hub, and these sectors came back quickly. But city development officials recognized that a culture of crime and violence festered in the poor, overcrowded slum neighborhoods that sprouted on Medellin's hillsides. They needed to do something significant to bring the residents of these neighborhoods into the life of the city.

As they studied the poorest barrios, officials recognized that because of difficult terrain, these neighborhoods were isolated—people had to walk long distances to reach business districts. To knit Medellin's neighborhoods together, officials designed and built a system of cables and gondolas that, like the lifts at fancy ski resorts, would carry people up and down the hillsides in style. The first line of the Metrocable, promoted with a code of behavior called Metrocable Culture, opened in 2004. The gleaming stations and cars became a source of civic pride, and hours-long commutes were reduced to minutes. Better still, the culture of cooperation and respect seemed to rub off on people, making the streets and alleys near stations more peaceful and, eventually, more prosperous.

We set out to visit the J line on an April morning when children were heading for school and workers were hustling to their jobs. It serves a neighborhood called Comuna 13, and is anchored at the train station named San Javier. There, officials had designated concrete walls to showcase an ever-changing display of graffiti artwork. One big painting showed two fists about to bump, and the slogan "Hip Hoppers Por La Paz" (Hip Hoppers for Peace). Other spray-painted murals depicted Santa Claus in his sleigh and cartoon characters. The art is well executed. Our guide told us that this concrete canvas satisfies artists' need for self-expression—in seven years of operation, the Metrocable has never had a graffiti problem.

The Metrocable system represents a successful demonstration of some basic theories of modern urban planning, which hold that citizens will respect public services of high quality, especially when they feel they have equal access; the idea is that people who can't pay for cars to get to jobs in other parts of the city will still have transportation that allows them to work. The metro culture also imbues citizens with a sense of ownership and personal investment; from the beginning, neighborhoods were part of planning the system, helping choose the sites for the stations as well as helping make improvements around those areas.

Station construction for the Metrocable included gently sloping ramps with switchbacks that make the walk from nearby streets less demanding and dangerous. The success of these improvements led the government to add outdoor escalators, shaded by brightly colored roofs, which further improved life in poor communities. The "electric stairs," as they are called, made it possible for people to climb more than two hundred feet in elevation in five minutes. Previously, the walk took thirty minutes. The escalators are built by laborers who live near them—and openings are big, celebrated events attended by civic leaders and hundreds of citizens.

Spurred by traffic, the areas around the escalators and Metrocable stations have also become magnets for commercial development and the construction of parks, schools, playgrounds, and libraries. Backed in part by money from the Gates Foundation in America, the five new libraries have been designed by world-famous architects and have become community centers as well as repositories for collections and Internet access points for residents. Each one is set in a park, and one was sponsored by the Spanish government. Spain's king and queen attended its opening.

Although violence has been reduced in the poorer neighborhoods of Medellin, it remains a problem. However, security is much improved in Comuna 13 across Medellin, and much of the credit for this progress goes to the transit system and related developments. Access to jobs increases incomes for families, and with more money, and pride, owners improve their homes and police the behavior of young people.

These neighborhoods are called *barrios informales* because they developed without any plan—a by-product of squatters who occupied the land and just built their own homes. Now the city is belatedly trying to add infrastructure. To do this, the government won the support and emotional commitment of residents by involving them in the planning, design, and construction stages—an inclusiveness that made the residents feel that the projects belong to them.

The widely publicized efforts made to include all citizens in the life of Medellin and to foster peace and unity put the city on our itinerary as we searched the world for stories that showed the Athena Doctrine at work. Here, some very brave men and women have responded to violence and chaos by opening their arms to bring people close. Similar stories were unfolding elsewhere in Latin America as innovators sought to deal with long-term social, economic, and political problems. The approach was consistent with the emphasis our survey respondents placed on community involvement. More than 82 percent told us "volunteering in my community" is important.

● ● ●

The Empresas Públicas de Medellín (Public Services of Medellín), known by the shorthand EPM, provides water, electricity, gas, and sanitation services to the entire city and some adjacent areas. By law, the utility must serve even the illegal homes of the barrios, which means that people who live in these makeshift communities enjoy a higher standard of living than people occupying similar squatter neighborhoods in other places. Everyone pays for his or her service, of course, but the public status of the utility means that its profits—about $450 million annually—can be tapped for municipal projects.

In the 1990s, peace brought the opportunity to deploy EPM funds, and crews set to work on roads, drainage systems, and public squares. Spending accelerated when an architect's son, Sergio Fajardo, was elected mayor in 2003. Fajardo, who believed that "our most beautiful buildings must be in our poorest areas,"[2] said that the new libraries, schools, transit, and a public science center would raise the aspirations of Medellin's poor, inspiring them to seek the education and skills to succeed as workers in the twenty-first century. To help, he increased education spending to 40 percent of the city's $900 million budget.

A mathematician with a doctorate from the University of Wisconsin, Fajardo was also a writer and broadcast journalist before he ran for mayor. His personal popularity, coupled with his independence (he belonged to no party), helped him shift enormous resources toward programs for the working class without provoking any real criticism. When he left office to become governor of the state of Antioquia, which includes Medellin, he was succeeded by a series of young chief executives with similar philosophies. When we got to Medellin, the administration of Anibal Gaviria was settling in after the mayor's election victory. He had named a team of deputies and department heads who were mostly in their thirties and forties and who seemed to consider themselves part of a can-do government.

One of the few Colombian women with a civil engineering degree, Margarita Angel Bernal runs the city's urban development agency—called EDU—and works out of a low, modern office building next to Plaza San Antonio. The plaza is named for the neighborhood's ancient domed church, but it is a classic example of the kind of pedestrian developments that modern cities build to encourage neighborly street culture. Its landmark is a large Botero statue of a bird, a symbol of peace that was damaged by a bomb during the era of terror. It is flanked by a new version, donated by the artist. On the day we visited Bernal, street vendors in the plaza sold coffee and tropical fruit, and families walked under shady trees, pushing babies in strollers.

Inside Bernal's office, a wall map that measured about eighty square feet showed were dozens of projects like the plaza had been built or were being developed across the city. For each one, EDU had convened local advisory groups that helped steer decisions in regard to every aspect, from choosing a site to selecting the type of materials used to build a school, a day-care center, a park, or a police station. Typically the projects include upgrades for streets, sidewalks, and even commercial storefronts to make a neighborhood more livable. Funding comes mainly from the municipal utility, but Medellin also uses tax dollars, and grants from state and national government; and it courts international donors who like to reward success.

For the most part, Medellin's redevelopment initiatives have been small to medium in scale. This modest approach has helped officials avoid the problems many large American cities created in the 1960s when big highways were built through old neighborhoods, and historic buildings were demolished. (Fixing the problems caused by the construction of a highway through Boston cost billions of dollars.) However, four months into her new job, Bernal was ready to unveil one proposal for a large development in the heart of the city, where an area filled with junk shops, garages, and lumberyards also shelters criminal activity. Set in prime real estate, this tumbledown district borders a government administration complex and makes locals wary of venturing downtown. The redevelopment scheme calls for several million square feet of commercial space and almost twelve hundred new condominium apartments, which occupants would buy with financing help from the city.

Like any big development effort, this one will require the acquisition of land from occupants who will need new places to live and work. Current owners will be given temporary digs and get first crack at space in the new development. Still, as might be expected, certain landowners are holding out for the best terms. They will wind up dealing with neighbors who are being enlisted to help manage the project. The principle guiding this project is shared responsibility, according to Bernal, who said that 82 percent of the property is owned by someone who rents it out. Because people who live there are directly involved, the end result, she hopes, will be improved properties and higher rents.

•••

Mauricio Facio Lince is a man who overflows with the ambition that Margarita Bernal finds deep in the character of Medellin. The second-highest official in the city government, behind Mayor Anibal Gaviria, Lince is thirty-eight years old, which makes him almost a senior statesman in the city's youth-oriented government. His office, high in a modern tower, overlooks a cityscape that includes skyscrapers that would suit Los Angeles, as well as nineteenth-century churches. From an outer wall that is floor-to-ceiling glass, he can almost see inside the bullfight arena—La Macarena—that squats in parkland just to the west.

A tall man with broad shoulders, Lince exercises considerable power in a Colombian system that puts substantial authority in the hands of big-city mayors, who run everything from schools to police and social services. Although it continued the transit and development programs begun by previous mayors, the Gaviria regime shifted more attention to schools and programs for the young, he told us. According to Lince, 62 percent of the budget of Medellin is *una puesta*—a bet—on the future, money that they are spending on schools and other programs for children. The schools are digital, complete with computers, and free for everyone. The libraries are community centers that offer everything from Internet to music programs, including 180 symphony bands for children. The idea is to change the culture of violence, money, and drugs and construct a generation of educated and involved citizens.

For decades public safety was Medellin's main political issue and a constant concern for ordinary citizens. Lince recalled that as a child, he attended daytime parties and dances that ended at three in the afternoon because parents didn't think it was safe to travel the streets after that hour. The police and the military played essential roles in Medellin's revival as they broke up drug gangs and defeated the armed leftist rebels of the Fuerzas Armadas Revolucionarias de Colombia (FARC). Lince said that although this fighting was a very masculine affair, rebuilding the society in a time of fragile peace will depend more on women.

Following an example set in São Paulo, Brazil, Medellin provides services to young mothers, helping them keep their children in school and out of criminal activity. According to Lince, the key is to change how citizens live together—and the ones to lead this change are women. In Medellin society, the figure of the mother, especially, is very respected—90 percent of the victims of violence may be men, Lince said, but they all have mothers, wives, sisters. And because the family revolves around the women, they can contribute significantly to security and stability.

City officials have created agencies to serve women and involve them in security projects, but independent organizations have played a larger role in peacemaking. This dynamic, which finds women leading protests and speaking out despite dangerous conditions, has been common across Latin America. In Argentina and Chile, for example, women were on the forefront of campaigns that pushed governments to reveal the truth about political murders and began a reconciliation process. Their efforts succeed because, as Lince said, women enjoy a certain deference and respect, and their vulnerability can be a strength.

In Medellin, and throughout Colombia, women head many of the organizations that do the dangerous work of confronting violent gang members and would-be revolutionaries, offering alternatives to the FARC and gang life. One of these organizations, Ruta Pacifica, brings women from the city to rural areas to join locals in protesting military actions and the activities of rebel groups. Another, Vamos Mujer, provides counseling, legal advice, health care, and other support for victims of violence. And Foundación Mi Sangre (My Blood Foundation), based in central Medellin, has grown from a small foundation helping victims of land mines into a large-scale peace education and action organization. The group's name comes from the title of a hit song and album by singer-songwriter Juan Esteban Aristizábal Vásquez. Known to fans as "Juanes," Aristizábal began Mi Sangre in 2006, after he became a superstar in Latin music. He continued to supply funds and promote its cause, but by 2012, the foundation had attracted dozens of allies, including corporations, universities, and foreign governments. Mi Sangre operated out of offices on a shady street in the Medellin main commercial district, called El Poblado. It was led by an activist named Catalina Cock Duque, who came to be one of Colombia's best-known advocates for change in a most unusual way.

• • •

By five in the afternoon, the weekday traffic in El Poblado, which means "the Village," is so heavy that pedestrians make quicker progress than anyone in a car. In this, Medellin's wealthiest inner-city neighborhood, big cars are a status symbol, and no one carpools. It's a sign of wealth and power to sit idling in a Range Rover or Jaguar. A few blocks east of Poblado Avenue, where boutiques and shopping malls beckon, the lights are on in an office that's been carved out of the second floor of a small townhouse. Inside, Catalina Cock Duque speaks perfect American-accented English to a caller on the telephone while tapping at a computer keyboard. Like many children of Colombia's leadership elite, Catalina attended school abroad. She earned a bachelor's degree at the University of Maryland and a master's at the London School of Economics. She returned home to pursue a mission she had begun at age sixteen.

"At that time, my father was the minister of mines and energy, and he took me on a trip to the coast where he was going to announce that the government was bringing electricity to a small town," recalled Catalina. "It was supposed to be something good for the people, but it turned out that they didn't want electricity. They didn't want television or any of the things that came from electricity. They just wanted to preserve their way of life, which is very holistic and traditional."[3]

The town that didn't want electricity was in a region called Chocó, which hugs the Pacific coast of Colombia. The native people, who descend from groups that lived along the coast from Peru to Panama, retain local languages and share the region with descendants of African slaves. Perhaps the poorest state in Colombia, the Department of Chocó depends on gold mining and logging in tropical forests. These activities pose both environmental hazards and opportunity for local people. When Catalina came home with her degree in 1999, she began Amigos de Chocó Foundation, which sponsored a marketing organization for small-scale prospectors dedicated to environmentally safe mining practices. The group grew to serve more than seven hundred families who supplied ecofriendly "Green Gold" to jewelers all over the world. Catalina went on to create the larger Alliance for Responsible Mining, which serves small-scale miners in four countries. In 2009, she accepted an offer to head Mi Sangre.

"There are two missions," she told us. "One is to heal the wounds of war. The other is the violence prevention for our young people through arts and culture." Mi Sangre reaches young people through music, theater, writing, and visual arts programs in hundreds of schools and neighborhood centers. This work and related projects are carried out by the organization itself and by others it helps fund and manage. On occasion, Juanes himself will participate, lending a bit of star power to an inspirational event, but for the most part, the work is done by teachers and volunteers. By 2012, the group had reached fifty thousand children. "Many people want to do something to help, but they don't have the options or the access. We provide that, and invite them to participate."

Mi Sangre heals the wounds of war by providing education, psychological assistance, and other services to victims of war, especially children injured by land mines. Catalina's approach is definitively feminine, emphasizing empathy, hope, communication, and inclusion as she works with all parties, including those who battled in the past, to promote reconciliation. "The man is a fist," she says bluntly. "The woman is open arms."

On the evening when we met, Catalina had just returned from one of the Casas de Paz (Peace Houses) that serve former revolutionary fighters who want to return to normal civilian life. More than thirty thousand men and women have laid down arms and joined civil society with the help of a Colombian Agency for Reintegration program that includes the Peace Houses. The one she visited was outside the city of Villavicencio, in a vast farming region called Los Llanos, where cattle ranches and big farms dominate the landscape. As she described it, the farmhouse and adjacent buildings housed a handful of fighters and their families, who stayed for several months. During this time, they worked with Colombian legal officials and received psychological and educational services. The goal of the project is to provide alternative ways of life for men and women who may have joined guerilla groups when they were children and have little understanding of ordinary life.

"What they have experienced can be very unusual," said Catalina, recalling stories she heard at the house. "I met one young woman who was brought into a guerilla group when she was still a child. She was forced into having sex with one of the men, and when she became pregnant, she really didn't even understand what that was. She didn't know that there was a child inside her."

This young woman arrived at the Casa de Paz with her child and a single thought about her life, added Catalina. "She just said, 'I want to be a mom. I want to be a mom. I want to be a mom.'"

Catalina said that similar, basic human drives motivated all the people she met at Casa de Paz, and she was taken aback by the lengths to which the former fighters would go in order to gain acceptance in ordinary society. "The idea is to put people who were in the FARC, people from the military, and people who were just bystanders all together to communicate. The guy who runs the program introduced himself by saying his grandfather had been kidnapped and killed by the FARC, but now he wants to help them."

The multiday program that Catalina attended involved extended meetings and exercises designed to bring people from different political, economic, and military perspectives together. It began with a mock fashion show with lights, pounding music, and former FARC guerillas dressed in women's clothes, pretending to work a catwalk. As they shed their inhibitions and caused their audience to roar with laughter, these retired fighters made people who might otherwise despise them reconsider them as human beings.

In later encounters, Catalina said, she discovered that "these were guys, kids really, who had been recruited at age nine or ten and went off to live in the jungle. They had known nothing but fear their entire lives. They were afraid of the military, they were afraid of their commanders, and they had no one to trust. They had also been without shoes, without food. Now all they really wanted was a chance to live in a normal home, have a job, and a family."

The gathering near Villavicencio was filled with exercises intended to break down assumptions and defenses and show people from all walks of life a way to imagine themselves in a country at peace. Much of this process involved storytelling. People who had lived in fear of the guerillas and had lost loved ones to attacks spoke in moving and emotional ways about the experience of life in a time of civil war. Guerillas who had left the jungle described their own feelings of torment over fighting they had seen, friends who had been killed, and the life they gave up in order to join the FARC cause.

As Catalina saw it, the storytelling helped people who had felt estranged and aggrieved instead feel empathy for each other, imagining how their life experience fit into a national narrative. "I am a pragmatic idealist," she said. "We were a society whose values were broken. Now people are listening to each other, there's hope, and there's a will to change that, to change the story." At Casa de Paz, the members of the reconciliation group that Catalina joined signaled their commitment by ending their work with a song, the Colombian national anthem.

Colombia's embrace of peace after decades of civil war has been a dream for most of the population. The process has approached fruition with the concerted efforts of the police and military, joined by a host of more feminine-style actors, including civil organizations like the government of Medellin and activists such as Juanes and Catalina. All these groups participated in a push for peace that culminated in 2011 with a new law to return land and make restitution to four million victims of war by 2021. In the meantime, reconciliation and peacemaking efforts will continue.

• • •

Colombia can muster the resources to accomplish its goals because it is the second-largest country in South America and has enjoyed significant growth for most of the last decade. Indeed, most of the entire continent escaped the economic crisis that affected the United States, Europe, and much of Asia starting in 2008. This trend has left people feeling optimistic. A 2011 survey of public sentiment across the region found that confidence in government had more than doubled since 2003, while economic worry had declined by half.[4] More remarkably, according to a more recent study, the most optimistic businesspeople in the world were in neighboring Peru—where through most of history, everyday people have struggled with high levels of poverty and limited public resources.[5] Inequality remains a stubborn problem in Peru, but the country's economic conditions have improved more in the past decade than any nation on the continent.

Compared with Colombia, Peru seems to have advanced on the strength of do-it-yourself efforts that have succeeded despite its grave political problems. The country has endured a long history of coups, including ten in the past century. In 1992, President Alberto Fujimori ended a stalemate with opposing politicians by suspending the constitution and shutting down the congress and the courts with military force. Today he sits in jail, convicted of human rights abuses and other crimes. Before, during, and after Fujimori, the country was plagued by civil war, as the government fought the often-brutal community revolutionaries of Sendero Luminoso (Shining Path). Remnants of the insurgent group remain active in rural and Andean regions, but three successful elections seem to have stabilized politics enough to motivate entrepreneurs and individuals to remake the country and its image. Emphasizing local culture, especially its food and food products, they have sparked a kind of renaissance, stimulating pride among Peruvians and worldwide interest in the country's blend of Pacific, indigenous, and European influences.

The leading light of the movement to promote Peruvian culture is Gaston Acurio, an ambitious chef who studied at Le Cordon Bleu in Paris and returned home at age twenty-seven to invent a new cuisine drawing from local influences. Among those influences are the Asian restaurants that fill Lima's Chinatown, the seafood pulled from the warm Pacific waters, and the many regional cuisines of Peru. Add a dash of Spain, a touch of France, and the ever-present influence of his grandmother—"food is feminine"—he says, and you have the cuisine that Gaston turned into a craze.[6]

•••

Anyone who arrives in Lima looking for Gaston Acurio need only mention his first name to a cabdriver or street vendor to be pointed toward one of his restaurants. Among his fans are millions of Peruvians who have never dined in one of his places. They love him nevertheless, because he has taught the world to respect the kind of food prepared in many Peruvian homes, and his success has fueled the development of a small but important industry. Hundreds of local men and women work at his restaurants, which serve everything from fast(ish) food to haute cuisine. Moreover, he has galvanized low-income youth from Pachacútec and other slums through his culinary schools, training them—at roughly one-tenth the cost of high-end culinary institutions—to become skilled, disciplined, and ambitious chefs. Thousands of people share in the wealth as food exports grow, and the entire country benefits from the boost he has given to tourism.

In a country with few international celebrities, Acurio carries the hopes and dreams of millions—and he is in constant demand. The best way to get a bit of his time is to show up at one of his restaurant sites while it is still under development. We met him in a glassed-in, ground-floor space where decorators were putting the final touches on Los Bachiche, a soon-to-open Peruvian-Italian restaurant in the fashionable Miraflores district. Acurio, dressed in black jeans and a black polo shirt, sat at a long table near the bar. He spoke to us between tasting different items from the menu, brought to him one by one by a staff chef.

"It used to be that people went to restaurants to eat and have fun. That was it," said Acurio, running his fingers through his curly black hair and sitting back in his seat. "I went to school and studied how to cook like this. It required a lot of silverware, a lot of napkins. It was mostly for rich people, and it was a wonderful thing as far as it went. But it was like theater, and only a few people could experience it."

Feeling unfulfilled by the traditional fine dining scene, Acurio gradually developed an approach to food that incorporated "creativity, beauty, ethics, and even stories." In 1994, he and his new wife, Astrid, returned to Lima to open a place called Astrid y Gaston, where they served locally sourced food from sustainable farms and fisheries. All the dishes were adapted from classic Peruvian recipes, including ceviche, many kinds of potato, octopus, and alpaca. Menu items were paired with playful stories—"a hairy crab, oppressed by the powerful people, joins the yellow pepper and hedgehog . . . long live the revolution!"—and the flavors and stories were changed with the seasons.

Astrid y Gaston was so successful that it inspired a new school of cooking, Cocina Novoandina (New Andean Cooking), and Acurio found opportunities to open additional outposts of Astrid y Gaston in Spain and across South America. The culinary school followed, supplying these restaurants with staff, and then came additional concepts. A seafood restaurant called La Mer grew to eight restaurants, including one in San Francisco and one in New York. The Acurios started a less expensive restaurant called Tanta, which serves quick meals prepared to his standards, and experimented with everything from juice bars to Chinese-Peruvian fusion. Many of the experiments became small chains, spreading their vision of healthy Peruvian food and cross-cultural relationships.

"The farmers who produce our ingredients, which we use all over the world, are mostly still poor farmers who support their family with sustainable agriculture," explained Gaston. "But the more successful we are, the more successful they are. And that success depends on trust. We ask the person who is sharing our food to try something new—alpaca, sea urchin—and because they trust, they do and they like it."

As the world noticed Acurio—*Portfolio* magazine called him the world's "next great superchef"—imitators arose in Peru and abroad. He welcomed local competitors to study his methods, copy his dishes, and even buy from his suppliers, because the tourist economy needed to draw more visitors. "When people come to one of my places and we are full, I give them a list of five restaurants that are not mine," added Acurio. "I know they will have a great experience at these places, and they may go home to New York or London and say they had a wonderful time in Peru and then their friends will come. Today we have 2.5 million tourists a year. Maybe we can get to 25 million."

Gaston applauds the spread of Peruvian recipes across Europe, North America, and Asia. As local diners come to love Andean food, demand for authentic ingredients increases, and subsistence farmers find new markets. "What is great is that we were able to seduce other worlds with our foods," he said with a smile. "We didn't believe we could make a product that the entire world would love, but we did."

As far as Gaston is concerned, his "product" is the Peruvian culture and all that it comprises. He may be communicating about it through food, but he believes that people feel the connection Peruvians feel to the mountains and sea, their deep commitment to family, their artistic sensibilities, and their yearning for respect and recognition. And, ultimately, the connection Gaston makes with the world advances the cause peace and progress.

"I grew up at one of the most expensive addresses in Peru," said Gaston, whose father was a senator in the national legislature. "I went to the school all the rich people sent their kids to, and I lived in a sort of bubble. But my father taught me that I wasn't special, I was lucky. When I was older, I had poor friends and rich friends. And I knew that I had a responsibility to do something for Peru, to make things better."

Through the turmoil of the Fujimori years and the country's struggle toward real democracy, Gaston kept working at his craft, growing his business and gaining fame. He is certain that Peruvian musicians and designers are about to gain the recognition he and Nobel Prize–winning author Mario Vargas Llosa have enjoyed and that a great flowering of culture is at hand. Noting that Peru has never won a war or dominated a global industry, he theorizes that in an era of peace, it may be the artists, chefs, performers, and writers who seize the world's attention.

"We want to conquer the world emotionally," said Gaston. "Let America and Korea be the technology countries. Let France and Italy be the luxury countries. We can be the country of diversity and magic, and the world will come to us."

•••

Thanks to Gaston Acurio, more of the world is visiting Peru, and Lima has been added to travel itineraries alongside archeological sites like Machu Picchu and natural wonders like Lake Titicaca. However, visitors to Lima rarely leave the upscale Miraflores district; when they do, they quickly discover a city where huge numbers of people live in shantytowns where security, utilities, and money are in very short supply. Roughly half of the people live below world standards for poverty, and almost 20 percent exist in "absolute" poverty, which means they live on less than $1 per day.[7]

For the poor, basic services remain the key to survival; and in Lima's busy streets, no one has done more to help them than the women's police unit founded by activist Silvia Loli. As the director of Women's House, a social service center in the middle of the city, Loli was well aware of the trouble women in Lima faced when they were raped or subjected to domestic violence and tried to work with the police. Cases were routinely shelved or dismissed by the police, who were overburdened and who placed violence against women at the bottom of their agenda. Certain that police services would improve if women were welcomed onto the force, Loli began pressing for them to be recruited. The idea gained some traction when public anger over corruption in the transit police reached a boiling point.

A small woman with dark hair, Loli holds several advanced degrees and is well known in political circles. In a lifetime spent advocating for the poor and the excluded, she has retained a kind of warmth mixed with an air of authority. This is a woman who knows how to grapple with difficult problems.

With a sense of wonder at what has changed in her country, Loli told us about the progress made in public safety. Early success in the traffic control service led to the appointment of a female ombudswoman for the police department, and women were added to security teams at soccer matches—because, according to Loli, men are embarrassed to act like fools in front of women. Data gleaned from police units that included women led to the development of offices for women inside police stations, where female officers served female victims. National lawmakers were persuaded to approve comprehensive legislation making domestic violence a serious offense, and families suddenly had recourse to the justice system.

Although men, women, and children benefit from the police reforms and new laws, the energy behind the changes came almost entirely from women. When we asked Loli about the overall progress Peru has made, socially and economically, she said that the country remains at a point where meaningful solutions are still generated from the ground up, by people who need to see immediate improvements in their lives and their children's lives. Large institutions that might pursue these goals on a grand scale simply don't exist.

To fill the need, Women's House operates counseling programs and legal aid clinics that accept everyone. (When we visited, an elderly man waited patiently on a sofa for someone to see him about a landlord issue.) Loli has also started agencies that provide job training as well as financing and technical support for women who want to start small businesses. The center has backed start-ups that produce ceramics and clothing, and others that provide services, such as small appliance repair.

Loli recounted the story of one woman who fled violence in her village and wound up in Lima, where she didn't know anyone. Loli and her team provided shelter and training, and the woman eventually applied for a job and became a cook. Loli recognizes that her country is still filled with much machismo, but believes that one by one, case by case, she and her team can help people create better lives.

•••

It doesn't get much more "one by one" than a one-room school that occupies the roof of an apartment building on a crowded street in one of the poorest cities in South America. This is where Carmen Zavala helps mothers with deaf children by teaching them sign language and the basics of reading, writing, and arithmetic.

Raised by an American mother and a Peruvian father who were deeply religious, Carmen watched her parents give up the comforts of life in the United States to run an outreach program for street children in Lima. Ernesto and Margaret Zavala started this work in the 1980s, bringing blankets, food, and clothes to the street corners and plazas where children as young as eight and nine begged for coins to buy aerosol products they could sniff to get high. Deaths were common among these children, and, as the Zavalas discovered, many suffered from disabilities. Some who had hearing problems had even developed their own version of sign language to communicate.

Working from a van, which they used to patrol the city at night, the Zavalas met hundreds of children. They eventually sold their property in America and began raising funds at churches. The money they gathered bought nine homes in Lima, which became shelters and social service centers. The program grew and grew—however, it also attracted the attention of gangs who objected to their presence in Lima's slums. Eventually, serious threats of violence ended their work. The Zavalas returned to America to educate their own children. Not surprisingly, after Carmen finished school and spent some time working at a Starbucks in suburban New York, she felt drawn to return to Lima, where she quickly found work as a coordinator for a medical aid agency. But although this service could provide medical services, it could not educate deaf children.

"In Peru, there are about ten certified teachers for the deaf who know sign language and about seven untrained deaf people who can teach sign language and act as models to teach children," said Carmen. "This is a city of more than eight million people. Obviously there are a lot of kids who are not being educated."[8]

Approached by a mother named Dahlia, Carmen was moved by her desire to help her son and charmed by the boy, Humberto. "He was seven, and smiled a lot. But besides 'yes' and 'no' and a few other things like 'sit down,' they didn't have any language they could communicate in. He didn't realize his name was Humberto or that his mother was his mother. All he knew was that this was the person who cared for him, and if she was gone, he freaked out."

Beginning with just one child and one mother, Carmen enlisted a teacher to help introduce mother and child to sign language. The model Carmen designed called for both of them to attend weekly lessons and to practice and make progress together. Eventually mother and child moved on to academic subjects.

Word of the scheme spread, and Carmen's effort grew to the point where she could work with mothers and children in pairs, every day of the week. The entire endeavor continued in her apartment and, on sunny days, on the rooftop deck. Humberto and Dahlia were working together when we met Carmen. They were joined by a girl, also deaf, who laughed as Humberto clowned for his visitors. "You must be *muy viejo* [very old]," he signed to us, "because you don't have any hair."

The smile on Humberto's face was the same smile any boy would flash after poking fun at an elder. It showed how much he valued communication. "That's progress," said Carmen. Count one more soul brought into the stream of life by another person's desire to make the world a better place.

Chapter 6

Kenya

*"In a world with less money, close personal
relationships are more important."* (82% agree)

Small-scale agriculture is the beating heart of Kenya's economy,
sustaining more than half its people. To understand this, you
must start at a place like J's farm. J owns just an acre or two, but it
is an impressive example of intensive and intentional small-scale
agriculture. On his sunbaked land, he produces more than enough
cassava, corn, and meat to feed his family. He sells the excess at
markets in the nearby city of Nanyuki, where travelers on Highway
A2 stop to snap photos at a big yellow sign that marks the equator.
The move from subsistence to trade has given J hope that his
children and grandchildren might attend school and find a life
more prosperous than his own.

When J spoke with us in early 2012, his voice echoed with
an optimism that defies Kenya's history of corruption and poverty.
Indeed, he was so positive about his prospects that he planned to
build a small cassava processing factory. Drought tolerant and easy
to grow, cassava root can be turned into a commodity that can
be stored for long periods of time, which increases its value. With
a small processing plant, J and his neighbors could even out the

fluctuations in their incomes and stabilize the food supply for their corner of the country.

J's hope and faith were built on a foundation that is both tangible—in the form of new tools and technologies—and intangible. First, the intangible. In the wake of the disastrous 2007 presidential election that led to corruption charges and deadly violence, Kenyans embarked on a broad effort to reform their political system. The result was a new constitution that promised to strengthen democracy, reinforce the rule of law, and extend equal rights to women. It was approved by a two-thirds vote in a peaceful and orderly referendum election.

Of course, the future cannot be predicted by a document, and politics in Kenya has been marked by paradoxes and contradiction. (The main proponent of the constitution was a prime minister who is both Kenya's richest man and a leftist who named his son Fidel Castro.) Also, for millions of Kenyans like J, politics and government are of little immediate concern. National leaders in Nairobi may anticipate growth spurred by a more stable democracy, but in the countryside, people are more focused on rainfall and soil conditions. And it is in the realm of these very basic concerns that Athena-style trust and cooperation, enabled by technology, are making a big difference in everyday life.

J is a case in point. We met him after our journey from Nanyuki along roads that became more rutted and narrow with every passing mile. Although the trip took two hours, the distance we covered was less than twenty miles. The last hundred yards was accomplished on foot, as we picked our way along a path that would have ruined the undercarriage of our van. We found J in a clearing, bustling about in a red fleece shirt and blue pants. He shielded his head from the sun with his hands and smiled broadly as he saw our intermediary, a young woman named Rose Goslinga. She is, for lack of a better term, his sales representative, and she is the one who made it possible for him to risk planting a new cash crop.

The title "sales representative" is inadequate to describe Rose's role because she has done so much more for Kenya's farmers than sell a financial product. Eager to do something to combat poverty in the country, Rose first focused her attention on the fact that many farmers held back on planting costly seeds or cultivating all their acreage. With a little more research, she discovered that many of these small-scale farmers were reluctant to risk bigger investments in seed and fertilizer because a drought or a flood could wipe out their crops. If she could figure out a way to limit their risk with insurance, just as big agricultural firms do in the developed world, they might make the moves required to get more out of their land.

Agricultural insurance is routine in richer countries, where it is often subsidized by governments. Kenya cannot afford such subsidies, and, more to the point, most of the country's farms are so small that traditional insurance schemes wouldn't make sense. "It would cost about $50 to visit each farm," explained Rose. "For that you would get a $5 premium."[1] If disaster struck and the farmer filed a claim, an insurer who made a second visit to verify the loss would incur $100 in expenses before writing a check to cover the losses.

To get around the cost of farm visits, Rose turned to inexpensive, automated weather stations that could measure wind, rainfall, and temperatures. One station might cover hundreds of farms. With a network of stations reporting by wireless telephone, great swaths of the country could be observed. Analysts, equipped with the right computer program, could take the readings from the stations and determine when farmers enjoyed the conditions to thrive and when their crops would suffer. In bad times, farmers wouldn't even have to make an insurance claim. They would be paid automatically and have the money to try again.

"I was always told that insurance was a numbers game," Rose said as she recalled her early work on her project. In other words, insurance schemes can work only when great numbers of people pay premiums that cover the occasional, expensive payouts for losses. Eager to build a program that would sustain itself, she set her sights on a large-scale endeavor. "We wanted to see if we could take it to hundreds of thousands of farmers."

Rose, who had accompanied us from Nanyuki to J's farm, was almost uniquely qualified to build a program to help make Kenyan farmers more secure and productive. With an advanced degree in economics and years of government service in Rwanda, she understood the workings of business, government, and finance. ("I could do the maths," she would say.) But it was her personal experience growing up in Tanzania that motivated her commitment to Africa and agriculture.

A child of missionaries who were themselves children of missionaries, Rose was born into a family with a generations-long involvement in efforts to aid human and economic development in poorer countries. Some of these projects proved fruitful; others failed. As a girl, Rose was impressed by a farm established next to the hospital where her father served as a physician. The place was run with labor from local people who earned credits they could spend on clothing from a hospital supply. Clothes were hard to come by in 1980s Tanzania, and Rose noticed that even the paid staff at the hospital put in hours at the farm because the pay was so desirable.

The farm at the hospital also imbued in Rose a deep appreciation for people who work the land and depend on the cycles of nature to survive. As she explained it, life in most African agricultural communities depends on the sun and the rain, as it has for thousands of years. "Farmers are only very happy if they have a good crop," she said. "And if it rains, everyone is in a good mood." Indeed, rainfall can make the difference between a generous Christmas and a lean one, and it can determine whether money is available to send a child to school. Historically, poor harvests came every three or four years; without crop insurance, the losses could be devastating.

With little doubt that insurance could make life better in rural Kenya, Rose turned to the technology of weather stations and wireless communication to make it affordable. Here she followed a path blazed by civil rights activists in the postelection crisis of

2007. The key development then was a program called Ushahidi (Swahili for "testimony") that allowed people to send in reports of violence by text message and email. The data produced maps showing the intensity and spread of violence around the country. The brainchild of a Kenyan-born American named Erik Hersman, Ushahidi provided better information than any government or media source.

Ushahidi's accuracy and ease of use proved the power and reliability of crowdsourcing technology, which would be the basis of Rose's insurance scheme. A second technology, called M-Pesa, would create a cashless, almost cost-free system for the financial transactions, including premium payments and claims payouts. M-Pesa (M is for "mobile" and *pesa* means "money" in Swahili) was introduced by the Safaricom wireless company in 2007 and quickly became a workable, almost universal substitute for credit cards, checks, and, most important, cash. With M-Pesa, farmers and others could make transactions at markets without fear of later being robbed and losing their income.

As these helpful technologies emerged and came into wide use, Rose met with lenders in hopes that they would include the cost of insurance in small loans they made to farmers purchasing supplies. She discovered that the great majority of Kenyan banks did almost no business with farmers because they didn't understand the way agriculture worked and considered the expense of making so many tiny loans too great. However, two large seed and fertilizer companies were willing to help. The multinational company Syngenta backed her through its foundation and by making insurance available through seed sales. Seed Co of Zambia also agreed to let farmers add insurance to seeds it sells across Kenya. These agreements transformed the small dealers who supplied farmers with their essential supplies into salespeople for the drought and flood coverage.

With all the groundwork done, Rose named her enterprise Kilimo Salama (Safe Agriculture) and enlisted a seed shop run by Lucy Muriuki to make the first insurance sales. Like other "agro-vets," Lucy offered the necessities that agriculture experts call "inputs" for the small farms that are the heart of the regional economy. As a longtime supplier, Lucy knew hundreds of farmers who had come to trust her. She always donned a white, doctor-style coat before opening her shop for business, and she listened carefully when her customers spoke of their problems and strategies.

"When I would learn of new technologies, I would pass them along," Lucy told us when we met her at her shop in Nanyuki.[2] As she explained it, a farmer who had success with medicine for rabbits or a pesticide for cassava would tell neighbors, and the circle of trust established by Lucy's expertise would open wider.

Trust was essential to the first insurance policy sales. Kenyans in rural areas had limited experience with insurance products. Many were wary of paying the premium and feared that they would not be compensated if they needed to make a claim. This fear was put to rest in the very first year of Kilimo Salama's operation, when the weather stations reported drought conditions and many of the insured farmers received payments.

As word of the insurance program spread, more seed dealers became salespeople, and thousands of farmers agreed to pay premiums to participate. Enrollment was expected to reach twelve thousand in 2013, and the Kilimo Salama staff grew from five to seventy during the peak season.

The technology used by salespeople has evolved to the point where farmers can step up to the sales counter at a seed shop, report the locale of the weather station nearest to their property, identify the crop they want to raise, and receive an immediate quote on the cost of insurance. This is all accomplished with cell phones that read codes kept in a book at the shop and fill an electronic "shopping cart" as a farmer considers his or her options.

Today, farmers across Kenya make Kilimo Salama's insurance a routine part of their seasonal planning. The repeat business has allowed the service to become self-sustaining, which was one of Rose Goslinga's primary objectives. She said she wouldn't have been interested in a charitable enterprise that subsidized an outcome that wouldn't be possible otherwise. "The idea is we've got to run it as a business," she noted. A farmer's willingness to pay indicates that "it has value."

The value is also evident in the lives of farmers like J, who can try new crops and techniques and expand production. The ultimate goal for everyone is to make farming so profitable that families can afford to send children to school, where they can prepare for work in different sectors of the economy. This kind of development is essential, as small farms cannot sustain ever-growing numbers of people—and Kenya's population is growing faster than that of any other country on Earth.

•••

In Kenya, as in much of sub-Saharan Africa, farmers have long lacked access to the kind of storage facilities, seeds, irrigation equipment, and financial tools needed to join the "green revolution" that swept much of the world following the invention of advanced grain hybrids in the 1960s. More recently, declines in foreign aid and boom-and-bust cycles in commodity prices have put additional pressure on African farmers.

In this environment, development and agriculture experts have begun to focus on helping small landholders do a better job with more modern and sustainable methods. On a large scale, the major industrialized countries, led by the United States, have pledged to spend billions of dollars on improving small family farms with the goal of raising yields. Allied with major private actors like the Bill & Melinda Gates Foundation, these programs aim not only to end hunger but also to avert security problems that arise out of extreme conditions. Hungry populations are vulnerable to political extremists, which means that developed countries make themselves more secure by helping Africa.

Of course, the job of helping small farmers inevitably comes down to individuals traveling the countryside, contacting farmers and providing them with education and support. At the forefront of this effort in Kenya and Rwanda is an organization called the One Acre Fund, which seems to pop up in every conversation about Africa, farming, and the future. The fund, which is named for the size of a typical sub-Saharan farm, partners with Kilimo Salama and is famous around the world for its "market bundle" program.

Imagined by Andrew Youn when he was still a business school student, the One Acre Fund is building a self-sustaining program to educate farmers and finance expanded production at their farms. Youn begins with a partnership between the fund and some existing community organization. (Typically these are social or support groups made up of women farmers.) After they attend classes on modern, sustainable techniques, the farmers get access to loans, advanced seeds, and fertilizer acquired in bulk to cut costs. At harvest time, they get help locating markets for their crops, or they get assistance to develop and use secure storage facilities so that harvests can be held until prices improve.

Beginning with grants and donations that amounted to less than $100,000 in 2006, Youn reached just a few hundred families with One Acre's "bundle." The experiment cost about $300 per family, but average output at the participating farms grew by 400 percent, and income tripled. With the idea working, Youn attracted funding to expand rapidly. According to the model, financing was made available to groups of farmers who pledged assets as small as a goat to secure their loans. If one member of the group failed to make repayment, the entire group would be ineligible for a new round of funding for the next season. This system created so much peer pressure that 98 percent of the farmers met their obligations. Loan payments could then be recycled as new loans.

By the time we arrived in Kenya in early 2012, One Acre was so big and efficient that its costs had been reduced to just $80 per year per family. Nearly one hundred thousand farm families were involved, and the fund employed, in all, more than forty directors and assistant directors in its many districts. They supervised more than eight hundred staff people, who formed the corps of individuals who could rise in the ranks to leadership positions.

One Acre's values are spelled out on its website and include, among others, humble services, hard work, and integrity. ("We do what we say, and our words match our values.") These values also require that people who are employed by One Acre spend virtually all their time in remote locations working directly with farmers and their families. This policy made it all but impossible for us to pin down a staff member in Kenya, but we did connect with One Acre's policy director Stephanie Hanson when she was in the United States.

During our discussion, at a coffee house serving a fair-trade Kenyan blend, Stephanie explained that One Acre isn't delivering a new set of ideals to farmers. Instead, it builds on a tradition of trusting relationships that has long guided life in rural Kenya.

"There's always been sharing," she said. "If your neighbor has a good crop and you don't, it's expected the farmer that had a good harvest will give some of it to you."[3] Traditionally, this sharing saved people from hunger and even starvation. However, a more formalized system that spreads risk more widely could increase the volume of food available to farmers with failed crops. At the same time, improved methods would reduce the number of bad seasons and give farm families a higher baseline standard of living.

The One Acre method is working so well that 80 percent of its expenses are paid by the fees and interest on loans paid by participating farmers. Demand for the fund's services is outpacing its ability to hire and train new workers. This is, of course, a good problem to have, and Hanson said that the organization's leaders are looking at some surprising role models, including the McDonald's hamburger chain.

"McDonald's is very good at standardized operating procedures," noted Hanson, "but is also getting better at tailoring itself to local markets." One Acre could succeed with a similar strategy that teaches partners in other countries to work almost like McDonald's franchisees, delivering the basic program with a local twist.

But although Andrew Youn designed One Acre to grow and thrive as a business might, the fund's ultimate goal is not the creation of an agricultural empire. Instead, Youn and his staff intend to improve the lives of farmers, their families, and the communities they serve. Worldwide, about eight hundred million of these people currently subsist on less than $2 per day. Improving their lot would go a long way toward reducing poverty, hunger, premature death, and social unrest.

With the antipoverty goals in mind, said Hanson, One Acre may eventually teach its techniques to a variety of for-profit, nonprofit, and governmental groups and permit them to adapt them even where the fund already operates. Under this concept, a bank could design a package of services that loan officers might offer in the same way that they offer financing for cars or small businesses. "If there is a viable market to serve smaller farmers, they wouldn't be partnering with us, but rather competing with us," said Hanson with a calm, matter-of-fact tone. "We think that's great because it means more options for the farmers."

• • •

The long-term payoff for Kenya from a program like One Acre would be seen in the rising health and education levels of the farm children who will soon be young adults. With its urban population growing at nearly 5 percent per year, Kenya will need more jobs in commerce and industry, and these positions require workers with sufficient schooling. However, many of today's adults in Kenya also need immediate access to work and incomes, and cannot devote years to study. For this segment of the population, one of the world's oldest aid groups—Catholic Relief Services—promotes a saving and lending scheme that serves people who are so poor that they cannot qualify even for the kind of microfinance loans popular in many parts of the world.

"More than credit, these people are in need of a safe place to keep their money," explained Guy Vanmeenen, whom we met at an office in the Westlands neighborhood of Nairobi.[4] The district is the type of well-developed community of offices, retail shopping strips, and residences you might see anywhere in the world. It is home to many aid organizations and the businesses that serve them. A Java Shop (Kenya's version of Starbucks) bustled with business, while a block north, the Phoenician Restaurant and Sushi Bar awaited the lunch crowd.

Belgian born, Guy is tall and slender, with dirty blond hair. His commitment to antipoverty work emerged during a backpacking trip through South America in 1989, where he was shocked by the conditions he saw in very poor communities. In Kenya, he works with people who are even poorer than most of the One Acre Fund farmers. These Kenyans have no access to financial institutions, but as Vanmeenen found, their communities enjoy a tradition of savings clubs. Sometimes as large as two dozen people, these community organizations meet weekly, collect very small payments from members, and then distribute the sum to individuals who each get a turn in the role of recipient.

Although the clubs allowed members to benefit from a periodic infusion of cash, no interest was paid on the savings, and certain obvious weaknesses were inherent in the informal system. First, if attendance varied, then the receipts and disbursements could vary in an unfair way. Second, the scheme could fall apart before every member got his or her turn to be paid. Third, it was inflexible and made no provision for emergencies or community interests.

Soft spoken but also passionate about his work, Guy used a yoga ball for a desk chair and rocked gently on it as he talked. He obviously admired the thrift and resourcefulness of the people he served. "People do save, even if they save by buying and caring for chickens," he said. He also believed that he could help the very poor take additional steps toward financial security. In villages and city neighborhoods, he helped formalize the savings clubs by equipping them with ledgers, lockboxes, and a lending plan. The lockboxes, which secure both contributions and records, were each equipped with four locks and could be opened only with keys held by four separate members of the club.

As safe as a bank, the box system reinforced trust that already existed among neighbors. The lending plan encouraged members to consider requests for loans and to set interest rates charged to borrowers. Accustomed to paying double-digit rates, sometimes on a daily basis, the cash box groups typically set rates that would reach as much as 30 percent per year. Most loans are repaid in a matter of days or weeks, so individual borrowers are able to clear their accounts by repaying principal and just a small additional amount. However, the groups see an average 27 percent return on their savings per year. For most small savers, these earnings represent the first gains they have ever seen from investment.

Besides the lending, most of Guy's groups also operate social benefit projects, which might fund some improvements for a community, and they offer emergency aid for participants whose families are struck by illness or some other crisis. Aid allocations are determined by group members, who are likely to be wives and mothers. Seventy percent of the savings group enrollees are female. "Women have more social skill and are more accustomed to coming together to solve problems," added Guy.

Remarkably, in seven years of operation, the savings club members have poured $8 million—often a nickel or dime at a time—into the lockboxes. Guy's next step involved savers in training programs that equipped them to help establish new groups. Certified by Catholic Relief Services, but operating as entrepreneurs, these consultants collect fees for helping people form and operate new groups. Because the trained consultants are paid by every group they serve, they have a stake in spreading the practice. In a self-perpetuating cycle of empowerment, poor people who are "microsavers" become microentrepreneurs.

Guy's ultimate goal is a financial system that is run by and for the most impoverished people in the world and that requires no outside funding or direction. "We're moving from a subsidized approach to a market approach," said Guy. "We have seven hundred private service providers, and they have recruited ninety apprentices." Fears that the private consultants might neglect the poorest people in their communities have been calmed by studies showing that they continued to serve the original, targeted groups. Soon the system could function so well on its own that Guy and the Catholic Relief Services bureaucracy will not be needed. He's okay with this outcome.

• • •

"It's about empowerment," he told us. "People now say, 'We don't have to depend on handouts.'" In fact, some of the savings clubs have decided to share their wealth with neighbors. In villages, they supply aid to widows and orphans on a case-by-case basis. "When the project ends," said Guy, "we will leave behind the capacity for people to do it themselves."

Empowerment based on group action seemed to be a trend in Kenya, one that recalls the rise of trade unions in industrial countries a century ago. The difference here is that the Kenyan economy is not industrial, but rather entrepreneurial. Those seeking strength in numbers must do so on a smaller scale and with their own resources. We found an example in a small, unspoiled forest within the city limits of Nairobi. The Ngong Forest Sanctuary is one of just a few urban forests in the world. It shelters hundreds of animal species and beckons the city's four million people with the prospect of an accessible retreat from noisy neighborhoods and traffic-choked streets.

We went to Ngong to meet with women who had pooled their money and purchased the equivalent of a franchise in honey production. Inside the forest, which was protected by rangers, they tend to bees with the same kind of equipment we saw in the Hackney district of London, at the start of our Athena world tour. Their honeybees lived in block-shaped "Langstroth" hives, and the women donned white suits, masks, and gloves to do their work. Smoke from little pots subdued the bees—"They look like drunkards," joked one of the keepers—and made them so docile that the hives could be opened.

While they worked, the Nairobi beekeepers talked about the prices paid for honey and the devotion required to make a go of beekeeping. They also recalled that before getting into this business, they made even less money collecting fallen trees branches in the forest and selling them as cooking fuel on the streets. That work was possible only because rangers gave them access to the sanctuary. When they finished work the day we visited, the women showed their gratitude and enthusiasm with a dance they had devised. Moving with the same seemingly random twists and turns shown by their productive little buzzing partners, they bent low to the ground, extended their "wings," and laughed with happiness.

The money harvested in the Ngong forest goes to a small factory operated by a company called Honey Care Africa. It's founder, Farouk Jiwa, is a fourth-generation Kenyan descended from Indian immigrants who came to the country when its railroad was developed and Nairobi became a center of regional trade.

Farouk began his adult life as a starry-eyed environmental scientist, who quickly became a business development specialist. The transformation occurred when he returned to Kenya from college in Canada and realized that his country's environmental problems required complex solutions. Although he was deeply concerned about the future of rare animals and their habitats, he recognized that protecting them required simultaneous work to reduce the poverty that drove so many people to exploit the country's natural resources.

On the one hand, "traditionally NGOs [charitable nongovernmental organizations] would come in and do lovely work over a period of five years, but it all ended when they left," Farouk told us.[5] On the other hand, "private sector companies come in and are exploitative, but they have a longer-term perspective than five years." The way Farouk saw it, Kenyans either got involved with aid projects that ended prematurely and left them high and dry, or teamed with business enterprises that reserved almost all the profits for themselves while scarring the landscape and using up natural resources. Searching for an alternative that would create long-term business activity, more equitable profit sharing, and benefits for the environment, he quickly settled on honey production.

At the time, most Kenyan honey, which holds a special place in traditional culture, was produced with methods that made the work difficult, the yield small, and the quality low. Not surprisingly, imported goods from as far away as Australia dominated the market. Returning to Canada for a master's degree, Farouk wrote a thesis that became a plan for reviving the Kenyan industry. The plan called for equipment designed to bring women into the business, and methods to ensure the consistent quality of what they produced.

Begun in 2000, Honey Care Africa reached out first to farmers, who paid to be trained, acquire equipment, and become part of its network. Field agents traveled the countryside in trucks equipped with hand-powered pumps to extract honey when it was ready. They paid producers on the spot. (Loan payments for supplies and equipment were deducted first.) The agents then delivered the honey to the processing plant, where it was pasteurized and purified and blended into one of three brands that were then sold to retail outlets. Farmers, who monitored the prices charged for their honey at retail stores, received an accounting of all the costs that went into the final product. Producers with four hives earned roughly $300 annually for about an hour of work per week. Added to other sources of income, this revenue has helped more than two thousand participants rise above the $2-per-day poverty level.

Twelve years after its creation, Honey Care is a stable, profit-making enterprise. Women make up 40 percent of its beekeeping force, and Farouk sees the benefits accruing to their children, who now live in homes with proper roofs and attend school every day. These improvements are due to his company and countless other enterprises that have blossomed since 2000. In 2011, the Kenyan economy grew by 5.4 percent, and the trend continued into 2012.

Considering the success of Honey Care Africa, One Acre, Kilimo Salama, and others, Farouk is very optimistic. In fact, he has targeted small retailers in rural villages for a branding revolution. With proper networking, training, supply chains, and branding, these small companies can improve their service and inventories in ways that will cut prices and raise quality. "The key is to be more nimble," he noted, "and more responsive."

The device that will make this happen is the wireless telephone.

• • •

Anyone who has visited Kenya in the last three years comes away with the realization that it may be the most wirelessly connected place in the world. Just about everyone from downtown Nairobi to distant farm villages walks around with a phone in his or her hand. (Kenya has twenty million adult citizens and twenty-five million active cell phone accounts.) And wherever people do business, many of the transactions are conducted via text messages on the M-Pesa system.

Trust in mobile technology may be higher in Kenya than anywhere else, thanks to Erik Hersman's crowdsourced Ushahidi project. We met Erik at a place called iHub, which he opened in a building on Ngong Road. Like the Lightning Spot in Tokyo, iHub provides space for technology innovators and interested parties to meet and collaborate. Although this incubator is Erik's major interest, he acknowledges the historical and political significance of Ushahidi, and he willingly answered our questions.

"What it was really about was changing the way information flows," he said as he recalled the debut of Ushahidi. "It has its own power and the ability to change the way people see the world."[6]

A big, mild-mannered man, Erik marvels at the way his technology has been adopted for use in crisis spots around the globe, including political uprisings in Iran and the Arab world. He's also amused to find that people are using Ushahidi to create maps of the best slopes to ski in North America and where to find midwives in the northeastern United States. As users discover that the information is reliable, he said, "it builds bridges of trust between communities and organizations." The big lesson from the Ushahidi experience, concluded Erik, is that "connectivity is power."

No institution holds more threads of connectivity in Kenya than the wireless provider Safaricom. With 65 percent of the market, Safaricom is also the highest-rated brand in the country. When the company launched M-Pesa in 2007, its executives understood that Safaricom was perfectly positioned to make it work. However, they had no idea that people would turn it into an alternative financial system.

The executives at Safaricom first imagined the potential for moving money via text message when they heard that texts were being used to send salary payments to police officers in Afghanistan. As CEO, Robert Collymore thought that Safaricom's customers might use M-Pesa to send money to friends and family across town or across the country. "The way people sent money then was to give it to a person to take it themselves, or to send it with a bus driver," said Collymore when we met him. "We thought that wasn't very efficient."[7] Delighted to have an instantaneous and completely safe alternative, Kenyans adopted M-Pesa immediately and then found many more ways to use it.

As M-Pesa exploded in popularity, Safaricom found thousands of people lining up at authorized agents and Safaricom offices, where they either deposited money into their accounts or converted credits sent by texts to cash. Safaricom recoups the cost of M-Pesa's operation through a small fee for withdrawals of cash. The maximum charged is 1 percent on withdrawals of $100 or more. Typical M-Pesa transactions are worth just a few dollars apiece, but by 2012, the system was handling two million transactions per day. Roughly 20 percent of the Kenyan economy flowed through M-Pesa.

The security and safety provided by M-Pesa makes the commercial marketplace a more trusting environment and encourages economic activity. Mobile phone providers in other African countries have begun experimenting with the system, and reg-ulators are hearing complaints from traditional financial services firms, which suggests that M-Pesa is having an impact. Collymore is delighted by the system's success, but he is eager to see text-based technologies yield even greater benefits.

Collymore believes that Kenya's infant mortality rate, which is among the highest in the world, could be reduced if health agencies paid for prenatal care and deliveries with M-Pesa. He has heard from NGOs who want to get involved in this kind of scheme and believes it would save the lives of mothers as well as babies. In a similar vein, he said, American emergency relief officials have approached Safaricom with the idea of providing food vouchers to refugees via text message. Cash and paper voucher systems are subject to rampant theft and extortion, he noted, but a text message sent to an individual aid recipient could ensure that people in need get the food, water, and medicines intended for them.

Beyond cell phones and finance, Safaricom is also looking at using wireless technology to educate Kenyan children with tablet computers, which would make a world of books, articles, and other materials available to students in the most remote villages. Considering a future in which Kenyans compete globally, Collymore sees technology as "the only way a child in Kenya is going to keep up with a student in a place like New York." When education depended on the purchase of millions of books and on salaries for teachers in thousands of schools, the vast majority of Kenyan children couldn't hope to compete. With wireless, Collymore expects they will.

• • •

Improvements in education, as well as in health care and finance, will be essential to the development of a more diverse economy and improvements in the Kenyan standard of living. As the hub of an East African economic community that is seeing rapid population growth, the country is poised for growth in manufacturing and services. At the end of 2011, World Bank officials were praising the country's government for its economic policies and predicting sustained growth at a time when Western Europe was falling back into recession and the United States was struggling to avoid the same fate.

Although heavy industry isn't well developed in the country, manufacturing does make up 14 percent of the economy, and a few bold entrepreneurs are keen to expand this figure with radical ideas. Joel Jackson, for example, plans to build extraordinarily rugged but low-priced vehicles for travelers who must cope with rural roads that are often no better than cart paths through the wilderness. His first prototype—Mobius One—proved he could make such a car for $6,000. A bigger Mobius Two was in development when we came to Kenya. Both vehicles were designed for simple manufacturing with off-the-shelf parts. The larger one could be especially useful for entrepreneurs who would use it to transport people and goods to isolated places like Jackson Kindori's farm.

Transportation "is a huge social challenge" throughout Africa, Joel told us.[8] However, he saw in this challenge a great opportunity to offer African consumers affordable cars and trucks that can stand up to their roads. Whether he could seize the opportunity to become the Henry Ford of Kenya, making vehicles where they will be used, remains to be seen. "Our hope is to have as much assembly as possible in Kenya," Joel told us. "Right now the challenge is cost, quality, and delivery."

If the company can get to the point where it makes and sells five thousand vehicles per year, said Joel, it will begin to transform the economics of transport across Kenya and affect the design and quality of its competitors' offerings. "For me, the most compelling thing would be creating meaningful change for millions of people," said Joel, as he reflected on the potential of Mobius. "I think we've got a really great shot at doing it."

The conditions that would help Mobius succeed—growth, a burgeoning middle class, rising consumer demand—also contribute to Kenya's improved relations with global trading partners. Here, as is the case throughout the domestic economy, technologies, policies, and relationships that build trust form the foundation of hope and well-being.

In the last decade, six of the ten fastest-growing economies in the world were in Africa, and international financial institutions expect that a rising middle class will make the continent the next great market for business. The developments that inspire this confidence have prompted hundreds of American corporations and their competitors from around the world to make investments in Africa. Overtures made by Chinese enterprises have caught the attention of American officials, who don't want the United States to be overshadowed anywhere in the world. Not long after our visit, Secretary of State Hillary Clinton arrived in Nairobi with dozens of businesspeople in tow, including executives from Walmart, Boeing, and FedEx.

The delegation was making a tour of the region, intent on showing that the United States appreciated its potential. Clinton, noting the essential role of democracy in the country's development, pledged support for 2013 elections.

During Clinton's African tour, a South African analyst named Chris Lanberg told the *New York Times* of an "unprecedented interest in Africa. Every single important country whether China, France, Britain, India, Brazil, Turkey, you name it, they are all queuing up."[9] As the world gets in line to serve industry and consumers, Kenya and its neighbors may prove that they deserve the nickname bestowed on them by the editors of the *Economist*, who have dubbed Africa "the Hopeful Continent."[10]

Chapter 7

India

*"It would be good if there were more
women in leadership positions in
government." (76% agree)*

In India, where cows are sacred, the *chamars* who scrape fat and hair from a deceased steer's hide and use chemicals to make it into leather occupy an unenviable position. They are Dalits, or Untouchables, and although legally protected from discrimination, they are still rejected by much of society. At school, Dalit children are often forced to scrub floors while classmates study. As adults, Dalit are lucky to find work. The least fortunate, among them many women, work every day collecting and disposing of human and animal waste.

Historically, a Dalit woman's fate has been absolutely sealed at birth, and in another time, Manjula Pradeep would have been a leather tanner or perhaps a latrine cleaner. Denied an education and every other avenue to more comfort or security, she would have been lucky to support herself and see her fiftieth birthday.

Determination and the legal progress of modern India brought Manjula into higher education and made it possible for her to earn a master's degree in social work. But in her province of Gujarat, tradition is so powerful that Dalits still face hatred, discrimination, and violence. In 1989, Manjula's cousin was killed by men protecting the "honor" of an upper-class woman he was dating. In 1993, a Dalit woman shocked the nation by demanding justice for her son who died in police custody. Manjula took up her cause, beginning a long career of confrontation with convention. She became a lawyer, brought cases on behalf of minority groups, and stirred enough conflict to require bodyguards after her offices were attacked by a mob. In her most famous case, she won justice for a Dalit student who had been raped by six of her professors.

From the inland industrial city of Ahmedabad to the rural coast of the Arabian Sea, Manjula Pradeep is loved and admired and disparaged and hated as the implacable conscience of Gujarat. Perhaps no one in the state has done more to bring outcastes and minorities into the social and economic mainstream. Because of her work, the political establishment considers her a troublemaker. Those she helps regard her as a fearsome warrior. But when we met her in the dusty courtyard of a rural school, we discovered a small, soft-spoken woman who wore a smock the color of marigolds and beamed with contentment. She brought us into a classroom where the words "World Wide Web" were written on the chalkboard and a teacher described the Internet in the local language, Gujarati.

"These children come here and are treated as people," said Manjula, noting that like students at the better Indian schools, these boys and girls will learn about technology, along with foundational academics.[1] They will be taught to speak English and to challenge those who would relegate them to second- or third-class status. To reinforce the ideal of equality, they all participate in the work of preparing meals with the head cook, who was cast out by her family when they learned that her husband had given her HIV. When the meal is ready, students take turns serving it from large platters and eat, sitting together.

For thousands of years, no one of higher status would eat or drink with a Dalit person, and the Dalit themselves would refuse to share with someone from a slightly lower rank. Given this history, the meals at the school transmit a deep and quietly subversive lesson to the students, establishing in them the impulse to question customs, assumptions, and authority. "When they get out, they know to question their situation in life and to push for equality," added Manjula. "It's a way to help the next generation."

Planted on a few dusty acres near the tiny rural village of Rayka, the Navsarjan Vidyalaya school hums with the voices of children and teachers and is governed by the schedule of lessons and mealtimes and the routine of turning classrooms into modest dormitories for a hundred students. It seems a world away from the industries that have powered the growth of India's huge cities—such as Mumbai, Bangalore, Delhi, and Hyderabad—and it shares little in common with the Bollywood–call center–billionaire image many people now hold of modern India. But in fact, the school and its students may represent India's best shot at a future that looks like the modern country of Indian dreams.

India dreams because, despite years of impressive growth in gross domestic product, the demographic facts of the national economy describe a country that will need millions more children to be educated like the students in Rayka. This is because, for all its progress, India remains an extremely poor country where 70 percent of the people live in rural isolation. India's future depends not so much on software engineers and industrial moguls as it does on the rural poor becoming middle-class workers and consumers who enjoy the kind of life promised by independence and democracy.

Noting that the country has but "a sliver of time, a matter of years, in which to seize its chances," Sunil Khilnani of the India Institute at King's College, London, recently wrote that India must choose between two fates.[2] One would tap its diversity as a source of innovation and bring every social group into the economy. The other would perpetuate the exclusion of women and Dalit and risk disaster as "those who are being left out" will eventually rise up in anger. Khilnani urged India to use its "political imagination, judgment and action" to find ways to spread the benefits of development and avoid dangerous inequalities.

Nowhere is the promise and peril in India more evident than it is in Gujarat, where we traveled to discover stories of innovators practicing openness—to other people and new ideas—in the pursuit of progress. It is, as Manjula said, "one of the most developed states in India," but it also ranks high "when it comes to human rights violations." The persistence of prejudice widens the gap between the haves and the have-nots, but it also leads to dangerous social and political divisions. "Much of the land that is being taken away by the corporate sector is from the Dalit and poor communities," noted Manjula. At the same time, Dalits struggle to find work at the facilities built on their former lands.

The ultimate symbol of the challenge India must overcome as it develops rises on a thousand acres in the Sanand region of Gujarat, fifty miles from the school in Rayka. There, the fourth-largest automaker in the world, Tata Motors, turns out the tiny Nano hatchback at a brand-new assembly line opened in 2010. Shaped and colored like Easter eggs, the cars roll off the line at a rate of ten thousand per month. Priced at about $3,000 apiece, the two-cylinder Nano is the least expensive automobile in the world. However, four years after its introduction, it has yet to gain a foothold in India, and exports have been nil.

Though billed as a project that would take the world car market by storm, Tata's Nano initiative was delayed when protesting farmers forced the company to abandon a plant in Bengal and build the one in Gujarat. Underpowered and lacking basic safety items like airbags, the car produced there was greeted coolly. In 2010, the New York Times called it "the car that few want to buy."[3] By 2012, when we visited India, the Nano had definitely failed to spark the revolution once predicted. Ratan Tata, Tata's chief, suggested that the car suffered from a kind of caste discrimination because it was perceived to be a car for the poor. "Whatever stigma has been attached to it, we will undo going forward," promised Tata.[4] He also reiterated Tata's plans to sell a small car called the Pixel in Europe and the United States.

The prospect of consumers in Western markets accepting a car from a company battered by negative publicity remains to be seen. In the meantime, Tata's Nano adventure has captured in a nutshell many of India's socioeconomic problems. Many sectors of the society missed out on the Nano project's promised opportunities. And the car's failure was thoroughly discouraging for anyone who hoped that heavy manufacturing would bring the country quick prosperity.

India's true development power may lie not in massive schemes but instead in creative and even daring efforts to improve social mobility for the typical Indian man or woman. Indeed, the well-being of women, as measured by employment, education, and health, is a widely established proxy for a nation's well-being. Although a member of the G20 assembly of major economies, India is the poorest in measures of per capita wealth and income, and Indian women rank last in measures of equality and welfare. According to a report issued by the United Nations, "Most women do not have any autonomy in decision making in their personal lives."[5]

If nations rise when the lives of women are improved, then a better India depends on the eradication of gender disparities as well as caste-based discrimination. No organization in the country is more closely identified with this cause than the Self Employed Women's Association (SEWA), a national group that began in Ahmedabad and is still headquartered there today. Its first effort secured fair pay and security for street vendors, who were being harassed and exploited by police and corrupt suppliers. Soon SEWA was organizing microfinance loans to help poor workers escape debt and establishing secure markets for craft workers. With the organization's help, women who sold goods in markets also gained access to selling space at reasonable rates.

Based in modest offices on the eastern bank of the Sabarmati River, SEWA offers services and support for impoverished Indian women who are often so isolated and accustomed to discrimination that they struggle even to imagine a better life. With SEWA's help, they learn the market value for their labor, handmade goods, or farm products, and can use this information to demand fair pay. SEWA offers education, health care, savings and loan programs, insurance, and housing. Members in the state of Gujarat number more than eight hundred thousand. Chapters in other regions bring the national count to more than 1.2 million.

On the day we visited SEWA's national headquarters, just a few women occupied the modest administrative offices, and computers hummed quietly in a technology center where members gained access to the Internet and vocational instruction. The real work of the organization was being done in hundreds of other places, including a new polytechnic school that serves four hundred girls in Delhi. The four top officials who agreed to speak with us don't often get the opportunity to reflect on their lives and on what they have accomplished in their work. The president of SEWA, Kapila Vankar, offered us her prayerful gratitude for our interest. Then she told us about her transformation from a dispirited and isolated woman into a leader, noting that she knew little of the world outside her house and had no identity as a worker.

Like many impoverished Indian women, she put in long hours of labor each day, but the arrangement was so informal that she could claim no set wage rate, schedule, or duties. And, like so many others, Kapila, who worked in tobacco fields and factories, accepted her insecurity and poverty as practically immutable.

From its very beginning, SEWA was greeted with skepticism by the women it was formed to serve, who are wary of outsiders. Mothers feared leaving their children at the organization's day-care centers, and laborers worried that they could be blackballed by employers. But with persistence and with the law on their side, organizers generally succeed, and this was true in Kapila's case. When she and her coworkers asserted their rights, they started getting regular work, and income increased. They also discovered that they were entitled to predictable schedules, periodic rest breaks, and meals that they had never before received.

Respected by others, Kapila began to get involved in decision making, both in her family and her village. Family and neighbors recognized her confidence and valued what she had learned in SEWA literacy classes and management seminars. With pride, she confessed that today villagers actually look up to her, and the *panchayat* (village leader) consults her on village matters, something that would never have happened prior to her involvement in SEWA.

Kapila's leadership was tested in 2003 when her village was devastated by a flood that marooned the entire community. After discovering hundreds of women huddled in the dark with their children, she helped them find shelter. Then, accompanied by roughly half of them, she approached village leaders to ask why the floodwaters had not been diverted by a drainage system, and what could be done to avert future disasters. The women heard that the contractors who had built the drainage system had made mistakes and paid fines for construction failures. After the disaster, Kapila pushed to use the money paid in penalties to correct the rainwater sewers. This work was done, and the remainder was enough to build the village's first high school.

The success Kapila described flowed not from an industrialist's dream to build a new car for the world but from something far more basic: the self-esteem she gained as she established an identity as a worker and then as a full citizen. Having touched millions of lives in the same way, SEWA moves India forward by empowering individuals who cannot even consider applying for jobs making cars or answering phones at a call center. For them, a better life begins in an organization that values them and nurtures them almost like family.

Other women aided by SEWA have relied on the personal strength developed in the sisterhood to take risks with new technologies that have helped them increase their output of crafts, textiles, and farm produce. In some cases, they rely on the organization's microlending to acquire equipment that helps them become more efficient even in the age-old occupations of weaving and salt making. These two occupations resonate deeply in Indian culture because of their connection to the renowned nationalist and human rights campaigner Mahatma Gandhi. During his long and highly inspirational struggle, Gandhi made and wore simple "homespun" garments to emphasize his affiliation with women and the poor. He also conducted a famous "salt march," leading thousands of people from Ahmedabad to the sea, where he made salt in defiance of a policy that restricted its production. Similar to America's Boston Tea Party, the march marked the beginning of a wide move toward civil disobedience and ultimate independence.

Gandhi was a native of Gujarat who established his ashram in Ahmedabad, and his presence hangs over the city even now, more than sixty years after his death. Although he is almost universally revered, people hold extremely varied opinions about his life and actions. For example, some Dalits recall with admiration how he helped outlaw "untouchability," whereas others regret that Gandhi insisted that the caste system remain legal. Similarly, many people are vexed by the conflict between Gandhi's personal attitudes about women—he had lots of destructive gender hang-ups—and his politics of inclusion.

As a folk hero, however, Gandhi stands secure as a symbol of the struggle for equal rights for women, the poor, and religious minorities. His ashram, which occupies a small campus on the riverside in Ahmedabad, is a sort of national shrine attracting visitors from around the world. When we were there, we watched busloads of Indian tourists arrive to inspect the modest red-and-white buildings, including the Mahatma's home (now a museum) filled with papers, photos, and artifacts. Most of the people who came off the buses stopped and kissed the feet of a statue of Gandhi positioned near the entrance to the site.

We visited the ashram to absorb a bit of history and connect with a group called Manav Sadhna (Service to Mankind). An organization with virtually no central organization, Manav Sadhna was founded by Viren Joshi, whose father had campaigned with Gandhi. For most of the 1980s, he lived and worked in the United States, where he was employed by the retailer TJ Maxx and then as a machine operator at an aluminum casting company. He returned to India and settled in Ahmedabad in 1989. He visited the ashram regularly for prayer and then took it upon himself to go into the city streets and talk with the children he found wandering on their own. What he heard and saw moved Viren to teach the children about hygiene and then arrange for them to bathe. He sewed buttons on their clothes and fed them when he could.

From his beginning as a spontaneous friend and mentor to street children, Viren went on to affiliate with the ashram, and created Manav Sadhna as both a service organization and an incubator of ideas that would serve the poor and bring them into mainstream society. As a partner with the Indian government, the group helps run seventy-eight schools in the slum neighborhoods of Ahmedabad and a residential school for the blind. With others, Manav Sadhna also offers technology training and Web-based college education at a computer center, and works in health, finance, and community development.

Impressive as its array of projects may be, what makes Manav Sadhna special is the distinctly Gandhian philosophy and modus operandi. Although it is actively involved in supplying some direct services, most of what the group does involves offering support for others. Without passing judgment or offering concrete direction, Viren welcomes anyone who wants to serve the people of the city or state at daily ten o'clock prayer sessions followed by open-ended discussions that can become miniseminars in both the practical and spiritual elements of service. The ultimate goal is to create a community that makes it possible for people to intelligently endure and succeed in a place where even the simplest tasks can seem impossible. As valuable as grant money and technical advice, emotional and spiritual support can keep people going when everything else tells them to quit.

After the prayer meeting we attended, we heard several people report on their activities. Some pointed to successes. Others asked for insights that might help them deal with difficulties. Two Australian architects, Ciara Tapia-Toms and Evan Drage, noted that hot weather seemed to be keeping construction workers away from the site where they were building a school, and they were worried about delays. Things were only going to get worse in a few days with the arrival of the raucous holiday called Holi, when people celebrate the arrival of spring by joyously pelting each other with brightly colored powders.

The few dozen men and women who sat barefoot on the floor and listened to the architects describe their concerns didn't volunteer a solution or suggest that they take any specific action. But they did listen attentively. And they reassured the Australians, who were volunteers from a group called Architects Without Frontiers, that their experience was normal and that faith might be their only option. And though they were scheduled to depart in a few months, the work they had done would remain, and others would carry the project through to the end.

The acceptance and patience urged upon the architects was offered as an antidote to the frustrations that are common to both Indians and outsiders who might follow Gandhi's example and try to achieve some substantive good in a place where obstacles are numerous and substantial themselves. Sitting in the crowd, a young woman named Mariette Fourmeaux du Sartel could recall her own experiences when she lived and worked in Delhi for a company called D.light, which makes and sells inexpensive ($8) solar lights that double as cell phone chargers. Ecofriendly and imagined as an aid to poor schoolchildren who live in homes without electricity, the D.light is a cause as well as a business. In India, Mariette met with some success as she teamed with others to distribute lights in rural areas, but also experienced some deep frustrations.

She found real encouragement when she visited Manav Sadhna near the beginning of her work in Delhi, after she had accepted a new job with Hewlett-Packard back in the United States.

"I had never experienced such purity of heart and purity of action, such generosity," said Mariette, when we asked her about Manav Sadhna.[6] The people at the ashram follow "an unaltered path from the heart to the hand," she added. "They think something and 'boom' they do it immediately. For me it goes from the heart to the head, which processes with questions of 'What if? What if?' They make an immediate expression of love, which is unfiltered."

The spontaneity and spirit of the people in Manav Sadhna accompanied Mariette to her job at Hewlett-Packard in San Diego, where she works in product development and is involved in HP's efforts to use environmentally safe and sustainable practices. "They really aren't interested in greenwashing," she said, referring to the way some corporations may claim to be caring for the Earth when they don't. Despite the firm's size and success, Mariette believes that it is a "heart-based" organization and that it is open to idealists and those who would seek to serve others.

On her own, Mariette has led a small group in her office to consider the spiritual element of their work through periodic group meditation. She also began a "random acts of kindness" project involving anonymous gifts and services for coworkers, who would receive a card informing them that they had been the beneficiary of someone's good deed and encouraging them to take a similar step for someone else. She soon noticed similar cards appearing in lots of different places around HP's offices—"and I didn't do it," she said.

Although they are small things, acts of kindness and group meditation can set a tone of harmony and inclusivity that will benefit people who work in groups toward a shared goal. "At HP there's something called the HP way," which she finds consistent with the Manav Sadhna philosophy of encouraging others. "With [HP's founders] Dave and Bill, that's always been there. They were actually very heart people. The past few years partially destroyed that, and now they are trying to rebuild it."

With her company returning to the openness and enthusiasm at its roots, Mariette finds that her priorities are affirmed at her workplace. She can rally her team by showing them that small steps can make progress toward big goals. "We have a pretty awesome grand vision," she said. "But what's the small stuff we can do right here right now, without having to get permission from our boss's boss's boss?" Mariette can draw a straight line from the ashram to the leadership style at HP, but the energy and inspiration of Manav Sadhna affect her life well beyond work. "My experience here has shifted everything," she said, explaining why she'll travel eight thousand miles to visit whenever she can.

Mariette's shift, in heart and mind, mirrors the process followed by Viren Joshi, who spent his early adulthood in America working in heavy industry but always wondering, "Could life be just for me, just working and education and getting a job and money and family, or could it be more than that?"[7] To find the "more," he traveled rural India searching for ways to serve others. He finally decided to help poor children, first by meeting their basic needs for food, shelter, and care and then through education. This was how Manav Sadhna was born. When he ran out of money, he returned to America, but never let go of his dream of service. A boss who discovered his divided loyalties offered a solution: work half of each year for a salary in America and spend half in India with Manav Sadhna. The compromise worked until 2005, when Viren's mission became self-sustaining and he could work at it full-time.

Over the years, the human services organization that began with a handful of street kids grew to include schools, kitchens, and dozens of "experiments" that allow people with skills, talents, and education to help each other. "People come to us and say, 'I want to serve,' and they might stay six months or a year." During that time, they are part of a generous community that now employs eighty former clients full-time and another two hundred part-time. They provide education to more than nine thousand students and meals to seven thousand poor children. All of this happens because of the intentionally inclusive and deliberately unmanaged "nonsystem system" embodied in the 10 amprayer meeting. "We don't have officers, managers, or supervisors," noted Viren. "We had one pay phone, but it didn't work half the time, so we took it out." Remarkably, "nothing we started has ever stopped for [lack of] money." Experiments might fail because of a poor concept or bad execution, but somehow, he added, material resources and talent are always available to see a project through until it proves sustainable or unsustainable.

• • •

Although some observers might reckon that Viren relies on faith and miracles to make things happen, he has in fact established a kind of market for helping, where ideas and projects find fertile ground but must grow organically. Those that thrive are ones that are workable and deliver something of value. Others either fade away or undergo refinement with input from the Manav Sadhna group. Anand Shah, for example, spent years working on an idea to bring safe, reliable supplies of fresh water to people who lack such supplies. This is no small problem in a country where three hundred million people have no access to clean water and as much as 90 percent of all illnesses are related to water or sanitation.

Born in Houston to immigrant parents, Anand was on the leading edge of a wave of young people with Indian heritage who wanted to do more for the country than donate money. As he told us, "Lots of young people in the Indian Diaspora wanted to do things in India."[8] To help these people "put their hearts and souls into action," he and his sisters created an organization called Indicorps that matched young people abroad with Indian organizations that needed their talents and labor. His theory was that "money follows people" and that therefore, Indian Americans who gain the experience of working in India will forever serve as ambassadors for effective programs that will always need help.

After turning over Indicorps to his sisters, Anand began working with a wealthy Indian family—the Piramals—who wanted help developing both businesses and activities for a charitable foundation. As he conducted his research, he spent lots of time in poor villages and neighborhoods and attended lots of prayer services at the Gandhi ashram. At the talk sessions after prayers, Anand presented many ideas to the group, and narrowed his focus to addressing the water problems in rural India. The project—called Sarvajal (Water for All)—became a hybrid of business and philanthropy. Sarvajal's approach differs from the many water development schemes that sent crews to drill wells in villages, installed pumps, and then departed. Too often these wells failed, and travel to the site was so costly that repairs were never made.

To overcome the problem of isolation, as well as difficulties associated with billing villagers for water services, Sarvajal developed a high-technology filtration system that would be franchised to local operators. The financial structure called for the cost of the machines to be amortized over a long period of time, during which villagers received clean water, and franchisees could draw profits from their payments. With the help of the Piramals, Sarvajal builds, installs, and monitors the machines remotely. Franchisees pay in advance to process a certain amount of water. If they aren't current with their payments, the device eventually shuts down. A franchisee with 175 customers can earn the equivalent of $430 per month. However, the business is viable if as few as twenty customers, who buy prepaid cards for the service, become devoted users. They pay a tiny fraction of a penny per gallon. Poor Indian families, who spend about 20 percent of their incomes on health care, can save comparatively enormous sums if they avoid water-borne illnesses through purchases from a Sarvajal dealer.

In less than four years, more than fifty franchisees had begun delivering water to tens of thousands of people. In the same time, Anand Shah came to appreciate the power of simply being the Harvard-educated young man who left America for India and the opportunities it could offer. "A lot of what I did didn't make sense," he recalled, "but there was power in being that guy who was doing those things. For example, I wrote a letter to the president of India and got an appointment to see him. I did all this stuff because it didn't make sense," yet others wanted to see him try.

On a grander scale, Anand sees India as a country that has shaken off the "big projects" mentality of its more socialist past when the public was told that "big things, big factories were going to take care of everything." Today, millions of entrepreneurs and organizers have thrown themselves into problem solving. Among them are many people who left India for America and Europe but returned in order to do something positive for their homeland. Others are, like Anand, children of the Diaspora who are intrigued by the land of their heritage and eager to apply their energies to its challenges.

So far, no new social or political ethos has arisen to replace the old socialism. India is, Anand added, "a peaceful chaotic country where there's an opportunity to originate" new ways of making progress. But so far, "no one has actually said that we *all* have a role to play. That discourse needs to come. I think it will."

•••

In the meantime, a seemingly endless number of inspired and creative people apply their own ideas to bring more Indian people into the mainstream economy where they can find more safety, health, and security. Nothing is more basic to this status than housing, and here an entirely homegrown outfit is taking on the immense challenge of sheltering people who have no ready access to the market for modern housing.

The founders of the development company DBS Communities were inspired by a book called *The Fortune at the Bottom of the Pyramid*, by the late C. K. Prahalad. In a nutshell, the book argues that huge opportunities for profit, and social good, await those who tap into the multibillion-person market represented by those who live on less than $2.50 per day. Goods and services priced to serve these customers will find almost limitless demand. In his book, Prahalad presents success stories in banking, health care, and consumer goods such as soap. He also offers a strong argument for businesspeople to consider what he calls PPP—purchasing power parity—to gauge a market's opportunities.[9] By this measure, someone who lives on $2.50 per day in India or China is a much more active and valuable consumer than an American with the same resources.

PPP takes into account huge variations in the cost of basics like land, transportation, raw materials, and labor. The founders of DBS Communities did the same thing as they considered building affordable housing in Gujarat, where construction workers earn modest wages, and materials such as cement cost less than they do in industrialized countries. Powered by these cost savings, DBS launched two housing developments in the city of Ahmedabad and one in the coastal city of Surat. Secured with perimeter fences and gates, the projects each feature multistory buildings that offer apartments as large as two bedrooms. Equipped with modern kitchens and baths, they will be priced between about $8,000 and $20,000.

The Indian market is filled with potential buyers who rent substandard and even slum housing but could afford to buy low-priced condominium-style homes. However, many of these people don't have bank accounts and have never taken out loans or credit cards that would establish a credit record. To overcome this problem, DBS approached nonprofit agencies that could help buyers gather documents for mortgage applications and put their finances in order. These agencies also counsel buyers on setting households budgets.

"We understand the customers much better," explained Rajendra Joshi, who founded a nonprofit development agency called Saath, which formed an alliance with DBS.[10] Like many Indian housing experts, Rajendra doesn't support wholesale slum clearance projects. Indeed, informal and substandard housing—crowded, often poorly built—is widely considered to be essential to the needs of hundreds of millions of people. However, the marketplace has failed to provide options for individuals and families who could afford to pay a bit more but still cannot afford a middle-class home of the sort widely available in more developed countries.

Historically, "whatever housing stock has been created [in India] has been for the upper class and upper-middle class," added Rajendra, who served us sandwiches and chai at a DBS office. To create a new approach, DBS and Saath "got together and said, 'Let's think this through. Let's find out what affordable housing should be like.'"

After consulting with groups of potential buyers, the partners determined that buyers who made $150 to $200 per month could afford new apartments ranging from two hundred to four hundred square feet. Economies of scale could be achieved by constructing hundreds of units at sites near existing slums, creating new communities that would represent a higher standard of living for people who had achieved a certain level of financial stability. The concept got a boost when new housing finance companies arose to serve lower-income customers. Rajendra saw, in this development, a chance to tap a "sustainable market" that was grossly underserved.

Rajendra had long experience using market forces to improve living conditions for the poor in Ahmedabad. One of his most successful projects involved using Saath funds to lower the cost of connecting households to the electric grid from $250 to $40, payable over time. When officials of the local utility discovered that a profit could be made delivering power to poor customers who signed up for the low-cost connections, they offered the same service without requiring a subsidy from a group like Saath. Once the idea was proven, "I [didn't] have to worry about looking for grants all over the place," said Rajendra. "The money is there" in the poor communities; "you just have to design the business model."

Because housing involves a valuable fixed asset and not a delivered service like electricity, Saath and DBS added some extra conditions to the market mechanism. They won't sell to investors or speculators "even if they come with a checkbook and want to buy one hundred units." Rajendra said his group is determined to meet the social goal of "filling the gap" between slum housing and larger middle-class homes. "We are consciously targeting people who need these houses." They are also adding services, including medical clinics, day care, and other supports that will make for sustainable communities.

But although the model used by the partners comes with elements of social support and aims to improve the welfare of poor people in Gujarat, it is a for-profit enterprise that aims to produce tens of thousands of homes. DBS anticipates a lot of competition once it proves that its strategy works. However, given the potential pool of customers—perhaps as many as half a billion—the market seems big enough for a large number of players.

On the day when we met Rajendra Joshi, we also visited one of the venture's building sites on the outskirts of Ahmedabad. There we saw four- and six-story concrete-and-brick apartment blocks rising next to crowded slums. Bags of cement, bricks, and iron reinforcement bars were piled up, and a security guard patrolled to protect the materials and tools. (As it was a holiday, no workers were present.) Our guide explained that 885 apartments would be completed in buildings equipped with modern kitchens and baths and served by elevators, which are a rarity in Ahmedabad. In almost every way, the place looked like a construction project you might see in the suburbs of any American city. The only thing missing was a welcome and sales center marked by colorful, fluttering flags and a billboard.

Of course, the scale and quality of the construction meant that banners and a welcome center were hardly required to draw attention to the development. The new buildings were flanked by unnamed neighborhoods of flimsy one- and two- story structures alongside rutted dirt roads where rainwater collected in deep puddles and children at play dodged noisy motorcycles. Behind the new complex of apartments stretched a swamp where wading birds wandered amid trash and human waste. In this area, without paved streets, reliable water supplies, and working sewers, DBS-Saath needn't advertise or solicit buyers. People are naturally drawn to the opportunity the development represents, and hundreds had applied to buy units even though completion was many months away.

Although DBS must complete and sell out a project to fully test its scheme, Rajendra and others who have seen the success even of programs that merely upgraded utilities and services in slums have great confidence. Those past projects were embraced by slum residents, whose pride and self-esteem were reflected in their own spontaneous efforts to improve their homes and their neighborhood. As he explained, even the streets became quieter and more orderly; "a positive cycle was set in place."

The DBS-Saath plan depends on pride of place and homeownership to create upward momentum for the poor and the development of a strong middle class in India. As a market-based strategy, it applies the kind of logic used by Anand Shah to involve people as paying customers who have a stake in a water delivery system. In both cases, success depends on the fact that real incentives are driving everyone toward the same end point: an India in which more people can raise themselves up. The desire for the social mobility represented by home ownership has always existed among

India's poor, added Rajendra. "The difference is that today they feel their aspirations are in reach." This feeling is reinforced by the growing economic energy in the country, democratic politics, and a powerful mass media that often transmits Horatio Alger–style messages of hope and social equality.

As a fan of cricket, which is the national sport, Rajendra reflexively turns to the national team for an analogy. "Until ten years ago, the national cricket team was mostly players from the big cities. They were upper-class elite players," he said. However, more recently, leagues and teams have been more open minded about seeking talent, and "the best players are coming from smaller towns and cities. They are hungrier than the others, and they perform better."

Hope and optimism echoed in Rajendra's voice as he described a country with a broader middle class made up of people who have worked hard and succeeded, in part, because they were able to invest in their own homes. Add to this story the notion of a national pastime, played with a ball and bat and open to all, and you hear the outlines of a familiar story. Somewhere else in the world, a country with a growing population and cities crowded with poor people relied on community service projects, individual ambitions, and the dream of home ownership to develop the most vibrant middle class on Earth. The people of this country were also devoted to a game that featured bats and balls and runs scored on hits. The main difference is that cricket allows for games that can last a day or more. American baseball only feels that way sometimes.

Chapter 8

China

*"Having and admitting failures is critical to
overall success."* (82% agree)

Aside from the most elementary comments about burgeoning
cities and rural poverty, nothing you can say about China in
the twenty-first century constitutes a simple truth. The country is
Communist, but it is also capitalist. (Hence the Rolls-Royces we
saw parked just blocks from Mao's tomb in Beijing.) Chinese businesspeople and political dissidents are hemmed in by the authorities,
except when they are free to innovate and agitate. China is traditional and modern, rich and poor, confident and insecure.

In Shanghai, China's largest city, supermodern skyscrapers loom
over squat older neighborhoods jammed with colonial buildings
and narrow alleys. Here you can buy Prada, Versace, and Dior at
a megamall called Plaza 66 and then walk a few blocks to visit
the museum at the site of the first Communist Party congress. The
paradox you find on the street is also apparent in national politics.
Communist leaders, who hold ultimate and complete authority,
have engaged in a decades-long effort to loosen controls on the
society and stimulate economic growth.

The party's strategy has produced spectacular increases in consumption, investment, and exports and a controlled increase in political dissent. Although progress on human rights has been too slow to satisfy outside critics, including the United States, the average citizen in China has enjoyed a rapid rise in her standard of living. This nation of 1.3 billion people has seen a 500 percent increase in gross domestic product in twenty years. More remarkably, all of this has happened without a return to the kind of turmoil seen in 1989, when a crisis at Tiananmen Square ended in hundreds of deaths when troops attacked protesters. This conflict apparently set the parameters for citizen protest and political action, which slowed but did not stop.

The balance of change and security seems to concern everyone in the country. "The typical Chinese person would say, 'I can deal with anything but chaos,'" explained PT Black, a longtime business and marketing consultant based in Shanghai.[1] "The government is very good at mass organization, and that keeps things from falling into chaos. They have also been pretty good at making sure there's a lot of space for an individual in China to lead a happy life." Indeed, in modern China it seems as though creative types and entrepreneurs can experiment and advance in any direction, as long as no law or rule prohibits them. "'Don't ask, don't tell' is a way of life here," added PT. "It's how things get done."

Any first-time Western visitor to China benefits from time spent with someone with knowledge, experience, and the ability to interpret the place with both respect and care. Few people fit the bill like our friend PT, who has devoted both his academic and professional lives to understanding China from the street level up. Indeed, PT is frequently consulted by journalists, government officials, and businesspeople who ask what China's leaders and its ordinary citizens might be thinking and doing at any given moment. In his work as an executive for a company called Thoughtful Media, he has focused on discovering and understanding the essence of contemporary Chinese culture and society. We asked him about the flexibility and creativity of Chinese entrepreneurs.

"There's a ton of creativity here," said PT, as we visited in his fashionable apartment in Shanghai's old French concession. This creativity can be seen in the explosive development of business since the Communist Party began loosening controls on commerce with the "open door" policy of 1986. However, after twenty-five years of economic boom, the Chinese definition of success has begun to shift, said PT. In addition to the pursuit of wealth and status, people with drive and ambition want to feel fulfilled and that they are creating a better way of life. As other experts have noted, the people of China seem to be yearning for a kind of spiritual fulfillment, which might be expressed in connection and service to others, or perhaps in the restoration of pre-Communist values. They seek to do this mainly through individual initiative and not through political organizing.

"Ten years ago, everyone may have been talking about politics and democracy, but that has changed," said PT. He now believes that America's struggle with terrorism has Chinese people considering "the dangers of democracy," while their own economic success has reinforced nationalistic pride. With these developments in mind, individuals are pursing "long-term creative ideas" that will move the nation toward a way of life that is free, prosperous, and safe in a distinctly Chinese fashion.

"The Chinese are the most successful race of humans in the history of the planet," noted PT. "China itself is an empire of many countries that is multiracial, multilingual, and held together by a central state that has brought six hundred million people out of poverty in twenty years. I'm not sure any government in history has ever done more for so many people, and so quickly. If you look at it this way, the Chinese have every reason to focus on developing themselves, their own markets, and their own country, and to believe that they can do a very good job of it."

• • •

PT Black's best advice to foreigners revolves around letting go of long-standing assumptions and opening their eyes to the breadth and depth of possibilities in the world's largest and oldest continuous society. When they do this, they see a place where conditions change by the minute and creative individuals can find outlets for their initiative.

A first-generation Chinese American, Calvin Chin immigrated to Shanghai in 2004, looking for a fast track to success. He found it in high-tech manufacturing, where China enjoyed big advantages over foreign competitors due to lower labor costs and government policies that aid the development of export-based businesses. Calvin joined a start-up called Semiconductor Manufacturing International Corporation (SMIC), which had grown rapidly thanks to partnerships with city governments eager for job-creating industry. Three hectic years later, after SMIC went public with an initial stock sale, Calvin left to work as a business consultant while he circulated among other people who felt a similar urge to do something more with their lives. He settled on the idea of creating a self-sustaining business that would do some good for society while also generating profits.

Calvin and his friends were motivated to find deeper satisfaction in life. "You notice that after all this economic growth, life can still feel empty," he told us.[2] The emptiness can be personal, as newly rich entrepreneurs discover that money brings only so much happiness, or it can be a matter of social concern. Although it sparked real excitement and fascination among everyday people, the rise of China's millionaire-billionaire class has also invited reflection on the inequality that can arise in competitive economies.

China is now a place "where you will see a young woman driving an expensive sports car past an elderly woman scrounging in a garbage bin," added Calvin. The concern young Chinese people feel about such disparities echoes similar sentiments you might hear in America. Young Chinese adults worry about paying for higher education and health care, and they feel deep anxiety about caring for elderly parents and grandparents. These concerns power an ongoing conversation about Chinese values and the definition of a successful and well-lived life. They may also herald a new development phase that nurtures innovation with a higher purpose.

Taking what he learned and what he earned with SMIC, Calvin cofounded an organization called Qifang, which pools small investments to provide tuition loans to college students. In a matter of months, Qifang arranged for twenty-five hundred students to get financing at interest rates that varied according to the student's credit worthiness. Not one borrower fell behind on his or her payment schedule, and Qifang attracted worldwide attention for its success.

Having proved that a social enterprise could work in China, Calvin handed Qifang to others, who set out to expand the service. His next initiative—called Transist—provides technical assistance and financing up to $1 million for start-ups that seek both "profit and purpose." The Transist team, which includes Chinese and foreign-born advisers, conducts training seminars including one three-day course called the Lean Start-up Machine, which shows students how to test and implement ideas for new enterprises. Transist also solicits proposals for funding, and has already put money into four promising companies. Three of these start-ups are concerned with Internet-based financial services; one, Unitedstyles, delivers fashions to consumers worldwide. Unitedstyles customers log on to the firm's website to design their own clothes, which the company then manufactures and delivers anywhere in the world. Unitedstyles prices are competitive—about $130 for a dress—and it uses the most modern, environmentally friendly technologies available to make its products.

Financing and know-how can relieve some of the anxiety felt by young Chinese adults who were raised in one- or two-child families and feel deep obligations to their elders. "When you have someone who may be responsible for taking care of two parents and maybe four grandparents, taking the risk to start something new is a huge gamble," explained Calvin. Without encouragement and a financial partner, potential innovators are likely to opt for a safe career with a huge company instead of pioneering something new. With this aid, hopes Calvin, they can pursue ideas that will make life better in China and, perhaps, around the world. He sees opportunities in education, health, security, food safety, and environmentally friendly technologies.

In all of Calvin's target businesses, the Chinese government has scaled back its presence, opened up markets for profit-driven concerns, but also left a leadership vacuum. "China has gone from a command-and-control economy to free market and from a system of state-owned property to privately owned property," he added. More recently, the government has reduced its role as a cultural arbiter, declining to define the values that should guide individuals and society. "Thirty or forty years ago, the government filled the space for values," he noted. Today Chinese people can set their moral, social, and commercial priorities. "A grassroots change in values is starting to pick up steam," he added. That change is expressed in the development of socially conscious businesses and, for the first time in Chinese history, the rise of philanthropy and private service organizations.

● ● ●

On May Day 2012, when almost every other person in China was celebrating the national labor holiday, Flora Lan met with us to explain how engineers, designers, marketers, and educators can make a profit by promoting environmentalism. For Western-ers, who associate China with tainted toothpaste and industrial pollution, the business model behind Flora's company, Greeno-vate, may seem implausible. However, Greenovate makes money by teaching Chinese firms how to deliver sustainable products and services while meeting international standards for labor fairness and environmental quality.

The firm benefits from a recent shift in Communist Party pri-orities. After a generation of almost unbridled growth in China, government officials have begun to focus on the quality of life experienced by everyday citizens, and not just economic develop-ment. Noting severe pollution problems, authorities in Guangzhou, China's version of Detroit, are moving to cut the number of cars on city streets by 50 percent. Similar policies are going into effect across the country to reduce traffic and improve air quality. At the same time, municipalities are making big investments in mass transit, parks, and cultural centers, all with the aim of improving public welfare. These moves are also seen as a response to a growing environmental movement, which mounted street protests in 2011 against polluting factories.

Just in time to take advantage of this new concern for the environment, Greenovate was founded by a Slovenian named Mihela Hladin. She first came to China with a European firm that did engineering for heavy industries. She noticed that the work was made more difficult by cultural confusion and a kind of ecological ignorance. As Hladin told an interviewer, "I kept bumping into the same challenge, which was that people are not educated or aware that you can't just buy trees. The river will not get clean in a week. I was sure that if the industrial owners I'd been working with had a bigger picture of their environmental impact, they would not continue doing things in the same manner."[3]

When her original project ended, Hladin stayed in China to create Greenovate. The firm was born as companies like Wal-mart and Apple began to insist that suppliers meet international environmental and labor standards. In the same time period, Chinese citizens began to protest pollution in their communities. When government authorities allowed these campaigns to continue, others sprouted, and more people began talking about how the good life in China might require safeguarding the air, water, and land.

The move from concern to action posed particular problems in a country where only government and private business were trusted to pursue big goals. In fact, China had almost no nonprofit organizations, and authorities had no basis for understanding or trusting what they might do. To get around this problem, Hladin made Greenovate a business, not some type of charitable enterprise. This flexible strategy allowed Hladin and her colleagues to work as environmental advocates—educating, advising, informing—in a way that fell outside the sweep of the government's regulatory radar. As a business, Greenovate can promote the public good without uncomfortable scrutiny, as long as it stays independent from the government.

Flora Lan told us the Greenovate story during a visit to the company's office in a residential Shanghai neighborhood. It occupies a two-story building in an alley where laundry hangs from lines strung high in the air, and children's voices echo down the block. Due to the holiday, her colleagues were not working. But Flora, whose family lives so far away that a quick holiday visit wasn't possible, seemed happy to talk about the value of social entrepreneurs and the steps they must follow to gain acceptance. The first involved establishing independence.

"When you work with government—the big elephant—people think you are a big elephant too," said Flora.[4] Her point is that Chinese businesspeople and consumers may depend on the government for certain services, but a close association with government could breed skepticism about Greenovate. Customers couldn't be certain of Greenovate's true purpose, or feel confident that their relationship with the firm would be secure and private.

Greenovate's clients range from manufacturing companies with heavy carbon footprints to a small restaurant where the chef wants to assure diners that he's offering healthful and ecofriendly fare. In her work with clients, Flora begins by reviewing their consumption of fuel, electricity, water, and other resources. She and her colleagues also examine waste streams and check to make sure that products are safe for consumers. When the review is complete, the consultants present a report to managers, and then stick around to oversee changes in technology and practices and to train workers.

For Flora, Greenovate's work is about more than a paycheck. As a social entrepreneur, "You can make money, and you can also make your happiness along the way," she noted. In Flora's case, the money is not substantial, especially when compared with the salaries of her Shanghai University of Finance and Economics classmates employed by major companies. And on the day we met, her happiness was tempered by the loneliness she felt being separated from her parents, who were celebrating the holiday back in her hometown. The day also happened to be her birthday. She smiled when a delivery man appeared with a box full of small gifts from her mother and father, and spoke proudly of how they had accepted her unconventional career choice.

Under China's one-child policy, Flora's mother and father had no other children, and thus their emotional investment in her may be higher than it would be if their family were larger. Like other parents their age, they also struggle with a kind of generation gap. Better educated and more assertive, China's young adults challenge their elders by voicing their opinions on politics and public affairs, and their dreams range far beyond a higher material standard of living.

"My parents consider themselves to be good citizens," explained Flora. As children of the Communist revolution, her mother and father reflected often on the words and priorities of leader Mao Zedong. "They listen carefully to what the government says. They are good, and they don't do outrageous things." Flora said her generation "doesn't talk about Mao, except if we make a joke. In my definition, a good citizen takes care of her fellow citizens. A good citizen is more aware of society and makes decisions that move the needle."

A distinctly Western expression, Flora's "moving the needle" refers to identifying a meaningful social challenge and mustering "a little courage to say I can think of a solution to that problem." Flora said that her parents are puzzled by the fact that she doesn't care how much money she makes. "But I have convinced them that I am happy doing this. It's something I can make impact with. It's how I want to live my life."

This focus on combining social good with career ambition is something Flora developed after hearing a lecture by Steve Koon at her university. Koon attended Harvard's Kennedy School, where he studied social enterprise, and was based in China, where he advised social entrepreneurs from across Asia. In 2008, he toured China speaking about the possibility of using business activities to improve communities. His target audience was the generation of young adults about to enter the world of work. To them he says, "Traditional philanthropists pride themselves on how many people they have helped. Social entrepreneurs hold themselves accountable for how many people in need they have not helped. The world needs more social entrepreneurs."[5] Flora found Koons's message of "mission-oriented business" so inspiring that she made it the model for her career.

Critical of what she calls the "conspicuous consumption" of the generation that preceded hers, Flora seeks greater reward from her work. She wants her life to be a kind of mission, devoted to a cause. When we asked what motivates this desire, she paused and then reflected on the small families mandated by China's population policies. She speculated that without siblings, she and her peers feel a certain loss. Describing her generation as water lilies "floating in a river with no roots," she said, "We are very lonely. We don't have brothers and sisters. We don't have community."

In Flora's fondest dream, her work will demonstrate the value of an independent business that pursues profit with a purpose—and word of Greenovate's success will echo across the World Wide Web. In this way, the social enterprise model could gain momentum, she added with a note of hope. "Instead of waiting for permission from the government," she said, those looking to shape a better China can find empty spaces where they can act assertively. The energy for this endeavor is already building in Chinese society. With enough communication, Flora believes, ideas for action will be identified, refined, and implemented to create better lives for individuals and a better country overall.

· · ·

If Flora Lan is a homegrown foot soldier in an army of peaceful change, David Wertime is a correspondent on the front lines of the campaign, issuing dispatches that inform the world. His company, called Tea Leaf Nation, publishes an Internet magazine by the same name, which offers Chinese readers and people around the world a smart account of fast-changing developments across the country. Much of what David and his colleagues report is drawn from postings on social media, but unlike similar sites, *Tea Leaf Nation* doesn't rely on computer programs—called bots—to do the gleaning. Instead, as the magazine itself explains, the staff "scours Chinese social media every day to spot trends, gauge sentiment, and carry major news stories one level deeper."[6]

The magazine's stories are reliably provocative. One issue contained the translation of a dissident writer's article "Plea for a Gentler China." Using the pen name Murong Xuecun, the author declared, "We have some rights in theory, but in reality, they do not exist. Income has increased in theory, but once you get to the market, you'll see that you can't even afford to buy meat. In theory, some people have risen up, but actually, they're still kneeling. In theory, you've moved a few mountains, but you've actually just fallen into a hole. In theory, you're the master of your country, but in actuality, you live in chains."[7]

Murong's liberal cri de coeur supported all those who would make China more open and democratic. But this isn't the only sentiment the magazine allows. In an earlier issue, *Tea Leaf Nation* noted a government crackdown on foreigners living and working in China illegally. In this case, there was great agreement, not dissent, as the magazine noted an upwelling of public support for the tough government action.

Reading through a small sample of the 114,000 comments to the recent news, *Tea Leaf Nation* found netizens to be roundly and angrily supportive of the measure. Many argued that this step was "overdue" and "better late than never." Others chimed in to call for similar measures in Dalian, Shanghai, and Guangzhou. The overall tone of discussion would surely be deeply troubling to anyone who has ever had to be an "outsider." One writer lauded the dangerous semantics employed by Beijing police: "'Clean up' . . . is really the right word to use. I feel like it's cleaning up trash from the street."[8]

The magazine's openness and breadth of opinion reflect the explosion of self-expression that can be found in Chinese social media despite periodic government attempts to rein in public discourse. David explained this when we met him in China's capital, Beijing, an enormous city of hulking, intimidating government buildings and avenues so long and straight they play tricks on the eye. (One day we set out for Tiananmen Square and gave up walking when, after thirty minutes, we didn't seem any closer to it.) Though less vibrant than Shanghai, Beijing is where the powerful state bureaucracy resides and much of the media is headquartered. Here too is where policymakers struggle to deal with the disruptive nature of the World Wide Web and social media.

"The Chinese government has tried a couple of times to cut it back," said David on the day we met him, noting that authorities occasionally delete controversial posts and the accounts of certain bloggers.[9] However, the state's efforts to manage the Internet have been largely ineffective, as the volume of postings from China's 250 million social media subscribers defies easy control. Indeed, officials generally had to choose between keeping the Internet "on" to allow for open debate and restricting it so severely that they would risk massive protest.

"They chose to let people have the megaphone and walk around shouting into it," said David. "And now they can't control what they say." Acting as a kind of filter for the megaphone, *Tea Leaf Nation* strains out the noise and transmits the messages that create a consistent reflection of the moment.

Poetically enough, the idea for Tea Leaf Nation arose during a long walk that David took with his friends visiting the National Mall in Washington DC. There, in the shadow of the Jefferson Memorial (Jefferson famously championed free speech), the three Harvard alums talked "about what mattered to us," recalled David. "We wanted to create something to bridge the gap between China and the West."

The idea was a natural for David, who had spent ten years in China, first as a Peace Corps volunteer and then as an attorney for giant international law firms. It also fit his coconspirators, Jimmy and Rachel. (Both declined to use their last names.) Jimmy was born and raised on the coast of northern China and was coleader of the Asian Law Society at Harvard. Rachel's family came to America from southern China, and before heading off to the Ivy League, she counted reading Chinese poetry among her childhood hobbies. Together, the three friends harbored passion for and curiosity about China. They also shared a deep desire to do something meaningful with their lives.

The project that emerged from their walk around the mall allows Jimmy, Rachel, and David to take China's social temperature every day. They review a variety of Weibo sites, or microblogs, in China, as well as other social networks. This "eavesdropping," as David called it, lets editors listen to "hundreds of people, getting their relatively candid opinions." The process reveals a population that is hardly as insular and detached as many outsiders imagine.

"There's a saying in China that goes like this: 'You only sweep the snow in front of your own house,'" explained David. However, he has found that in their online habits, Chinese citizens tend to issues far beyond their own doorsteps. Scandals in city and regional governments generally attract a flood of harsh comments, and authorities seldom censor the posts. When we visited China, thousands of people had recently used the Internet to join a national campaign on behalf of an extremely wealthy woman named Wu Ying, who had been prosecuted for fraud. Although the superwealthy often inspire skepticism and envy, Wu became a cause célèbre when a Chinese court found her guilty and sentenced her to death.

"What moved me is that people were courageously tweeting en mass about how unjust this was for someone they never met who probably was a criminal," said David. "They felt it was unfair to sentence someone to death for an economic crime. China's government never said exactly why, but the high court overturned the death sentence. The fact that these people thought they could save her life and wanted to do it was just amazing."

The bigger picture David and his colleagues paint in *Tea Leaf Nation* reveals a China that is alive with criticism, dissent, and creativity aimed at making life more interesting and rewarding in the openings that the government allows. In the short run, their accomplishments will be modest and mostly in the margins. But in a few cases, the push for a different China, one that allows for more creativity, direct action, and citizen problem solving, comes from people with higher visibility who could have more substantial change in mind.

• • •

If a single word can be used to describe anyone, for Bessie Lee it is *confidence*. A calm self-assuredness shines in her eyes when she greets you, and it rings in her voice when she says that a better

Chinese society won't come from the "efficient machine" of the Communist state. Instead, it will come from private enterprises, which are just beginning to shape public tastes, attitudes, and behaviors. "Because of the size of the market, there are so many people I can influence and impact... It's very exciting and very emotionally fulfilling," she said within minutes of our meeting. "I want to be here, in China, doing a China-only job."[10]

Bessie's loyalty is remarkable for many reasons. First, she is the daughter of parents who were born in mainland China and fled to Taiwan when the Communists rose to power in 1949. Her father, who died before reforms would allow him to return, could only keep his homeland alive through the practice of old traditions. He marked the holidays in the old style and prepared special meals to celebrate his link to the ancient China. He couldn't have imagined the modern, dynamic country Bessie discovered when she began to visit and then claimed as home in 2002.

As she became chief executive for the Chinese division of GroupM, a global advertising and media firm (also a division of John Gerzema's company), Bessie entered an enormous market where her industry was just beginning to develop. The opportunities for growth were almost boundless, and so were the opportunities for shaping a team that would produce the highest-quality work. As she studied the talent, Bessie discovered a certain hesitancy when it came to innovation and creativity. In her analysis, China's isolation and its education system had quashed the impulse to challenge the status quo, which is the main way that breakthroughs occur in any field. "That's common in Asia, not just in China," she said. "But in China it was probably more severe because China opened up to the world much later."

For decades, the impulse to conform inhibited investors, recalled Bessie. They were quick to put money into new companies that copied tried-and-true products from abroad, but reluctant to back a Chinese investor or entrepreneur who came up with something completely new. "Thinking out of the box and challenging authority are new concepts," she added. Recognizing the value of these concepts, Bessie decided she could best serve her company, and best serve her new home country, by "building an environment that encourages people to be creative."

We met Bessie for lunch at a restaurant in Shanghai called Zen, where every table seemed to be occupied by customers who did business while sampling small dishes of exquisitely prepared dim sum. (We had, among other items, pork ribs, egg soufflé, crispy tofu, greens, and fried shellfish.) The fashion was up-to-the-minute, and among our fellow diners were plenty of executive women. Although workplace discrimination against women has not been totally eliminated, its absence is one legacy of the Cultural Revolution that Bessie considers a substantial advantage for China as it moves forward. However, this plus is diminished by other social factors that limit the expression of the feminine strengths that are vital to the future economy.

Women who came of age in the 1960s and 1970s may have felt comfortable with authority and achieved rough parity with men, but the tenor of the times limited their creativity. One superficial sign of this dynamic, said Bessie, can be seen in fashion. Before China opened itself to the world, "women weren't supposed to pay attention to fashion, to make-up, and to hairstyles," and this attitude reinforced conformity. At its worst, the conformist norm put loyalty to the state above all else. "Anyone caught bad-mouthing the party and Chairman Mao was to be reported, even your loved ones, your parents and spouse or children." Those who were reported for expressing dissent "were dragged out in the street, kicked and humiliated." Children who saw this going on "were told to try to be quiet. Don't try to stand out in the crowd. Be as quiet as possible."

Women who experienced equality under the old regime may have felt that they had equal access to education and jobs, but they were equally repressed. As quiet citizens who feared standing out in a crowd, they were not likely to use their talents and strengths to create a dynamic, expanding economy. As freedom increased and constraints were eased, some adapted well, but real Athena-style flexibility and creativity would be expressed by their daughters. Among China's most successful innovators, Bessie can point to dozens of very successful women, including 30 percent of the billionaires on the government list of its richest citizens. She described for us some of the most highly regarded women in China:

Hung Huang is director of the country's first design museum and counts 2.5 million people as followers on social media. Her mother taught English to Chairman Mao. Her daughter grew up to be a celebrated author, publisher of a fashion magazine, and proprietor of a blazingly successful clothing store.

Wang Yinxiang is vice chairman of Air China and a top official in the Communist Party. Moving between government and industry, she is one of the most visible figures in China's fast-growing aviation sector.

Hu Shuli is founder of the influential news magazine *Caijing*. Defying government pressure, she has provided thorough coverage of natural disasters in China, including critiques of government responses. One prominent American journalist called her an "avenging angel" for the Chinese public. Inside the country, she's called the "most dangerous woman" in the nation.

Zhang Xin is cofounder of SOHO China, which has become the largest real estate developer in Beijing. She and her partner, her husband, took the firm public with a stock offering on the Hong Kong exchange. The issue was the largest initial public offering for a realty company in Asian history.

Jiang Qiong Er is CEO of Shang Xia, China's first luxury consumer brand, which offers high-end goods with the quality and beauty to match Hermès. In fact, Hermès was Jiang's partner in the development of her firm, which is the biggest luxury clothing and home furnishings company in the giant Chinese market. Local artisans are employed to make every product in the company's line, and the firm is credited with helping end China's association with cheaply made goods.

The women who are best known for their success in modern China all come from the post-Mao generation that reached adulthood in the 1980s and came to believe that the reforms that allow for creativity and a modicum of dissent are real. In almost every respect, they resemble the female leaders found in other major economies. Unlike their parents, Bessie told us, "they are being equipped to innovate, think critically, and think creatively." They also understand that they possess what Bessie calls the "soft power" to effect change in China in ways the government cannot control. This is done through media and through the creation of corporate cultures that reward divergent and ambitious thinking.

The coming decades will see China further develop its domestic economy (which Bessie compared to the European Union), where diversity presents a challenge to companies that seek to serve the entire market. Business success in such a setting requires great flexibility to reach all the corners of a country where commerce is conducted in multiple languages and both infrastructure and cultural norms vary dramatically. In China, a salesperson can deal with cautious Muslim customers in the morning, hypercompetitive Hong Kong go-getters in the afternoon, and staid party officials in the evening. In each case, conversations and negotiations will be conducted according to distinct and separate unstated rules.

On a social level, Bessie believes that Chinese people will become better informed about the nation's problems, including poverty and inequality, and "will get to see the country is not as harmonious as we thought." Indeed, disparities in education, employment opportunities, health care, and infrastructure define the nation. Addressing these social challenges will require a devotion to something more than accumulating wealth for oneself, she added; and of necessity, Chinese will have to learn to take the initiative on behalf of their neighbors, their communities, and their countries. Just how this will happen is a worry.

"Unfortunately, the only thing Chinese people aspire to right now is money," said Bessie, noting that the communism that produced dependency has given way to a capitalism without a balancing interest in public service or charity. The government is aware of a values gap that must be closed if people are to become concerned, engaged citizens, she said. "The government went to the media and said we want programs that promote this good spirit. We no longer want to see strange singing and dancing every night. That's only going to go on two programs a week. We want more education" to encourage selflessness and generosity.

Chinese people are used to listening to government messages, "and [the government] might as well leverage that," added Bessie. But over the long run, civic virtue will only emerge as a replacement for government largesse if a private, philanthropic movement—call it a *caring sector*—is built by China's rich. This is happening, said Bessie, under the leadership of a "new elite. They are much better educated and properly educated," she said. "They are very successful, and young people look up to them. And they will use their own ways to spread their values."

• • •

It is no surprise that the person leading the development of a caring sector in Chinese society is often described as the Oprah Winfrey of China. Yang Lan, a wildly popular television talk show host, is also coowner of a media conglomerate with divisions that include newspapers, television production, Web content, and magazine publishing. One of the hundred wealthiest people in China, Yang may also be the most famous. Her main program, *Yang Lan: One-on-One* presents the most celebrated figures in national and international affairs. However, like Oprah, she also explores social problems, with an eye toward finding solutions.

Eager to do something positive for China with her wealth, Yang created a family charity, the Sun Culture Foundation, in 2006. Guangshen Gao, who was hired to help run the foundation, told us that initially it lacked any central purpose and that Yang funded projects that caught her eye and seemed worthy, although forest preservation became one recurring interest. Yang was also very eager to use her fame and access to "influence the influencers" who might also use their private wealth to benefit the country.

China has no shortage of needs for philanthropy. Despite its rapid development, the country is still home to hundreds of millions of people who live in poverty, lack modern housing, and have trouble accessing quality education and health care. However, more than fifty years of Communist rule had left the country with no independent social service sector to do what government could not. "There was no culture of philanthropy," said Gaungshen.[11] The real problem with China's lack of a charity sector became obvious to all after the 2008 Sichuan earthquake, which left 4.5 million people homeless. Relief efforts, almost exclusively the government's domain, were slow and inadequate and revealed a shocking lack of preparedness. Chinese people responded generously, donating to private relief efforts. However, after the disaster was over, the public learned that 85 percent of the money donated had ultimately gone to the government because the private aid organizations had not put it to use.

"The truth is, we just didn't have the capacity," recalled Guangshen, who is thirty-eight and was educated both in China and the United States. "I used to work in corporations and for the government," he said. "But I grew up with people who believed in hope and in taking responsibility and in trust." Certain that those qualities could be expressed best with privately backed service organizations, he made the unconventional choice of committing himself long term to an enterprise that had no track record or clear plan for the future.

To build nonprofit capacity, Yang and Guangshen established a training program that brought dozens of foreign experts to China to conduct seminars for local nonprofit organizations. By the time we met Guangshen in 2012, more than five hundred people had been through this program. To encourage the creation of more foundations and charities, Yang also sponsored a trip to New York for a select number of what Guangshen called "super-high-wealth" individuals, who met people involved in major philanthropies, including university trustees and family donors such as the Shrivers, who have been involved in the Special Olympics for decades.

Although the trainings for workers and administrators were successful, the Sun Culture Foundation discovered that the potential philanthropists "are not used to listening to experts," recalled Guangshen. "They prefer to talk with people they know." To get around this problem, Yang invited America billionaires Bill Gates and Warren Buffett to China for a session with the same group. This meeting was a hit, as the participants got a chance to meet two of the most prominent men in the world and learned from them directly about the ways they used their wealth to benefit others. "They talked a lot about family and values," said Guangshen. "That was very important."

Gates and Buffett have famously started a project they call the Giving Pledge, which brings together the wealthiest Americans, and others, to support philanthropy. Those who sign the pledge agree to devote a substantial portion of their wealth to charity. They also agree to lend their expertise to causes, so that charitable organizations can benefit from both their intelligence and experience. In China, Gates and Buffett spoke about the Giving Pledge and told the Chinese tycoons that if they invested themselves, they would find the experience more meaningful than simply writing a check.

The contacts between the rich and famous Chinese and the rich and famous Americans also helped Yang and Guangshen see the differences in the groups. In America, the one hundred wealthiest men and women average age sixty-five. About 30 percent of them come from families that have been wealthy for generations, and the majority were quite familiar with philanthropy long before they got involved directly. In China, the average age of the hundred richest people is fifty-one. None of them come from family money, and none had any real experience with charitable giving.[12]

The wealthy Chinese were also far less diversified in their holdings than the Americans. Real estate forms the bulk of their wealth, and this fact made them feel less secure. Indeed, the Communist Party continues to play a big role in land prices and development. The routing of a highway or the choice of a factory site can change property values instantly. Recently, local Chinese officials have cut back on their construction spending because they fear they may overbuild and be left with expensive, vacant development. This slowdown could have a direct impact on the personal wealth of the richest one hundred.

Guangshen said that the insecurity of China's moneyed elite, coupled with deep public suspicions about the wealthy—many Chinese people think that the rich become so through cheating—makes potential donors feel hesitant. They don't want to put their names on buildings or create highly visible charities because they don't want to have a high public profile. This is true for roughly two-thirds of the men and women Yang Lan has asked to help build a private caring sector for the country. These same people also want to avoid attracting too much scrutiny by the government. "Normally the government pays no attention to small gifts," explained Guangshen, "but if the donation is huge, they want to know why it's being made and what it's for."

Despite the obstacles, the impulse to give, and to do so constructively, is growing among the Chinese elite, and the Sun Culture Foundation has honed a special pitch to get individuals started. It tells them that "no government, whether it's a democracy or a dictatorship"[13] is equipped to support the kind of experimentation that is needed to find out what might work and what will not. Likewise, "business is not a good choice to make these kinds of pilot programs because they have to see the potential for results,"[14] and often the most intriguing models for delivering services come with real doubts about how they will work in the field. This is precisely where nonprofit, foundation-supported enterprises come into play. Free of bureaucratic pressures or profit demands, they can test projects in urban neighborhoods and rural communities and arrive at distinctly Chinese models through trial and error.

Moving these people to the point where they will give freely to such experiments will take time. As Guangshen explained it, Communist rule has "practically destroyed" a Chinese middle class that valued this kind of citizenship and traditionally embraced a help-thy-brother ethic.

"No matter what dynasty," said Guangshen, "we had this middle-class sector in the country for thousands of years. They knew how to be honest and trusting, how to take responsibility. These people were the cultural root of China." Tragically, added Guangshen, land reforms and the Communist revolution meant that several generations were not taught these values. "Today Chinese people are true individuals. The ones who get rich get rich by some individual effort. They don't trust the market system or the legal mechanism. They only trust themselves."

With trust in short supply, Bill Gates's suggestion that China replicate the Giving Pledge "just isn't possible yet," said Guangshen. "Bill wants to see this happen, but here we are not very aggressive. We can invite people to come and share and learn. We believe in this slow kind of development. If people learn and understand, then it is not necessary to push."

Experienced in both nonprofit development and Chinese society, Guangshen is probably right about taking a slow-growth approach to big-ticket philanthropy in China. However, events beyond anyone's control may push the country as a whole toward a culture of caring much faster. A case in point occurred a few months before we visited China, when a little girl was hit by a delivery truck passing down an alley in southern China. The child, who was so small that she was not visible to the driver, fell under the truck's wheels and was killed as it rolled over her. A surveillance video of the incident made it onto the Internet. Public outrage over the hit-and-run accident was doubled by the fact that more than a dozen people walked past the child and didn't stop even to check her condition.

The hit-and-run death was widely associated with a decline in Chinese values and sparked a nationwide conversation about citizen responsibility and moral values. Guangshen will continue to actively build philanthropy and an infrastructure to care for people in need, but he suspects that the real energy for this effort will come from an awakened public. In China, people are talking "about the future of human society," he noted. "Will we be like the bees or the ants, and just do what we have been organized to do? Or will we be a society of people who have freedom and use that freedom to do something more? We are going to find out."

Chapter 9

Sweden, Germany, and Belgium

"People are more open to sharing their feelings
than in previous generations." (77% agree)

Sweden's version of Mardi Gras comes with creampuffs. On Fat Tuesday in Stockholm, they are as common as plastic beads at a New Orleans parade, and so airy that you hardly feel weighed down by the first five or six. When we arrived on this holiday, Maria Ziv met us with a plate of these pastries—called semla—and steaming cups of coffee. After a shivering walk, these treats made us feel welcome—which was appropriate, considering that it's Maria's job to make the entire world feel welcome in Sweden.

As marketing chief for VisitSweden, the national tourist bureau, Maria might also be expected to guard the country's image and control how it may be broadcast. But we went to see her because she and her government colleagues have deliberately ceded control of the national Twitter account @Sweden to citizens who use the handle to say what they will to the entire world. Each week, a different person controls the stream, writing with almost no restrictions or oversight.

The experiment in crowdsourced messaging arose from a multi-year effort to develop a plan for Sweden's national brand, explained Maria. "Instead of there being one voice, we thought, 'The Swedes are the voice of Sweden, so why not just hand it over to them?' You have to have guts, I guess, to just cross your fingers and hope it goes well. But we have a pretty strong sense of who Swedes are."[1]

The Swedes who stepped forward to tweet turned out to be rich, poor, straight, gay, male, female, and varied in many other ways. Among the early popular favorites were a priest, a sheepherder, and a lesbian truck driver named Hanna Frange, whose comments included a rant about the odor emanating from a livestock hauler that passed her on the road. "Damn you, piggie truck beside mine!" she tweeted.[2] Others wrote about food, culture, snow, and the differences between Nordic and North American elk.

The openness inherent in the campaign reflected the core values government officials had identified when they set out to define Sweden and its people a few years ago. Along with "open," they also selected "innovative" and "caring." Certainly the experiment was innovative. No nation had ever before turned over its tourism message to the public. And it depended on the volunteers caring enough to represent the country with thoughtful comments. Swedes are "interested in other people's opinions, they love their country, and they're pretty humble as well," said Maria.

Except for a handful of tweets, the messages sent in the first months affirmed the government's faith. This success was consistent with the mature level of social engagement that can be found in much of Europe. In Stockholm, Brussels, and Berlin, we discovered how a long tradition of civic action inspires people to the heights of Athena-style innovation. However, few of these examples were as visible as the VisitSweden campaign, which was attracting attention around the world—followers were logging in from more than a hundred countries—and making Swedes swell with pride.

"We had an international audience in mind, to show we are very open, confident—not screening and not controlling," said Maria. However, she added, the intensity of the global response was unexpected. "People were surprised that other people were interested, because what they are writing about is very normal stuff we take for granted. They get an outside perspective on their own culture that generates pride." A similar project that promotes Swedish food led a generally humble citizenry to realize that they actually possess a cuisine that is worth talking about. Swedes, it turned out, cook as well as the French and the Italians.

Remarkably, the officials who embarked on these sharing initiatives didn't even consider asking for permission from the highest level of government. It is in the Swedish nature of things to simply open up conversations and include as many voices as possible. It is, by law, a democratic society. Government is subject to strict public records laws, which makes most information available. On average, about 85 percent of voting-age adults go to the polls, and the ballot always includes the option of "none of the above" so that dissatisfied citizens can register their feelings.

"We did ask the foreign minister what he thought of the Twitter campaign," said Maria. "He was actually criticized [online] by one of the curators. We asked him if he saw a risk in handing out the account. He answered and said, 'No, this is great. Sweden is the sum of everyone.'"

And everyone in the country seems to have a growing interest in both self-expression and discovering the perspectives of their neighbors. When we asked her to explain this phenomenon, Maria cited the pioneering psychologist Abraham Maslow's "hierarchy of needs," which suggests that people who satisfy basic requirements for survival invariably turn to higher-order moral and social concerns. In this case, she believes that Swedes and visitors to their country hunger for direct connection, whether it means sharing a week, a day, or an hour with each other. Tour buses are out. Welcoming visitors to your home is in.

The @Sweden campaign isn't without its hiccups. In June 2012, a woman in control of the handle tweeted remarks that were perceived as anti-Semitic. The controversy was widely covered by the news media, but the team at VisitSweden left the tweets intact, uncensored. "When things are not as you think they are, you get curious and you want to know more" about Sweden, a spokeswoman told BBC News.

"You learn a lot from the dialogue," Maria told us. "Maybe as we become so far up the hierarchy of needs, we want to satisfy those last questions about who am I? How am I different from others? We wanted things that were superficial for a while. But now we've got this hunger to learn about others."

• • •

The Swedish pursuit of higher-order rewards is enabled by a remarkable combination of capitalism and social programs that have created one of the highest standards of living in the world. Although a member of the European Economic Union, Sweden never adopted the Euro currency and thus escaped the pain of the monetary crisis that began in 2008. As measured by the Gini index, which charts social and economic equality, Sweden is number one in the world.[3] The country consistently ranks at the top in measures of health, welfare, education, and security. And although Swedes pay high taxes to achieve this status, they live in a free-enterprise economy that also rewards innovation and hard work. In short, the Swedish state assures everyone a certain base level of support, but it's also possible to excel on your own.

In such a setting, people feel quite free to experiment with almost every kind of human endeavor, beginning with early childhood education. After our visit with Maria, we trekked to the Egalia Preschool, where 350 children are served by seventy-six teachers who studiously avoid gender stereotypes. Here, robots are piled with dolls in the toy boxes, and play kitchens are painted in primary colors, not pink and lavender. Here, a teacher calls out "friends" rather than "boys and girls" to bring a class to attention. When a boo-boo occurs, empathy is applied in equal measure whether the victim is male or female.

When it was founded in 2010, the preschool attracted criticism from outsiders concerned about gender stereotypes and perhaps an antimale bias. In fact, the school's staff is more concerned with equal opportunity than identity. Teachers at Egalia are determined that every child feel free to select toys, costumes, activities, and interests without considering whether he or she is making a proper choice for a boy or girl. It's about freedom and flexibility, not political correctness.

The Egalia school looks like any other preschool in the developed world—except, perhaps, a little blonder. On the day we visited, children scampered in the hallways, a song drifted out of one classroom, and somewhere, someone was whining in a tone that means frustration in whatever language you speak. Founders Lotta Rajalin and Anders Bengsston, comfortably sitting in a classroom's tiny chairs, told us that as young teachers they had believed they were offering children every option possible to decide who they were. However, when they thought deeply about their work, they realized that ingrained concepts of masculine and feminine influenced them in unexpected ways.

"We started to film each other working with children and made observations," recalled Lotta.[4] Through the films, they recognized very big differences in the way they treated children. "A big difference was that often we talked a lot with girls and explained things and used many words to reach their emotional side," said Lotta. "But to boys we were very direct. 'Stop it!' 'Go there!' 'Sit here!' 'Now you did this, you have to do that!'"

Indeed, Lotta and Anders came to believe that boys were so neglected when it came to communication that they grew into young men with limited vocabularies and inferior language skills. In an age when communication is a necessary social and vocational skill, this deficit was alarming.

"Of course the girls get better language skills," said Lotta. "They also get better results in the school, even in the university, and in their whole life." This is especially true in the emotional realm, where accessing and expressing feelings are essential.

Anders and Lotta observed that adults tend to unconsciously steer boys and girls in different ways—and with each subtle difference, they signal what is appropriate or acceptable. To reduce these signals and allow children to find their own way, they consciously offer the same kinds of supports and limits no matter whether a student is male or female. Toys of all sorts, from dolls and carriages to trucks and tools, are made available without regard for gender, and no one who crosses the old gender lines is stigmatized. Boys are comforted. Girls are challenged.

Although Egalia is a new project, Anders and Lotta have been working on gender-neutral education since 1998. They have noticed that although some effort is required initially, teachers soon find that they reflexively change their styles to make sure that gender isn't determinative. Sometimes a princess comes to the rescue of a prince. Sometimes the birthday cake is baked by a dad.

The shift seems natural to those who are part of it, but many outsiders, especially older people, struggle to understand why it's necessary. (Critics say the school is involved in "neutering" children and creating confusion with distorted language.) Lotta likens the situation to the nineteenth-century movement that freed slaves around the world. Emancipation was considered unnecessary and absurd until it was accomplished. Then it was accepted as such an obvious choice that slavery seemed clearly wrong to everyone.

"This is how it is when I talk to teenagers," said Lotta. "They come to the school and say they don't understand what the big deal is." The end goal is an adult person who sees free choices and possibilities everywhere. Instead of being constrained by half the options—male or female—they can adopt and express anything they choose.

To us, it seemed that the hallmark of the school was not its gender neutrality but its thoughtfulness. Nothing done at Egalia escaped examination, evaluation, and reconsideration. It was easy to imagine that this process could become overwrought, but the potential benefits far outweighed the possible problems. How much better would things be if everyone learned how to share, collaborate, negotiate? How much more creativity and innovation would come from a society that encourages the blend of feminine and masculine in every imaginable way? How much happier would individuals be if gender didn't limit their development?

• • •

The desire for self-determination is not merely a Western or Eastern phenomenon, and it is not just a consideration for those who have achieved a certain level of wealth and security. All of human history can be seen as a long struggle for greater human rights and dignity. The most striking recent demonstration of this desire—the Arab Spring—began in Tunisia in late 2010, where massive protests eventually led to the first free elections since 1956. The movement quickly spread and brought about the end of dictatorships in Egypt and Libya. As unrest spread from Mauritania to Oman, authoritarian leaders responded with a variety of reforms. Although big victories were few, the movement became almost permanent, and protests flared and subsided across the Middle East. In Syria, opponents to the Assad regime embarked on a long uprising that was met with military force.

In Sweden, where the annual Nobel Prize reminds everyone of international affairs, interest in freedom and peacemaking runs especially high. However, the founders of Bambuser weren't actually thinking about foreign affairs when they created a service that allows anyone to stream live video from a mobile phone to the World Wide Web. Jonas Vig and Måns Adler actually imagined parents streaming soccer games to grandparents, or newly married couples live-streaming the fun of their wedding reception to friends a world away.

True, plenty of games and parties appear on the Web thanks to Bambuser, but the site has also hosted reports showing young Arabs protesting dictatorships across the Middle East. Young people (and it was primarily young people) used the site to expose violence and brutality that professional news crews weren't able to capture. Bambuser users were credited with sending out the first video of the violence against freedom activists in Syria. The service is now a target of cyberattacks from repressive regimes trying to control the news. This hostility is perhaps the best measure of Bambuser's impact.

We met Jonas and Måns in their workplace, which occupies most of an upper floor in a downtown Stockholm loft. On the street level, an Asian market offered the Bambuser staff ready access to all the noodles they could want at lunchtime. A few doors away, a bar called the Viper Room offered them a haven where they could unwind after hours. Måns, whose fluffy red hair looked as though it was about to fly off his head, had the scruffy look of a fellow often present at closing time. Jonas, who has short-cropped brown hair and wears neat business casual clothes, looked like the guy who was negotiating a partnership with the Associated Press. (The arrangement was sealed weeks after we met him.)

The founders came up with Bambuser as they worked on their final project at a management school in Denmark. They started with the realization that technology was wiping out the heavy costs long associated with broadcasting. Soon, they thought, anyone in the world could present video on the Internet. "We then had two questions," recalled Måns when we sat down to talk. "One was, what would people choose to broadcast, and what would people choose to view?"[5]

As they considered these questions, the two men realized that although Bambuser users might not reach ten million people with their broadcasts, they might connect with ten, and those ten mattered very much. For example, a father who is traveling abroad would much rather watch his daughter's game on the Internet than a major league contest on television. As an audience of one, he was intensely valued by his daughter. And as a broadcaster, the mother sending out the signal from the sidelines enjoyed the highest rating possible from her target audience. "It's the small things that keep us together," adds Måns.

Bambuser—an old Swedish word for an unskilled sailor—grew slowly in the first year or two after its founding in 2007. Use expanded exponentially after 2010, as wireless phone companies made their data networks faster and less expensive to access. Civic journalism streamed on Bambuser alerted the world to unrest in Egypt before international news organizations made it a big story. The site's value to human rights activists became evident as authorities confiscated cameras and computers and erased video. "There was one human rights guy who used our server so they couldn't erase it," recalled Måns. The recordings included scenes of police brutality. "They brought the police to trial for using excessive force," he reported, and the video evidence proved the claim.

As the uprising in Egypt unfolded, the small Bambuser staff in Stockholm found itself in the middle of events more than a thousand miles away. Videos shot by amateurs came in at a rate of more than fifty per hour. As they were posted, they were then viewed inside their countries of origin and around the world. In some cases, a person at the leading edge of a protest march sent out live video images of conflicts with police that were viewed by fellow marchers walking behind them, connected to the Web by their phones.

Eventually Egyptian authorities shut down public access to Twitter, Bambuser, Facebook, and other social networks. Then they blacked out all Internet service for six days. The move deprived the world of the powerful raw images that had empowered protests, but it also signaled the value of an accessible, international video-sharing service. After the Mubarak regime was toppled, Jonas attended a conference in Egypt where Bambuser users told attendees that the service had saved lives. In one case, a protester who was arrested kept streaming audio from a cell phone he tucked in his pocket. By the time he was brought into a police station, an enormous crowd had gathered to demand his release. He was freed almost immediately.

Bambuser's role in the Egyptian uprising was unusual. In fact, the founders estimate than 99 percent of the material streamed on the site is of no interest to anyone outside a small group of friends and family. However, the experience provoked Jonas and Måns to think more deeply about how cameras can open up the world. From a democratic standpoint, they say, citizens could start demanding that the video streams produced by government surveillance cameras be made available to the public in real time. A policy that allowed this to happen would flip the power dynamic of surveillance, allowing individuals to use the cameras to keep track of officials. Under such a system, the definition of public space would be expanded dramatically, and officials would be held accountable in the same way as citizens.

If live video services evolve to make the world into a public space, it won't be the first time that a technological advance produced unexpected results. Jonas recalled reading a biography of Thomas Edison that reported on his original phonograph patent. In his application, said Jonas, Edison wrote that he expected his device would be used to record the voices of the dying, so that their loved ones could hear them after they were gone. Although some people may have used the machine for such a purpose, the phonograph actually enabled the modern music industry, which allowed culture to spread faster, and farther, than ever before. The phonograph made the world into a closer community and led to the development of film and then broadcasting.

Bambuser's technology may spur change comparable to the transformation sparked by Edison. If it does, the key will be the users, not the hardware and software, and they will benefit from some essentially Swedish concepts of citizenship and engagement. The country was one of the first in the world to guarantee free speech, and its highly developed welfare state is a nationally popular emblem of the country's spirit of cooperative effort and civic morality. Bambuser is democratic and egalitarian, enabling anyone with a cell phone to communicate with the world. It also makes every participant in a social or political debate remarkably vulnerable. The powerful become vulnerable to the reporting of everyday citizens. The citizens open themselves up to criticism from all the people who view their videos. All of this communication over an open forum requires a high level of confidence, responsibility, and trust. All these factors suggest that Bambuser is ideal for those who want to live and act according to Athena values.

"We have a very strong sense of responsibility, and a passion for transparency and honesty," said Jonas.[6] Bambuser technology is reducing the cost of achieving transparency and honesty for people who want to take responsibility for conditions in their countries. With live streaming technology available in abundance, Jonas said, reports on events and ideas will flow in great numbers even from the poorest countries. The job of assessing and evaluating all the information will fall to the consumer. "We don't want to validate or verify," added Måns. "That is up to you." Of course, this task will be aided by the message marketplace, where ideas and claims compete freely, and every voice can be heard. Today, Jonas and Måns are even training citizens in the Middle East to use Bambuser as an election monitoring tool.

• • •

If Bambuser constructs an ever-expanding web, connecting everyone and everything to allow for a limitless variety of expression, ResearchGate acts like a funnel. This service collects input from a universe of contributors, all to help individual scientists and their teams make research breakthroughs, especially when they reach dead ends and roadblocks. The idea was born when Ijad Madisch, a Harvard-trained virologist, got stumped on a project, as happens to all of us from time to time. But when he reached out to his colleagues for help, he was promptly chastised. Big-time scientists were supposed to project an image of supreme competence, they told him.

Thankfully, Ijad felt secure enough in his scientific talents that he happily sought collaborators who might be stronger in a certain technique or a discipline. But despite his willingness to reach out for help, he found the scientific community almost impossible to navigate. He could search publications for articles and then try to track down authors who published research related to his, but this process was tedious and imprecise. What science needed, he realized, was a global community where the work could take precedence over ego. So he started one.

We met Ijad at ResearchGate headquarters in a nondescript office building in what was formerly East Berlin. Now part of a unified city, the area is a place where rents are low and space is relatively abundant. It is filled with start-up companies and the young energetic people who devote themselves to making new ideas work. Recently blessed with an infusion of cash from investors, ResearchGate occupied several floors and had grown to more than seventy employees. Modeled after a Silicon Valley start-up, the company gave every one of these employees an ownership stake and stocked the workplace with food, drink, and amenities to make everyone comfortable.

On the day we arrived, Ijad was bustling from desk to desk, monitoring the flow of traffic from the community's two million members. A bit of an absentminded professor, he had forgotten our appointment, but instantly welcomed us for a tour and a long conversation. He began by making sure we understood the difference between "stupid networking" and the type of "smart networking" he hopes to create.

"Stupid networking is like going to networking events, which is useless," he said bluntly.[7] "Who goes to networking events? Only people who are not well connected. The people who are already connected don't need to go, and they are too busy."

Smart networking, in contrast, occurs "when you create something of value that makes people want to come to you." For most scientific researchers, time has the highest value, and networking can save you lots of it. "I always tried to network when I couldn't get a problem solved," recalled Ijad. "Instead of working four or five months to solve something, I'd try to find someone who understood it already and could explain it to me in a couple of hours."

With his own experience in mind, Ijad imagined a sophisticated kind of Facebook that would allow scientists to create interconnected groups that would generate a cascade of communication about real research challenges. Ideally, it would allow people from different disciplines and with widely varying skills to consider problems that normally fall out of their purview. ResearchGate, which Ijad built with the help of Web developers, permits all of the relationships and cross-pollination that he hoped for, and it archives millions of pieces of information, including news items, blogs, and articles. Members, who reside in two hundred countries and must be affiliated with a university, hospital, or research institute, register with their real names and contact information. They also provide a detailed accounting of their education, experience, interests, and publications. All these data help members locate individuals and groups who might answer their questions.

In its most recent year, more than twelve thousand questions were broadcast to ResearchGate members, who made more than 1.6 million connections and shared more than eight hundred thousand articles. Often the sharing took place across scientific specialties, breaking the barriers that exist between, say, physicists and biologists or chemists and astronomers. Ijad saw this blending of specialties as a return to science as it was conducted before the twentieth century, when researchers were true generalists and polymaths, making discoveries across subject and interest areas.

Behind these numbers are individual scientists, many working in isolated labs, who use ResearchGate to access literature, find collaborators, share techniques, and even hire associates. We asked if the network has produced any spectacular results. Ijad said that dramatic breakthroughs are not the intent. "Scientific research is mainly a matter of solving a series of small problems," he explained. "Every small result is contributing to the big result."

For Ijad, efficiency is the main point. However, he also delights in destroying the stereotypes people associates with scientists. Turns out, scientists are often good communicators who are sociable and eager for friendship. They are competitive, but also collaborative. And they are far less critical than Ijad had feared. "I expected negative things, with people saying, 'Ah, you're stupid,'" he told us. "Instead it's really helpful. People ask, 'Did you try this? Did you try that?' Scientists are generally good people who try to help." The helpfulness is balanced by real ambition, which powers the dogged pursuit of answers that matter. Here, Ijad has much in common with the community he serves. He hopes that ResearchGate will be so important to the world that his team will one day receive a Nobel Prize.

• • •

If they gave prizes to insurance companies, Friendsurance would surely win. Headquartered a short distance from ResearchGate and within sight of a remnant of the Berlin Wall, the company is based on an ingenious scheme that promises to make its customers safer, healthier, and happier while saving them money. It accomplishes these goals by letting people form their own buying groups for basic insurance products.

The idea taps the age-old concept of group insurance—long used by corporations, unions, social organizations, and others—to spread the risk of big claims across many different buyers. This reduces the overall cost. But Friendsurance also works the other side of the equation, reducing risk through peer pressure that encourages participants to behave themselves. It works because the groups are made up of people who know and trust each other and agree to join together.

Tim Kunde, the young innovator behind Friendsurance, is like other European entrepreneurs who strive for a combination of social and financial rewards. However, he is not a technology pioneer like Ijad or a media provocateur like the people at Bambuser. He is the product of a classical business school education, and he cut his teeth as a consultant to a not-so-exciting company that made dry soups. His breakthrough idea involved harnessing the power of friendship to save people money and make their lives less susceptible to losses.

"People pay the same insurance premiums at the start of the year and then we give them a payback at the end of the year," explained Tim when we met.[8] The refunds, which can total as much as 50 percent, are based on the number of claims against the insurance made by your network of friends. "If there are claims, you get less back. If your network is average, or better than average, you get money back." Insurance underwriters who back the friend groups benefit from this scheme by shrinking their administrative and potential fraud costs.

"What fascinates us is changing an old, traditional industry," said Tim, who is thirty-one and could have gone into any of a hundred different businesses. (Tim's the kind of guy who rides his bike to meetings—as he did on the day he met us—despite frigid temperatures and rainy conditions.) "We're not thrilled by insurance," he said with a smile. "What interests us is looking at it from an outside perspective."

From the outside, Tim saw that consumers didn't understand that they could gain from acting in a responsible way. Much of the cost in the business is related to fraudulent and "gray area" claims that are made when clients fail to act carefully or misrepresent the circumstances of an accident or theft. This kind of behavior is more likely when people see their relationships with insurance companies as anonymous or adversarial. "All they want to know is that they pay a premium and for that they are safe. They try to get their premium back by making a claim. The insurance company is anonymous. If I commit fraud or it's in the gray zone, it's a big company and they won't notice. People don't feel accountable," Tim said.

Likewise, Tim noted, traditional insurance companies are not sensitive to the actual needs of their customers. "They sell you what they can sell you, and it's not tailored to your needs. But people want that kind of service. There was a campaign by an insurance company that rebranded itself by saying they were going to be on your side and not against you. At first it was a huge success. But they didn't change the way they did business, and it went away."

Friendsurance adds accountability to the insurance process by linking premiums and rebates to one's network of friends and acquaintances. Auto insurance buyers, for example, can think about their friends and consider who is a safe driver and who takes risks when he or she is behind the wheel. They can then build a group as small as five and as big as sixty to seek the best coverage. Once the deal is made, friends naturally feel a moral duty to behave well, and this feeling is reinforced by peer pressure. No one wants to be the guy whose fender bender (or something worse) wiped out the refunds that would have been paid to the rest of the folks in the group.

●●●

Well-knit groups that function in an open and cooperative way can represent Athena values even when they engage in a pursuit as mundane as insurance or, in the case of Berliner Seilfabrik, traditional small-scale manufacturing.

Located on the outskirts of Berlin in a plain and functional factory building, Berliner Seilfabrik was built to make elevator cables. The company did well under the leadership of David Koehler's father—but then a proposal from an architect who designed playgrounds changed everything. "He had the idea of building [play structures] with three-dimensional nets," recalled David.[9] A craftsman at Berliner Seilfabrik found a way to make soft but sturdy rope that could withstand weather extremes and be configured into a variety of shapes. Today the firm markets its playgrounds worldwide (our hometown of New York City has several) and offers two new product lines every year. It hasn't produced an elevator cable in many years.

Although the company makes a fun and happy product, Berliner Seilfabrik caught our attention because it's a great example of a type of firm—the *mittelstand*—that forms the backbone of the sturdy German economy. These middle-size manufacturers, which employ between fifty and two hundred workers, have thrived despite the Great Recession—and they do so with a real Athena style. "One of the main secrets is innovation," said David. "We look all over the world for trends, and we move quickly to take advantage of them. We can do something in six months that would take a larger company years to do."

Focus is another advantage enjoyed by mittelstand companies. Berliner Seilfabrik makes a niche product inside an industry that is already specialized. David puts great effort into maintaining quality, and this is easier to do when a workforce is small and employees stay with the firm for a long time. Some of his workers have forty years with Berliner Seilfabrik, and their experience means that whenever a problem arises, someone on the factory floor has seen it before and knows what to do. Similarly, the small and dedicated workforce seems like a family, even to the boss.

"I'm not that quick with hiring and firing, like the bigger companies are," said David. "Everyone calls me by my first name. I know the story behind every face. We really try to stick together when things are tough, and I'm happy to give an upgrade on salary when things are better. But it's not all about the money. We're not just interested in a return on investment. The key factor is that you like to go to work. People like the way they are treated. They know we are making decisions for everyone's future."

The product itself helps everyone feel good about the enterprise. "We talk a lot about the children, how to add play value for kids, how to strengthen their development so they get ready for life," said David. A net structure requires climbers to plan their steps to achieve a goal and to proceed with enough caution to avoid failure. Deploying these mental and spatial skills yields a feeling of accomplishment and even triumph when the child reaches the top.

The company's employees also know that their products, with worldwide distribution, are providing safe play options for children in South America, Asia, and Africa as well as Europe and North America. Although David handles most of the international travel for sales, he shares the experience by making detailed reports to his workers, explaining which elements of a playground engaged children the most and passing along admiration and criticism from school and park officials: "I tell them how people reacted to the new product they developed. Let them be part of the whole process. And when possible, I include them when I go to a show or exhibition. If I get an invitation because I'm the head of the company, I take someone with me. Everyone is part of everything here."

Everyone is part of the decision making at Berliner Seilfabrik, too. "We used to make big decisions on our own, within management," said David. "Now we include the designers, salespeople, even production. We show them the proposed brochure and say, 'Is this something you can go with?'" Remarkably, almost every worker in the company feels confident expressing an opinion. And David is counting on those informed opinions to see the firm into the future, where competition will require even more openness, cooperation, and shared sense of purpose.

• • •

By inviting inputs and even criticism from every one of his workers at Berliner Seilfabrik, David made himself vulnerable, but he gained from the collected wisdom of his workforce. Tim and Ijad created entire enterprises that make a virtue out of shared information and experiences. That these examples of entrepreneurial spirit can be found in Europe may surprise Americans and others who assume that the continent's tax regulatory systems pose almost insurmountable obstacles to creativity.

The classic critique focuses on slow-moving bureaucracies that inhibit innovation. Surely the clichés are based on some measure of truth. Social welfare states can become sclerotic and dysfunctional.

But within government, we see some examples of cooperation, long-term thinking, and innovation that would make even the most cynical observer more optimistic about the future.

In Berlin, the ultimate emblem of the Athena Doctrine may be represented by the diplomacy practiced at a complex called the Felleshus—a Danish word meaning "house for everyone." A complex of six low-slung, modern buildings, the Felleshus is home to diplomatic missions from five countries whose officials share common space and support staff, and move freely from office to office in their pursuit of common understanding and goals.

In stark contrast to the Felleshus, the shuttered Syrian embassy sits across the street, enclosed by barbed wire and marred with graffiti.

Not surprisingly, the Felleshus nations—Finland, Denmark, Sweden, Norway, and Iceland—are all Nordic and share much history and heritage. They also lead the world when it comes to social mobility, economic opportunity, and the advancement of women in all sectors of society. On a bureaucratic level, the combined embassy reduces cost and streamlines relationships. "Economically and socially, there has been much easier integration" because of the Felleshus, said Leo Riski , a Finnish official who was our contact at the embassy complex.[10] "It's much easier to do business. People can trust each other," whether they are selling goods, traveling, purchasing properties, or even emigrating for employment.

The idea for the embassy complex arose after the fall of the Berlin Wall, when Germany's capital was moved from Bonn to Berlin. The architecture emphasizes transparency, with plenty of glass and open space, but also cohesion. A fencelike copper band, fifteen meters high and weathered to a greenish patina, joins the building together to symbolize the shared interests of the five nations. It is visible from the street and reminds visitors that they are entering a sheltered space of mutual support.

As he spoke about the impulse that brought nations together at the Felleshus, Leo cited the lessons of World War II and Europe's experience with the Cold War. During these periods, the cost of conflict and isolation became apparent to all. When both the hot war and the Cold War became history, people saw openings for new structures. "In times of crisis, people tend to think about themselves only," he noted. But when peace was certain, they could think expansively. One outcome was the European Union, which, for all of its faults, promoted understanding and security.

"Germany understood it can only be free when it is accepted inside Europe," said Leo. For this reason, the EU remains popular in most of the capitals on the continent. The same is true for the Nordic alliance, captured in the spirit of the Felleshus. "We know that we are safer when we are together," he added.

The Nordic countries are also far more effective in reaching the public and the diplomatic community through the Felleshus than they would be acting independently. Alone, each country might have a dozen staff occupying a quiet building rarely visited by outsiders. Together, they can present more than a hundred public events each year, making the Felleshus a hub of activity and a lever of influence. "Whether we save a penny or not, we have a bigger impact when we are together."

• • •

The public good realized by the Felleshus flows from policies that recognize the limits of independent action and the shared interests of nations that occupy the Nordic region. According to the calculus Leo Riski offered, as member countries ceded some of their individual identities and prerogatives, they gained much more than they lost. The same equation governs the work of the world's largest international federation, the European Union, as it works to integrate economies and societies from Ireland to Cyprus and from Finland to Spain. Although the EU has had its problems, especially with monetary policy, the union has fostered peace, encouraged trade, and brought the people of the continent closer together.

Although the EU's mandates are limited, the union does approach global environmental issues with a single voice. Under this mandate, EU officials have played a growing role in safeguarding rivers, lakes, and oceans. Recently, the EU Commission's Directorate-General for Maritime Affairs and Fisheries made waves with a program that pays fishermen to fill their nets with the plastic refuse that litters the sea and haul it to shore, where they will be paid by the pound. The program pulls value out of money that was previously given outright to fishermen who had met their annual quotas.

Other maritime initiatives led by the EU include mapping out the ocean floor in preparation for mining, and developing aquaculture to replace depleted species with farm-raised fish. The impetus for these initiatives can be traced to public awareness and concern about sustainability. (For example, more than seven hundred thousand British citizens recently signed petitions to stop fishermen from discarding fish they didn't want to bring to port.) Leadership for these international initiatives comes from Maria Damanaki, born and raised on the island of Crete, where the sea is a constant presence and fishing has been a way of life for thousands of years. "If you look at the sea every day, you have to think about it," said Maria on the day we met her in Brussels.[11]

In her work as head of the maritime affairs and fisheries directorate, Maria must find consensus among twenty-seven nations and then deal with non-EU states that share maritime resources. "The fish don't care about boundaries," she noted as she described coordinating with North African states to monitor the Mediterranean, and with Russia in the Arctic. "We cannot combat illegal fisheries without the United States or Japan," she added. "My ambition is to have an international certificate for legal, sustainable fishing. This would have to be developed in the framework of the United Nations. But step-by-step, it could happen. The needs could be addressed."

Because she is subject to constant scrutiny, Maria must operate in a way that is so transparent that nations and interests groups know exactly where she is headed with policies. "The only option is to be completely sincere," she said. "Telling a lie works for a moment or a month, but then it falls apart. We have to change our vision, the way we do our jobs. People know. They may be very angry, but if there's a solution, they want to use it."

The solution, which has been embraced by the EU, imagines the resources of the sea as a type of capital, comparable to money in a bank. "I'm like a banker," said Maria. "I have natural capital, and I have to make the best use of it. I have to safeguard the survival of this capital for the future. If I spend it all in one year, a lot of people will be happy—but next year there will be nothing. But if I am careful, nature can take care of this capital, reproduce it, and make more for fishermen and the public."

Maria finds support for her role as a regulator in an informed public, including diners who demand that restaurants serve sustainably acquired fish. To maintain this support, she stresses the value of ocean resources, especially as Europe runs out of arable land and accessible minerals: "We have exhausted our land, so we must turn to the sea for new growth and new potential." In turning to the ocean for food, energy, minerals, and other kinds of wealth, humanity has a chance to get things right, she adds. Striking the balance would be "easy for a dictator," she said with a wry smile, "but we have to persuade our citizens." Persuasion begins with acknowledging that "we politicians don't know everything. We have to admit that. We have to work with scientists and data and with citizens. It takes money and time, but at the end of the day, it secures the future."

Maria uses the word "secure" because societies cannot remain stable without secure access to food, energy, and mineral resources. Safeguarding the seas, therefore, is not a simple matter of environmentalism or the sentimentality of a woman who grew up on an island. It is a matter of survival that depends on popular support across the world. Here, Maria is certain that the EU's methods of inclusion, unity, and transparency offer the best option for survival. "To feel more secure, people need to feel that they belong to a group, a nation. It's true especially for young people. They have to see their future inside the society, not outside it. Of course there are outsiders. There are always outsiders. But if there are too many outsiders, this is a disaster." As an Athena-style institution, the EU attempts to bring more and more people inside a community big enough to address problems that span the continent and extend to the seas.

Chapter 10

Bhutan

*"In a world with less money, happiness is a
more important measure of success."*
(80% agree)

It was, from the start, a radical idea: What if a country's status
depended not upon wealth or power, but happiness? asked the
king of Bhutan. Could the well-being of citizens be the true measure
of a nation and its leaders? If so, how would that assessment be
made? And who would chart the results?

All these questions and more swirled in our minds as our Druk
Air flight approached the one runway in the country that can
handle an Airbus jet. Due to the elevation (seven thousand feet)
and the looming Himalayas, landings at Paro International are so
difficult that only a handful of pilots are certified to attempt them.
Fly-arounds are common, but on the day we arrived in Bhutan,
conditions were good, and we touched down on the first try.

The easy landing came after months of vague discussions
with officials in Bhutan, who control foreign access to a country with a paradoxical combination of warmth and resistance.
They were intrigued by our topic—Athena values and Bhutan's

development—and certain they could speak to it, but no one would confirm an interview before we arrived. The Bhutanese government is wary of visitors who seek something more than the tourist experience—which meant that no one in the country returned any of the inquiries we sent from the States.

Given how difficult it had been to arrange our trip, we expected to have problems connecting with folks when we arrived. Instead, every door we tried was opened for us, and every person we met patiently answered questions that seemed incongruous, if not impossible to answer. When we asked local media expert Siok Sian Pek-Dorji whether she was happy, she seemed taken aback.

"Am I happy?" she answered. "What do you mean by 'Am I happy?' How do you define happiness?"[1] With some encouragement, Siok allowed that she might be happy, "[but] for me it would be closer to contentment, no problems, no major health issues, and a sense of fulfillment. A sense of being rooted."

Similarly, a member of parliament named Tshering Tobgay hesitated when asked about the country's deliberate approach to social and economic change, and then said, "Perhaps it's the power of Buddhism in us, the understanding that nothing is permanent. Change is the only constant. So most of us don't feel overwhelmed. We take it as a part of life."[2]

Tshering's equanimity and Siok's puzzlement were echoed wherever we went in Bhutan, for here is a country where people take for granted that every moment demands flexibility and that individual happiness is always bound to the well-being of the community. In our brief experience there, Bhutanese struggled to speak about themselves in concrete ways, but understood the ideals that guide the nation's careful creep into the modern world.

"Most of [the Bhutanese] say that they are happy because they evaluate their financial level and then other aspects, like the balanced use of their time, the community, and social bonding," explained Karma Wangdi, a research officer at the government's

Center for Bhutan Studies.[3] But as he considered his country's future, he worried about Bhutanese adopting new priorities. "Possibly the main challenge that we face," he told us, "is increasing our desire for material comfort."

In a country where people get by on an average $6,200 per year, runaway materialism hardly seems a reasonable concern. But in Bhutan, no element of daily existence, or national life, goes unexamined. This cautious consideration is a matter of policy formulated by a succession of highly respected monarchs who are both political authorities and interpreters of Tibetan Buddhism. For generations, Bhutanese kings have permitted only the most gradual modernization of the country. With the introduction of each new technology and social concept, including democracy, officials have painstakingly weighed the benefits against complex ancient values. They do not assume that "newer" equals "better" or that "modern" is the same as "advanced."

The overriding principle of the national religion stresses personal enlightenment for the benefit of a universe full of interconnected souls. In this view, individual achievement is encouraged, especially if it produces a benefit for all of creation. The local culture also promotes a remarkable level of mutual respect. Historically, Bhutanese men and women have known substantial equality in marriage, community affairs, and commerce. Indeed, the feminine spirit is highly regarded in Tibetan Buddhism, and property in Bhutan is passed from mother to daughter.

The tradition of rough gender equality served the Bhutanese well as they became a nation in the early seventeenth century. For centuries, geographical isolation and poverty—coupled with the country's strong self-image—helped preserve Bhutan, even while every other Himalayan kingdom disappeared. However, even mountain ranges couldn't protect Bhutan from satellite television and the lure of the Internet. In 1998, noting the approach of the modern world, King Jigme Singye Wangchuck handed almost all of his powers to a prime minister and parliament. This shift was followed a year later by the introduction of television and the World Wide Web. In 2008, the country held its first parliamentary elections.

Bhutan's careful steps into the modern world have included public education for all, widespread instruction in English, and partnerships with Western academics who have helped develop local media and a so-called happiness index to track the country's well-being. Refined to survey nine areas of national concern, from the contentment of individuals to the quality of the environment, the index considers economic factors as well as such metrics as antidepressant use and divorce rates.

Many countries around the world have used the index to conduct population studies, and it has inspired an entire field of research complete with country-by-country rankings. A 2011 "World Happiness Report" issued by the United Nations supported Bhutan's balanced view of what the king called "development with values."[4] Many organizations, from the Gallup poll to the New Economics Foundation, have adapted the index to rank countries by happiness measures. (Bhutan is routinely left out of such reports, due to its small size.) Developed countries, including the United States, Canada, and the Nordic nations, generally score well in such surveys, but so do many less developed places, such as Costa Rica and Mexico.

In Bhutan, we found that officials were concerned about improving economic conditions and reducing poverty, which stood at 23 percent when last measured in 2007. Tourism and hydroelectric exports to neighboring India have brought revenues into the country, and some of this money has gone toward raising the standard of living. But as material conditions improve, officials seek matching gains in the physical, emotional, and spiritual well-being of the population. In 1998, they established gross national happiness (GNH) as the centerpiece of the county's development plans.

"GNH can be summed up as the common aspirations of the Bhutanese people that must act as a compass to guide the development of the country," said Karma Tshiteem, secretary of the Gross National Happiness Commission.[5] The definition called for economic improvement with "a balance in the spiritual, emotional, and cultural needs of our society, based on the simple belief that all our people want to lead a happy life, that it must be the purpose of development to create those conditions."

We visited Karma at the national government's administrative center, a massive building called the Tashichhodzong in the capital of Thimphu. With less than one hundred thousand residents, Thimphu is Bhutan's largest city. It is nestled in a valley along the Raidak River, where rice paddies still produce red rice and farmers tend yak herds. It is a quiet, low-rise city. The tallest buildings are just five stories high, and the traffic at major intersections is managed by white-gloved officers.

Built, rebuilt, and refashioned over hundreds of years, the dzong is a whitewashed fortress of high walls and towers capped with multiple roofs. Rectangular in shape, it encloses a broad stone-paved courtyard. The buildings that house government offices, including the happiness commission, surround this open space. On the day we visited, the courtyard was busy with men and women dressed according to a national code that governs the use of traditional attire as formal. Women wore long dresses called kiras. Men appeared either in monks' robes or tunics—called ghos—which were tied with a cloth belt.

Karma greeted us wearing a red-and-black gho over high black socks and black lace-up shoes. A man with a slight frame and weathered face, he smiled broadly and spoke in a deliberate way, choosing his words with care. As we talked, it became clear that he sees an intrinsically Buddhist desire for balance and harmony motivating his countrymen to tread gently toward the future.

"The conventional things that most governments focus on are certainly important, even for the Bhutanese," said Karma. He then ticked off a number of essential concerns, such as employment, health care, education, and "law and order." Beyond these basics, he said, government officials have used surveys and other types of research to discover that people also "care about four other dimensions which are totally absent in the policymaking framework and considerations of most governments. These are psychological well-being, cultural diversity, community vitality, and time use." (Time use refers to the time a citizen can or must devote to work, relationships, leisure, and other interests.)

In addition to these concerns, said Karma, happiness research has identified values that Bhutanese people share. They include, he said, "love, respect, looking after your parents, respecting your elders." In a culture that acknowledges change and reveres flexibility, these values are "permanent," added Karma. "This is a very strong tradition we have. If someone asked us, 'When you grow up, what do you want to be, what will you do?' The first answer will always be, 'I'll look after my parents and repay their kindness.'"

Two-thirds of the Bhutanese people, who number fewer than eight hundred thousand, still live in rural areas. They raise rice and tend herds of yak according to practices that date back thousands of years. "Everyone knows everyone," said Karma, "and everything is done together with strong social networks of people helping each other. Community is very strong, whether it's constructing houses or farming crops, because labor shortage is a big problem; so you have to help each other. Those practices actually continue."

In such a setting, where the forces of nature demand cooperation, and individuals cannot escape personal responsibility, people must live according to certain codes in order to survive. More important, transactions of every sort—social, commercial, professional—are conducted in a very personal and face-to-face way. Indeed, one couldn't build, from scratch, a society more capable of promoting harmony. But this is not to say that Bhutan is a paradise. Indeed, considering all their harmony—and perhaps because of it—one wonders if the Bhutanese will ever experience the creative flame that comes with friction. This thought came to mind when we met parliamentarian Tshering Tobgay.

●●●

As leader of the tiny People's Democratic Party (PDP), which holds about 10 percent of the seats in the parliament, Tshering is officially the head of the loyal opposition. But the word to stress here is "loyal." Tshering doesn't appear to be opposed to anything offered by the dominant Peace and Prosperity Party (PPP). But then, no one in the PPP seems to have anything to propose that falls outside the long-standing agenda set by the king. In fact, if the politicians are like most citizens in Bhutan, their commitment to democracy is highly conditional.

According to every person we questioned in the country, the move from monarchy to democracy was resisted by most Bhutanese, who would have preferred the continued rule of the king, whom they described as wise, benevolent, and fatherly. They wouldn't have gone along with the change, except for the fact that the king ordained it. His motivations appeared to include concern about the country's status in the eyes of the world. He bet that a democratic Bhutan would find more friends and protection, with national sovereignty at the forefront of their priorities. (Look at Tibet.)

"All of us were quite cautious, to put it very very mildly," Tshering told us as he recalled the transition announcement. "Everybody wanted the king to stay on. But His Majesty the fourth king, and our current king, who was at that time the crown prince, toured the country and explained that we have to have a multiparty democracy if we are to insure and sustain the future of a strong country. But everybody was resisting."

The two sources of the public's resistance, noted Tshering, were fear of political corruption and satisfaction with the king's rule. "Democracy conjures up all sorts of evils of politicians and political parties and corruption," he said. However, "Our Majesty the king made it very clear that we can't have leadership determined by birth. It has to be by merit. And for Bhutan it has to be democracy."

A midlevel civil servant at the time, Tshering had been educated in Boston and Pittsburgh, where he saw in American life a reminder that the single-minded pursuit of economic growth is not sustainable—and even if it were sustainable, "it's no good." With this belief in mind, he "took the plunge" into politics in 2007. His purpose was to help the king's dream of a happy democratic Bhutan come true.

"If we actually loved him and if we trusted him, then we've got to fulfill his vision," he explained. "This is why I left my job and then started forming a party." But "we didn't have a political ideology to sell. And without a political ideology, it's really difficult to start a political party." Because both Tshering's party and the PPP supported all the king's policies, the election was a popularity contest, which Tshering's opponents won handily. (He was just one of four members of the PDP elected.) But because his main goal was to help establish the new system, not to achieve an electoral victory, he felt successful. The next step will be finding something to debate with his colleagues.

"I think a healthy democracy needs vibrant debate, yes? Because the purpose of democracy is supposed to be the development of the people. It is to achieve a larger goal—which is to uplift, or rather fulfill, the aspiration of the people. And in a democracy, debate is required, transparency is required, accountability is required."

In Tshering's analysis, the real challenge facing the Bhutanese involves coping with a great political opportunity that they did not earn the traditional way, but received as a gift. "Democracy is [usually] a result of internal strife and civil war, revolutions," he said. "This is the stuff of democracy. Democracy is not easy. It is difficult. People fight for it. So we've got to understand what it is, and we have to understand that, we have to accept that it is our responsibility to make democracy work."

Considered from a distance, Tshering's description of a happy country struggling to cope with new freedoms may sound implausible. But this problem seemed real to the people we met in Bhutan, who accept the king's premise that the future will require more of them. "The problem … of the proverbial benevolent dictator is that we don't do anything; we take everything for granted," explained Tshering. "And they feel they don't need to do anything. Democracy transferred responsibility, ownership to the citizens. In spite of all that, because the going has been so good 'til now, these citizens are reluctant to participate in the democratic process."

• • •

While parliamentarians may focus on the lofty aspects of responsibility and self-rule, more prosaic problems must also be addressed as the country becomes more modern and more urban. Although Thimphu is small by world standards, it has developed quite rapidly from a scattering of riverside hamlets in 1960 to a center city of seventy-five thousand and a metropolitan area with almost one hundred thousand residents. The people we met in Thimphu often volunteered worries about young people losing touch with tradition and succumbing to the influence of mass media and consumer culture. They also spoke about the side effects of modernization, which, like the side effects of a medicine, often require their own treatment.

Plastic packages are a case in point. Until their country began to open up to the world in 1990s, the Bhutanese had rarely seen plastic bottles and packaging. Unfamiliar with materials that won't biodegrade, people discarded empty containers the way they might discard an apple core or an orange peel, expecting it to be quickly absorbed by the Earth. Soon cities and towns, especially Thimphu, had a serious litter problem. Kama Wangdi and his friends addressed it with art. (Note that his name is Kama, not Karma.)

As founders of VAST—Voluntary Artists' Studio, Thimphu—Kama and his fellow artists set out to educate local children, who received no art classes in their schools. In the spirit of Tibetan Buddhism, they were soon engaged in projects intended to produce works of art and benefit their community. A group of students adopted a public square that needed renovation. After soliciting donations, they made art projects out of broken benches and fences, repairing them with flair and restoring them to public use. Next, they collected plastic trash from the streets to turn into art objects.

Trash art became a staple of the periodic exhibitions at VAST, and students went on to find new ways to serve others. Some of their projects, such as a rice bank to help people in two villages stockpile harvests, were completely homegrown. Others were inspired by concepts first tried in other countries. For example, the students had recently begun soliciting requests from people who are sick and would like some bit of assistance that would make life easier. Inspiration for this project came from the Make-A-Wish Foundation in America.

As Kama explained to us, the city kids who worked on the Make-A-Wish concept quickly discovered that it would require more than choosing to "spend some time with these old people."[6] To make the project work, "you need some money." To sustain their project and the entire VAST endeavor, they devised an auction and gala called Giving Night. "All the artists will give five paintings each," said Kama. "We put on the show and then we invite people, and they buy at a discount rate. We made money to sponsor this group."

Kama explained all this during a long conversation at the VAST center, which is located on the edge of Thimphu in a building next to a big archery field. (Archery is Bhutan's national sport.) With its white walls and wood floors, the VAST building could be a gallery anywhere in the world. The walls were filled with pieces left over from a recent Giving Night auction, including paintings of rural Bhutan as well as representations of Buddhas and Hindu gods.

The Giving Nights brought both residents of Thimphu and foreign visitors to the gallery and showed the students how a wider community could contribute to their efforts. Kama called it "Engagement art ... filling them with sharing, you know?" The students gain an even greater sense of engagement when they take weeklong trips into the countryside to offer classes and do service work in impoverished villages. In many of these places, they encounter a way of life that is both culturally rich and materially poor. For the Thimphu students, the visits are both eye opening and heartwarming.

The experience of engagement art can bring students to a more realistic understanding of the happiness Bhutan seeks for all its citizens. True happiness, in Kama's estimation, includes recognizing the truth that there "are a lot of things that we are not really happy about." Topping the list is "the gap between the haves and have-nots." The mere fact of inequality doesn't demand that Bhutan's young feel a loss of hope. This is not Kama's point. What he wants his students to grasp is that an optimistic, hopeful life requires a full understanding of the work that remains to be done. He added, "We need to work harder, I think. Harder and harder."

•••

In stressing hard work, Kama Wangdi sounded a bit like a Western businessperson or an entrepreneur from any other country in the world. Clearly, the Bhutanese quest for happiness makes room for commitment, labor, and personal growth. We heard another echo of the outside world at the Bhutan Center for Media and Democracy where, as we arrived, Siok Sian Pek-Dorji was fretting over her computer while a young member of her staff leaned in to help. A similar tableau of frustration can be found anywhere in the world. We found this one in a house nestled in the trees and hills that ring Thimphu. Far from the city and marked only by a tiny sign hung near the door, this is the hub of press development in Bhutan. Here a small staff of Bhutanese and foreigners work to persuade a country that a free press is valuable and essential.

The work involves public forums, which are held across the country, to educate people on the role of the press. It also includes seminars and workshops on journalism and citizenship. Young people, who have come of age with television and the Internet, are most receptive to the programs, said Siok. But even they must have that "ah ha" moment, as she said, when they realize that they bear a responsibility to assess and even study the information they receive to judge its value.

"We don't just talk about learning to read media or learning to analyze, you know, but to judge how reliable information is. That's one component. The other is the whole notion of citizenship. Does it mean that we just sit and accept everything? Or can we do something about what is happening?"

By doing "something," Siok means actively participating in the media. Her organization supports nonfiction and creative nonfiction writing workshops, filmmaking classes, and blogging instructions for anyone who is interested. "We've noticed that some of them have actually started contributing to the press," she said. "A few have started blogging, and they've started writing." To promote this kind of citizen journalism, the center distributes this work to colleges and schools to say, "Look, you don't have to wait until mainstream media comes to report about you."

Siok and her team work in a context that is hard for anyone in the media-saturated developed world to imagine. Bhutan's first local radio station was a student-run affair that began operation in the 1970s. The country's first newspaper was not published until 1986. Television came in 1999. Bhutan has no press tradition at all, let alone experience with free and competing news outlets. Until recently, important developments were discussed person to person, and news spread fast, said Siok. Today, the country has eleven newspapers, seven radio stations, two Bhutanese TV outlets, and all the video that satellites can deliver.

The people of Bhutan could argue that in the old days, when the country had a single newspaper, the system worked well. As Siok recalled, the paper could report on a problem like a supply shortage at a hospital, and "by ten o'clock, His Majesty went to visit the hospital to check." More recently, she said, competing news organizations take a more aggressive stance, emphasizing their "watchdog" role. As the news media increasingly function less like partners of the government, even their advocates worry about them going too far. "If all the press does is just to focus on the negative, what is there that's inspiring for the rest of the people?" asked Siok.

At the moment, said Siok, Bhutan's press focuses most of its attention on government and the country's problems, and little on positive stories. She considers this practice to be the product of a "hard-hitting male" perspective. Too many reports by young journalists lack the sophistication and balance they need, she said. The basic tenet of journalism is that "if there's a news story, be as balanced as you can. You shouldn't be offensive. You should just state the facts," Siok said. In the current era of new press freedom, this kind of fact-based reporting is hard to find, she added. As a result, government officials "get upset and uptight." Instead of having a king responding to a problem with immediate action, the country gets politicians who resent being shown up by the press.

As the Bhutanese learn to judge news reports and features, they are also coming to grips with entertainment television and the phenomenon of reality programming. Many people are baffled by competition shows like American Idol, said Siok, because the judging seems cruel. Bhutanese prefer that "everybody should be a winner," she said with a soft laugh. "Everybody should be great."

As Bhutanese recoil from the likes of Simon Cowell and pity the singers who endure his critiques, they are determining, through their consumption, the types of media that will thrive and the types that will fade from the scene. Like democracy and all the other elements of modernization, the development of mass media in this country will depend on the active choices made by people inclined toward generosity, trust, kindness, and empathy. Siok sees these choices as momentous and unavoidable. And she hopes they are made in a cautious, Bhutanese manner.

Looking forward twenty years, Siok thought about her country's identity. "Hopefully it'll still be an independent nation," she said, after taking note of Bhutan's giant neighbors, China and India. Although the forces of "materialism and commercialism are very strong," she hopes that Bhutan will progress "with some of our spiritual heritage intact." Somehow, she said, the young media makers on the rise in Bhutan will come to "appreciate some of this." In the end, they could use their freedom to preserve what is uniquely good about their tiny homeland. "The honor and privilege of being here in the early days of democracy is tremendous," she told us. "It's up to them to use that opportunity right, to build this so-called future."

• • •

Somehow it seems right to us that Bhutan's leading advocate for a free press also worries about responsible journalism. What else would you expect in a country where the politicians struggle to find things to argue about and the artists self-consciously seek to help others with their work? This is a country that missed the Industrial Revolution and sat out the global competition between capitalism and communism. Now its leaders are attempting to sample the best of the modern, technological age in such a deliberate way that they might avoid the alienation and disparities afflicting much of the developed world.

A brief visit to Bhutan, made at a single moment in the country's long transition process, can yield only a limited understanding. No amount of exploration could answer every question that an outsider might ask. Indeed, it would be impossible to say whether the loyalty people express to their king is genuine. And how could one prove, or disprove, the Bhutanese claim to happiness?

In most global reports on economic activity, Bhutan ranks in the bottom third, sometimes the bottom quarter. Somalia, Niger, and even Haiti hold higher spots in measures of gross domestic product. When the numbers are crunched on a per capita basis, things hardly look any better, with Bhutan still in the bottom half, behind Guiana, Algeria, and Albania. About a quarter of Bhutan's population is deemed poor by the United Nations, and Bhutan ranks second highest among Asian countries in a UN ranking of income inequality.

Bhutanese people, however, don't seem to regard themselves as suffering or deprived. This phenomenon was confirmed in a recent study by Japanese and Bhutanese experts who conducted a broad and deep study of the country. They discovered that people in Bhutan feel content if their health, relationships, spiritual lives, and families are all in good shape. Work and financial conditions also played a role in their reporting, but among the top ten factors, they were the only two that related to material well-being. In other words, money mattered, but it was not determinative.

In the conclusion of *Gross National Happiness and Material Welfare in Bhutan and Japan*, Tashi Choden and Takayoshi Kusago write, "Those who perceive higher social support availability tended to show better subjective well-being status . . . Similarly, those with more emotional support, i.e. having someone who shows love and affection, someone to have a good time with, and someone to get together with for relaxation, tended to show better subjective well-being status. Also, people who consider themselves more spiritual tended to show higher levels of subjective well-being."[7]

The report by Choden and Kusago was issued as part of a joint project of the Center for Bhutan Studies and Osaka University, but the locals didn't really need social science. A few thousand years of experience informs the work of the Gross National Happiness

Commission, and secretary Karma Tshiteem was confident that his country would get it right.

To help us understand, he added a caveat to the Buddhist notion that constant change is the foundation of life. Change may be inevitable, but it can be met with certain immutable, positive values. Among the ones Bhutan seeks to preserve, said Karma, "are conservation of the natural environment, our sense of community, looking out for neighbors, and looking out for fellow countrymen." Karma noted that these concerns are "soft" and "very conspicuously absent in the important considerations of most governments, who instead focus mostly on unemployment, stock markets, and stuff."

Although Karma expressed them in slightly different words, the Bhutanese values that he described dovetail nicely with the Athena Doctrine as we found it practiced around the world. Like people in Japan, Peru, Kenya, and Germany, the Bhutanese are experimenting with ways to create sustainable development that will benefit all. However, they are considering one element of human experience that no one else mentioned anywhere in our worldwide tour: time.

People can argue about resources like food, energy, and land. But no one disputes the fact that every living creature dies, and this means that for each one of us, time is finite. Similarly, if you ask anyone in the developed world to discuss the things that make life stressful, you will eventually get to a complaint about time. Simply put, everyone feels as though he or she has too much to do and too little time. Busyness afflicts us like an epidemic. Exhaustion is a universal complaint.

Dig a little deeper, and you'll discover that most folks fear that instead of making things easier, technology actually increases the demands on their time. Cell phones, computers, and other devices divert our attention. Friendships, partnerships, family relations, and even our own inner hearts are neglected as our time is filled with electronic chatter and the extra work we take on in order to "make it" according to some conventional definition.

"Time is life," said Karma. "It's the single most precious resource. Not a second of it can be got back . . . [H]ow you use it is going to have a huge impact on societal outcomes, on the well-being of individuals in terms of the joy and meaning they get from life. It's very important that we keep this on our radar as we make policies."

Noting that French voters have resisted longer workweeks and delayed retirements, Karma argued that people everywhere weigh the loss of time spent at work against the value of the income they earn. This may not be done in a conscious and deliberate way, as it is in Bhutan, but it is done nevertheless. "The correlation between the money and happiness after a certain point is actually very weak," he added. "The first few dollars have a huge impact, especially in our part of the world where there is so much poverty." However, after basic needs are met, said Karma, additional income brings less contentment, and people tend to value their time more.

Officials in Bhutan have identified three general uses for time—work, rest, and leisure—and set the ideal for a happy life at one-third for each purpose. According to this scheme, each day would have eight hours of work, eight hours of rest, and eight hours of leisure. As the government assesses national conditions, it tracks whether people actually live this way. "And our surveys show that Bhutan today is very close to that ideal," said Karma. This balance may explain why so many say they are content with their lives.

Can this sense of happiness be achieved by other nations? Karma posited that because it depends solely on the choices made by individuals, the answer must be yes. "Can the individual change?" he said. "Very easily. You could be on that treadmill, keeping up with the Joneses and going at it 24/7, and then one day say, 'This is not for me.' And then you can make the radical shift. So if the individual can, why can't the country?"

Motivation for such change can come from anywhere, and it's often in the form of a kind of crisis, added Karma. "There's nothing more powerful for making these things happen than some outside force that actually awakens you from the stupor of … empty prosperity because it's a prosperity of only money, but at the cost of all the other things which actually you really care about."

●●●

Clearly, the prosperity envisioned by the Bhutanese is deeper and more complex than simple wealth. In the crisis caused by the Great Recession, they are not alone in the search for new definitions of development and progress. Everywhere we went in our worldwide tour, we saw feminine, Athena-style practices employed in both the pursuit and achievement of happiness. In most societies, but especially the more industrialized ones, we saw that this movement was led by innovators who typically inspired others to join their efforts. In Bhutan, innovation wasn't required. Whether in art or media or policymaking, a balanced, inclusive, and human-scale approach to life was the starting point for everyone. Karma sees this quality as intrinsically Bhutanese.

"A positive bend of mind," weights the balanced Bhutanese perspective in favor of happiness, he added. "You run to catch the bus, but if you just miss the bus," he explained, "don't rant and rave and curse the driver. Do whatever you can with that moment because that moment is precious … Wait for the next bus, or just walk. That's the best to do. To some degree, I would say Bhutanese are born with [this] positive outlook. We are very concerned about things being auspicious. We like to have a ceremony for everything, but everything is auspicious. So you're having a wedding, and if it rains you'd say, oh, the gods are blessing us with flowers, and if the sun shines, you say, what good weather. You know," laughed Karma, "if you have that kind of outlook, I think you're likely to lead a happy life."

Conclusion

The Age of Athena

We live in a world that's increasingly social, interdependent, and transparent. And in this world, feminine values are ascendant. Powered by cooperation, communication, nurturing, and inclusiveness, among others, institutions, businesses, and individuals are breaking from old masculine structures and mind-sets to become more flexible, collaborative, and caring. Our data show that this change is deemed necessary, and is welcomed, by strong majorities in every country we surveyed.

In the year we spent traveling the world to see the Athena Doctrine in action, we discovered that the most promising innovators of our time depend on feminine traits and values to make their lives, and the world, better. We found this to be true whether we spoke to people who were solving political problems, seeking profits, or striving for happiness in their private lives. As a result of our experiences, we contend that *feminine values are the operating system of twenty-first-century progress*. By embracing feminine values, all of us can double the resources applied to problems and expand our potential for growth.

This shift toward the feminine does not portend "the end of men," but it does suggest a natural balancing that vastly increases the capacity of both men and women to solve problems and create a good life. In our surveys, 81 percent of people say that *man or woman, you need both masculine and feminine traits to thrive in today's world*. From this point of view, an embrace of feminine qualities can be thought of as a *competitive advantage*, not unlike a breakthrough technology or a major market insight. Our research indicates that individuals who include feminine strategies in their decision making are twice as optimistic about their future.

Men versus women is not a zero-sum game. Men can be as caring as women, and women can be as analytical and assertive as men. Our gender is who we are, not what we can be—and we must all see feminine values not as belonging to one gender but as a new form of innovation for today's world.

Athena values also bring benefits on a macro scale. When we compare our survey results with data related to economic status and quality of life, we see that countries whose citizens think in a way that balances masculine values with feminine ones have a higher per capita gross domestic product (GDP) and higher reported quality of life. Growth and development, whether economic or social, thus seems to be predicated on including feminine values in both personal and public affairs.

Wise, courageous, humane, and cooperative, Athena represents the best in all of us. We think this is exciting. We certainly felt energized by what we saw in the city of Holon, in the offices of WhipCar, and in Gaston Acurio's dining rooms. In each of these places, we saw feminine traits produce successes with very broad benefits. Athena businesses make profits while creating lasting and mutually beneficial relationships with customers and communities. Athena governments serve all constituencies. Athena nonprofits find self-sustaining ways to do good. We therefore believe that the best way to advocate for the rights of women and girls is to have men model their approach. Together we can create better businesses and improve our society as a whole. Women—and the men who can think like them—are creating a world we'll all want to inhabit.

The Implications and Applications
of the Athena Doctrine

As we saw across the globe, the implications for the Athena Doctrine run far and wide, and an embrace of these feminine values can change the way of the world—for the better—at every level of society. Most notably, Athena-style values can have a profound impact on leadership, innovation, organizational management, career management, and change management.

Leadership

We believe that the essence of the modern leader is feminine. In our surveys, people around the world challenge the incumbency of masculine structures and the ways of men in restoring trust and solving the most intractable problems we face today. As you lead, you'll need to think about your own style and how much you're willing to adapt. We'd encourage you to take confidence in this emerging style of Athena leadership. It is by no means mainstream, but the men and women you've met in this book are doing some amazing things for their organizations by refusing to play to business conventions and protocol. Here are a few of the skills and approaches they take.

Nurture and empathize. More than ever before, leadership is about being expressive and empathetic. The capacity to listen and relate to others and their points of view is critical because almost any business operates in a delicate ecosystem of partners, customers, and interwoven supply chains. Any company, regardless of its position or geography, can suffer from the domino effect of volatility that begins somewhere else. Athena-style leaders understand this codependency and often approach their relationships with extreme care and understanding. For example, Shai Reshef at University of the People couldn't overlook that 80 percent of his students are in nations that are in the bottom 20 percent in terms of GDP, often without a means of accessing the Internet continuously. He designed his curriculum and coursework to be downloaded in Internet cafés. Leadership is often described as passion. We'd describe it as devotion: if you want to lead, you have to relate to the world in which your business lives.

Put others before self. We were consistently inspired by the way in which the leaders we met framed their business in terms of a vision and purpose higher than their own. In our surveys, one of the traits least correlated with leadership was pride (seen as masculine), whereas loyalty and selflessness (both feminine) were among the highest. In this era of mistrust of power, a leader must dismantle ego, and focus on contributing value to society—rather than extracting value from it. Ijad Madisch in Berlin aims to advance scientific discovery through collaboration among the world's greatest minds. Catalina Cock DuQue in Medellin seeks to restore peace through human understanding. Government leaders are ruled by a similar dynamic. As President Peres told us, "Leaders need to adapt to a new season in the world. Leaders are servants."

Promote a positive culture. The concept of culture is often thought of as a "soft benefit," yet many people—especially Millennials—view it as anything but: in our surveys, 67 percent of people said they would work for *less money* at a company whose values and culture they believed in. Eriko Yamaguchi began with a deep desire to eradicate poverty. The values of Motherhouse are woven through its business model and marketplace approach. Assertiveness, competitiveness, and even aggression still exist and have value; these traits were shared by many of the entrepreneurs we met. But where innovation, problem solving, and creativity are the marks of a growing business, a strong culture is the foundation beneath them.

Practice inclusive decision making. The Athena-style leaders we met managed in a very transparent and open way. They invited input from every direction and especially from the bottom up. General Barbivai carefully listened to soldiers working at checkpoints in order to reduce hostility and the potential for conflict. This open and transparent practice broadens a leader's perspective and often fosters a higher level of engagement among employees. This is not to say that decisions are reached entirely through consensus. It would have been impossible for Örn Bárður Jónsson and his fellow constitutional draft writers to take into account every comment from every citizen. Yet by engaging the Icelandic people and inviting representation from the crowd, the Icelandic government was able to regain its countrymen's trust, confidence, and goodwill.

Be patient and see farther. When it comes to leadership, people placed the strongest premium on patience and the ability to plan for the future. People intuitively understand that short-term thinking dominates most decision making. But the Athena leaders we met often expressed their vision in terms of a long-term time frame, serving as builders of the future rather than simply custodians of the present. They were also keen negotiators, credit sharers, and inclusive leaders who could be flexible in order to bring people together. As society increasingly realizes that nothing perfect happens overnight, leaders must possess the talent to think and speak about long-term horizons, rather than simply short-term gains.

Innovation

Innovation is often one of the most elusive and sought-after traits in business. Here are a couple of insights that we feel are worth your consideration as you think about ways to be creative.

Empathy as catalyst. At MIT, professors and students have built a body suit that simulates for its wearers the degenerative effects of old age. The suit limits range of motion and dulls the senses in a way that helps students walk (literally) in the shoes of a senior citizen. Its use has many potential applications, from understanding how best to display items in grocery stores to developing new products and services for aging baby boomers. Today, empathy is a new route to innovation and growth in business. In the traditional masculine model of business development, executives envision a market and push out a product to serve it. The Athena-style approach is the opposite. It requires that innovators understand how their customers feel, and then develop ways to serve them. To accomplish this, they must immerse themselves in local markets and delve deeply into the social, economic, and cultural context that frames marketplace behaviors. Empathy is the starting point for exploring social needs and building a closer connection with your customer. But it can also be an entirely new avenue for breakthrough innovation.

Praise rather than criticism. In many of the interviews we conducted, we heard about how ideas came through experimentation, observation, and collaboration. Unfortunately, the masculine constructs of testing and analysis often kill good ideas before their time or stifle the group dynamics that may allow ideas to germinate. As companies search to optimize their innovation, they would do well to look in the mirror. Are you as an organization rigid or nurturing when it comes to championing ideas? Are you encouraging and shaping, or criticizing and controlling? Companies often confuse ideas with innovation. Innovation is the process of implementing ideas. But both ideas and innovation suffer in companies that attempt to apply a masculine analytical lens to what is soft, vulnerable, and sometimes not easily understood at first.

Organizational Management

Feminine values can significantly influence, for the better, the way in which organizations are structured and managed. Key elements of the Athena style suggest ways to encourage cohesiveness, shared purpose, and a productive spirit.

Winning is plural. In a masculine construct, winning is typically considered a zero-sum game—one wins; the other loses. But lasting change can't come at the hands of one person. Sustainable reforms depend on collaboration and agreement. If a great many members of your team don't embrace change, it won't hold. Today, as even the smallest firms buy and sell across the globe, business is far more collaborative, which makes "winning" a group construct for customers, suppliers, owners, managers, workers, and communities. Tomorrow's success depends on solutions that engage and champion the success of others. Winning organizations will cultivate the progress of their customers, colleagues, and community as much as they cultivate their own. Even people's careers will be more closely tied to the success of others. In the long run, we will see that the real winners are those who invoke the feminine skills of sharing credit and consensus building as they move assertively toward shared success.

Built for glass. Modern-day vigilance has been amplified, courtesy of technology. Cisco Systems estimates that by 2020, fifty billion devices will transmit data to the Internet, creating a stream of information that can be tapped by consumers, business competitors, public officials, and the press. In this age of connectivity, masculine-style hidden backroom dealings will inevitably fall prey to highly observant sensors that will force things out into the open. In this "glass house" environment, organizations must be designed to be as open as possible, keeping its dealings honest and above board. The Felleshus in Berlin, which pulls leaders from different nations together under one roof, is a great example of the power of transparent structures.

To build cohesion and get things done. In most cultures, the masculine archetype calls for men to explore and discover resources to enrich society. But in an era of finite resources, decisions about allocation are just as important as new discoveries. Traditionally, women have excelled at sharing resources and balancing the needs of individuals to provide the greatest benefits for all. This deep appreciation for group dynamics is essential to building sustainable systems and infrastructure. To build consensus and get things done, societies, businesses, and families need Athena-style long-term thinkers who are patient and flexible. In our surveys, loyalty (seen as feminine) trumps personal ambition (considered masculine) as a prized leadership trait. In order to effect long-term change, leadership requires fidelity to cause over promotion of self—much as mothers serve their families so that future generations will benefit.

Career Management

How we relate to others, the empathy we show, and the way in which we communicate all critically impact our success in the workplace. By appropriately leveraging feminine traits, men and women alike can better achieve their career goals and ambitions.

Fairness prevails. Be fair to others, and they will be fair to you. Sad to say, fairness is an easy way to distinguish oneself: nearly three-quarters of the people in our surveys feel that one of the major global crises today is that the world is becoming less fair. The cruelty that still exists in society can be diminished by the incorporation of feminine values. Central to femininity is a desire to be fair and to be treated fairly. Ego is a huge liability in this context. It has brought about selfish risk-taking and codes of conduct and control that place humanity in the backseat to self-interest and greed. People have had enough. Fairness begins with you. Your career will ultimately be a reflection of your character—how you treat others, how you work with people, and whether you have integrity. Dismantle your ego and strive for modesty and kindness. Champion fairness as a core value in your organization, and you'll have happier, more secure and creative people as a result.

Vulnerability as strength. Our society has long operated on the assumption that failure is shameful. In a masculine world, you would cover up failure, point fingers, and even disrupt progress to protect your own reputation. However, fear of failure denies you opportunities for experimentation and positive change. Trapped inside this fear, you can see neither opportunities nor looming dangers. As we learned from many of the innovators we met, past failure is essential to future success. This idea has become so main-stream that those who haven't failed are looked upon skeptically. In our surveys, 86 percent of people believe that having some personal failures is critical to one's overall success. Openness and humility are portals to new relationships and new opportunities and ways of seeing the world. Likewise, your recognizing and engaging with the vulnerabilities of employees makes them more trusting and open. Vulnerability is today the most important agent of change management.

From affluence to influence. New forms of emotional and psychological currency are beginning to replace masculine concepts of power and esteem. In our global survey, 91 percent of people said they'd rather their child be happy than wealthy. Today's young adults especially share this feeling: 83 percent of these Millennials said they would rather be respected than wealthy. Today, being "rich" in part means having an opinion that's sought after and having the ability to spread influence through networks. This change is best illustrated by the young people in Tahrir Square who used Bambuser to help topple a dictator. In this dynamic, the feminine inclination to form communities has become increasingly important. Power is reallocated to the person in the middle, the one who is a conduit of information rather than a hoarder of it.

Selflessness as selfishness. If you don't share, you are roadkill. In our survey, 78 percent said that a successful career today requires collaborating and sharing credit with others. You must build networks, help people, and view your career through a long-range lens. In building your career and reputation, you must recognize that your social network is part of your business model. In Kenya, we met women farmers who are literally putting their fortunes and futures in the hands of others in order to work together for the benefit of all. By collaborating, sharing credit, and working together, they prospered as a group and as individuals.

Change Management

The masculine constructs of awards, stature, and recognition are out of step with today's reality: when you are managing change, nothing is perfect or ever finished. Here are a few ways to contemplate managing (or at least surviving) change.

Always learning. Agility has become an inherent social skill. As our data showed, competitive advantage is shifting to those who embrace agility: 75 percent of our respondents said they believed that "you have to be more nimble and adaptable in order to thrive today." As a manager, you must move swiftly, try lots of things, and be willing to abandon those that aren't working and to try other, new things. You must learn on the fly. Often we see that the best navigators of change are those who see the world through the lens of others, learning from different perspectives. Jonas Vig and Måns Adler studied how Arab youth were using Bambuser and employed what they learned to radically adjust their mission and business model. Our data show that as developed countries evolve from industrial to service economies, people are recognizing that feminine skills—communication, listening, being flexible—are becoming more essential. The leaders we met never stopped being students; they used every source of information available and were willing to make changes based on what they learned.

The Athena Doctrine and the Next Generation

Fortunately for all of us, the young adults who will determine the well-being of future societies seem poised to live up to the Athena Doctrine. Among our respondents, these young adults were less rigid in their definitions of masculine and feminine and more likely to appreciate the full range of human strengths and talents. We believe that this starting point makes them more resilient, more willing to experiment, and more open to unconventional ideas. We found a case in point in San Francisco, where Marc Spencer explained that his success was inspired by failure.

"We had three ice cream shops that sold Ben and Jerry's ice cream and employed about twenty-five kids," said Marc.[1] "We had the backing of REDF [the Roberts Enterprise Development Fund], and they were hanging in there with us. But even though we had good foot traffic, we couldn't make it work. What we discovered was missing was the store owner, the sole proprietor, who you find at every successful ice cream shop," recalled Marc, who is head of Juma Ventures, which owned the shops. "It takes the dedication of someone like that who will put in all the hours because he or she has to make it succeed. You can't do it with kids working part-time. It was a big lesson for all of us who want to know what works and what doesn't."

Spencer and the people who run the REDF have for decades pursued solutions to tough problems like poverty, failing schools, and unemployment. The fund is philanthropy with a twist: it mainly backs job-creating projects that are poised to become self-sustaining. These social enterprises aim to help people who face the most difficult challenges—including disadvantaged youth, the homeless, recovering addicts, and ex-convicts. Begun in 1990, REDF has helped create more than sixty-five hundred jobs, and most of its projects have indeed become self-sustaining.[2]

When Juma Ventures gave up on the ice cream shops, the managers applied what they learned to a new business, this time selling food and drink at Bay Area ballparks. The jobs were perfect for the high school students Juma wanted to serve, who had both the energy to run up and down stadium steps and a desire to earn and learn.

When we visited San Francisco in the summer of 2012, Juma was employing about fifty high schoolers drawn from the toughest high schools in the city. At AT&T Park, where the Giants play, they ran espresso bars scattered around the stadium and hawked food and drink in the stands. In addition to pay and tips, the workers accumulated college savings in a plan they funded themselves and with the help of Juma, and they received academic tutoring and counseling. In more than a decade of operation, the business has become self-sustaining, with revenues in excess of $1 million per year. One hundred percent of the vendors have graduated high school, 70 percent have gone on to four-year colleges, and 70 percent of those have earned degrees.

We met some members of the 2012 crew at the ballpark on a day when the Giants faced their nemesis, the Los Angeles Dodgers. Guided by their boss, Jeronimo Martin (his official title is enterprise director), we visited a food-prep line where sandwiches were assembled, and we met vendors who sold iced tea and lemonade in the bleachers. On the mezzanine, we met Joanna Sodillo, who told us that she had worked her way up to one of the most coveted Juma jobs, behind the cash register at an Emerald Nuts stand.

"The thing you learn about here is hard work," said Joanna.[3] "There will be a hundred people who say no to you for every one who says they want what you are selling. The thing you have to do is not give up. You learn that here."

Out in the stands, Jeronimo introduced us to a young woman named Weidong Guo, who was too busy scaling the steps and calling out to customers to answer our questions. Young women often tally more sales than the young men who work for Juma, but managers never consider gender when making assignments. Performance is all that matters, in the stands as well as on the field. When we met her, Weidong was locked in fierce competition with James Luo, who was winning over the crowd with his hustle. As he dashed past us, James told us he intended to have a "good day," which meant $100 in tips and commissions, in addition to his $40 base pay.[4]

The hustle we saw in Juma's young workers is matched by managers who have expanded the business to ballparks and arenas in Oakland, Berkeley, and San Diego. This success is a credit to the Juma concept—a business with higher purpose—and to the confidence REDF expressed with its financing. The foundation was created to put wealth to work in ways that would produce innovations and lasting benefits. It is the ultimate Athena mission, and it is led by a woman whose skills could have been taught by the goddess herself.

A former state and city official, Carla Javits has also been a successful entrepreneur and advocate for the homeless. The daughter of the late U.S. senator Jacob Javits, she grew up listening to discussions of weighty issues and meeting people who tried to solve them. She recalled that as a child, she often heard her father begin conversations with the question, "What can we do for New York?" His question begged for new ideas, to be tested with great energy, in hopes that they might make life better for all the people he served.[5]

"What we are trying to do is create a new tier of businesses that offer work opportunities to more people," said Carla when we sat to talk in her office. "We're talking about employing people who face really tough challenges." Progress toward this goal "is not linear," she said, but she has noted an uptick in interest among investors who want to do more than just make more money.

"We're talking about 'impact investment,'" said Carla. "The real problem is, we don't have enough great ideas for them to invest in." In fact, although economic conditions seemed to inhibit investment in other sectors of the economy, Carla insisted there is ample capital available "for people with cool ideas who have the hard and soft skills to make them work." One investment under consideration by REDF was a fresh-food processing facility, located between farm country and the city, to serve schools, hospitals, and other big buyers who would prefer to use local produce. Another proposal under consideration would employ long-term jobless people in property services for hotels and apartment communities.

For workers, communities, and investors, the "new tier" of business emerging from REDF and similar foundations around the United States offers an unexpected solution to tough problems. "We were challenged to close the gap between the old concept of business, which was all about making money, and the old concept of philanthropy, which was about feeling good. The idea is to end the bifurcation, to say you can do business and still feel good about the contribution you're making."

In our view, REDF and Juma have succeeded in creating a new kind of economic engine, one that serves all stakeholders. Their achievement depended on leadership that ignored gender stereotypes and valued happiness as much as aggression. Along the way, they created a robust example of the Athena Doctrine in action. It's enough to give anyone hope for the future.

More Information

If you would like to join the Athena Doctrine conversation and community, you can go to www.theathenadoctrine.com and to Facebook/The Athena Doctrine. You can also follow @johngerzema on Twitter and John Gerzema on Google+. All the data, videos, and other excerpts are also available at www.johngerzema.com and www.michaeldantonio.net and at http://tedxwomen.org/speakers/john-gerzema/. You can learn more about our interviews on the Athena Doctrine Tumblr page, www.athenadoctrine.tumblr.com.

There are numerous organizations that promote the interests of women and girls worldwide. Several of them lent their voices and support to this book, and we are grateful. They can use your support.

United Nations Foundation—UN Fund for Women

> http://www.unfoundation.org/how-to-help/donate/fund
> -for-un-women.html

Dell Women's Entrepreneur Network (DWEN)

> http://content.dell.com/us/en/business/women-powering
> -business

Coca-Cola's 5by20 program

> http://www.thecoca-colacompany.com/citizenship/5by20/

Goldman Sachs 10,000 Women Program

> http://www.goldmansachs.com/citizenship/10000women
> /index.html

Leading Women
  http://www.leadingwomen.biz/
Cherie Blair Foundation
  www.cherieblairfoundation.org
Vital Voices
  www.vitalvoices.org
Women for Women International
  http://www.womenforwomen.org
Soroptimist
  http://www.soroptimist.org/
Live Your Dream
  www.liveyourdream.org
Plywood People
  www.plywoodpeople.com
WE Connect
  www.weconnectinternational.org
Woman Deliver
  www.womandeliver.org
Wage Cooperatives
  www.wagecooperatives.org
2020 Women on Boards
  www.2020wob.com
Alliance for Women in Media
  http://www.allwomeninmedia.org/
Be Present
  www.bepresent.org
Beirut Girl's Geek Camp
  http://www.facebook.com/GeekCamp/info
ASTIA
  www.astia.org

Channel Foundation

    www.channelfoundation.org

Corporate Voices for Working Families

    http://www.cvworkingfamilies.org/

Make Mine a Million

    http://makemineamillion.org/

Forté Foundation

    http://www.fortefoundation.org/

Girls Who Code

    www.girlswhocode.com

La Pietra Coalition

    www.lapietracoalition.org

Pace Center

    www.pacecenter.org

Prosperity Candle

    www.prosperitycandle.com

Society of Women Engineers

    www.societyofwomenengineers.swe.org

Notes

Introduction

1. Gerzema, J., and D'Antonio, M. *Spend Shift*. San Francisco: Jossey-Bass, 2010.
2. Howe, N., and Strauss, W. *Generations: The History of America's Future, 1584 to 2069*. Washington DC: Quill, 1992.
3. Ann Danylkiw, author, personal interview with John Gerzema, Nov. 2011.
4. Janet Walkow and Christine Jacobs, Leading Women, personal interview with John Gerzema and Michael D'Antonio, Nov. 2011.
5. Arterian Chang, S. "Outsiders and Outperformers: Women in Fund Management." *Finance Professionals' Post*, Apr. 5, 2010. http://post.nyssa .org/nyssa-news/2010/04/outsiders-and-outperformers-women-in-fund -management.html.
6. Curtis, M., Schmid, C., and Struber, M. "Gender Diversity and Corporate Performance." Credit Suisse, Aug. 2012. https://infocus.credit-suisse.com /data/_product_documents/_shop/360145/csri_gender_diversity_and _corporate_performance.pdf.
7. U. S. Bureau of Labor Statistics. "Wives Who Earn More Than Their Husbands, 1987–2011." *Labor Force Statistics from the Current Population Survey*. Washington DC: U.S. Department of Labor, May 2012. http://www .bls.gov/cps/wives_earn_more.htm.
8. Dewan, S., and Gebeloff, R. "More Men Enter Fields Dominated by Women." *New York Times*, May 20, 2012. http://www.nytimes.com/2012 /05/21/business/increasingly-men-seek-success-in-jobs-dominated-by -women.html?nl=todaysheadlines&pagewanted=all&_r=0.
9. Lofquist, D., Lugaila, T., O'Connell, M., and Feliz, S. *Households and Families: 2010*. 2010 Census Briefs. Washington DC: U.S. Bureau of the Census, Apr. 2010. http://www.census.gov/prod/cen2010/briefs/c2010br-14.pdf.

10. Roberts Enterprise Development Fund of San Francisco. "About REDF." 2011. http://www.redf.org/about-redf#accomplishments.

11. Pioneer Human Services. *A Chance for Change: Annual Report 2011*. Seattle: Pioneer Human Services, 2012.

12. Mondragon Corporation. "Corporate Profile 2012." Mondragón, Spain: Mondragon Corporation, 2012.

13. Flecha, R., and Santa Cruz, I. "Cooperation and Efficiency in Economic Contexts." *Analyse and Kritik*, 2011, *33*, 157–170.

14. Kim, P., and Bradach, J. "Why More Nonprofits Are Getting Bigger." *Stanford Social Innovation Review*, Spring 2012. http://www.ssireview.org /articles/entry/why_more_nonprofits_are_getting_bigger.

15. Adelaide Lancaster, cofounder, In Good Company Workplaces, personal interview with John Gerzema, Nov. 2011.

16. "Transcript of Dilma Rousseff's Opening Speech at the United Nations General Assembly." Sept. 2011. http://brazilportal.wordpress.com/2011 /09/22/transcript-of-dilma-rousseffs-opening-speech-at-the-united-nations -general-assembly/.

17. U.S. Bureau of Labor Statistics. "Women's Earnings as a Percent of Men's in 2010." *Editor's Desk*. Washington DC: U.S. Department of Labor, Jan. 2012. http://www.bls.gov/opub/ted/2012/ted_20120110.htm.

18. Catalyst. "Women on Boards." 2012. http://www.catalyst.org/file/725/qt _women_on_boards.pdf.

19. Forbes. "The Forbes 400: The Richest People in America." Sept. 2012. http://www.forbes.com/forbes-400/.

Chapter 1

1. All quotations from Vinay Gupta, cofounder of WhipCar, are from an interview with John Gerzema in Nov. 2011.

2. All quotations from Tom Wright, cofounder of WhipCar, are from an interview with John Gerzema in Nov. 2011.

3. All quotations from Katie Mowat, founder of Grannies Inc., are from an interview with John Gerzema in Nov. 2011.

4. All quotations from Holly Jones, employee at Grannies Inc., are from an interview with John Gerzema in Nov. 2011.

5. All quotations from Anna Pearson, founder of Spots of Time, are from an interview with John Gerzema in Nov. 2011.

6. Secretary of State for Environment, Food and Rural Affairs. *The Natural Choice: Securing the Value of Nature*. Natural Environment White Paper, June 7, 2011. http://sd.defra.gov.uk/2011/06/the-natural-choice-securing -the-value-of-nature/.

7. British Beekeepers Association. "Importance of Bees." http://www.bbka
.org.uk/.

8. Jha, A. "Bees in Freefall as Study Shows Sharp US decline." *Guardian*, Jan. 3,
2011. http://www.guardian.co.uk/environment/2011/jan/03/bumblebees
-study-us-decline.

9. All quotations from Zoe Palmer, founder of the Golden Company, are from
an interview with John Gerzema in Nov. 2011.

10. All quotations from Gustavo Montes de Oca, enterprise manager at Hackney
City Farms, are from an interview with John Gerzema in Nov. 2011.

11. Perry, N. "Spirit of the Beehive." Sept. 2011. http://www.bbc.co.uk
/programmes/b013r2gv.

12. Ibid.

13. Montes de Oca, G. "Flooding the Moral High Ground." Dec. 2011. http://
gmdeo.com/2011/12/02/flooding-the-moral-high-ground/.

14. All quotations from Giles Andrews, CEO and cofounder of ZOPA, are from
an interview with John Gerzema in Nov. 2011.

15. BrandRepublic. "Richard Duvall, Co-Founder of Eff and Zopa, Dies." Oct.
2006. http://www.brandrepublic.com/news/.

16. Quotations from Julien Callede, cofounder of Made.com, are from an
interview with John Gerzema in Nov. 2011.

17. Ning Li, cofounder of Made.com, personal interview with John Gerzema in
Nov. 2011.

18. Emily Bolton, director at Social Finance, personal interview with John
Gerzema in Nov. 2011.

19. All quotations from Cherie Blair, founder of the Cherie Blair Foundation for
Women, are from an interview with John Gerzema in Nov. 2011.

Chapter 2

1. All quotations from Halla Tomasdottir, cofounder of Audur Capital, are from
an interview with Michael D'Antonio in Feb. 2012.

2. United Nations Development Programme. "Human Development Index."
Human Development Report 2007/2008. http://hdr.undp.org/en/media/LP2
-HDR07-HDIlist-E-final.pdf.

3. Mitchell, D. "Iceland Comes in from the Cold with Flat Tax Revolution."
The Business, 2007. http://www.cato.org/publications/commentary/iceland
-comes-cold-flat-tax-revolution.

4. Kudlow, L. "Iceland's Laffer Curve." *Wall Street Journal*, Mar. 12, 2007.
http://online.wsj.com/article/SB117330772978430098.html.

5. Valgreen, C., Christensen, L., Andersen, P., and Kallestrup, R. "Iceland:
Geyser Crisis." Copenhagen: Daske Bank Research, Mar. 2006.
http://www.mbl.is/media/98/398.pdf.

6. Karmin, C. "Danish Economist Isn't Very Cool Among Icelanders." *Wall Street Journal*, Apr. 29, 2006. http://online.wsj.com/article/SB11462707 1540139472.html.

7. Ibid.

8. Walt, V. "A Meltdown in Iceland." *Time*. Oct. 8, 2008. http://www.time .com/time/world/article/0,8599,1848379,00.html.

9. Bárður Jónsson, Ö. "exPORT Mountains Inc." Sept. 2008. http://ornbardur .annall.is/2008-09-23/islensk-fjallasala-hf-export-mountains-inc/.

10. All quotations from Örn Bárður Jónsson, minister and author, are from an interview with Michael D'Antonio in Feb. 2012.

11. Woodard, C. "Will Social Safety Net Survive Iceland's Crisis?" *Christian Science Monitor*, Jan. 22 2009. http://www.csmonitor.com/Business/2009 /0122/will-social-safety-net-survive-iceland-s-crisis.

12. All quotations from Katrin Oddsdottir, lawyer, are from an interview with Michael D'Antonio, Feb. 2012.

13. "The Day the Women Went on Strike." *Guardian*. Oct. 17, 2005. http:// www.guardian.co.uk/world/2005/oct/18/gender.uk.

14. Bennett, C. "So You Think Women Would Have Saved Us. Think Again." *Observer*, Feb. 21, 2009. http://www.guardian.co.uk/commentisfree/2009 /feb/22/women-politicians.

15. All quotations from Salvör Nordal, professor at University of Iceland, are from an interview with Michael D'Antonio in Feb. 2012.

16. Constitutional Council of Iceland. "The Constitutional Council Hands Over the Bill for a New Constitution." July 2011. http://stjornlagarad.is/english/.

17. Ibid.

18. "Besti Flokkurinn – The Best Video – Subtitles." May 2010. http://www .youtube.com/watch?v=xxBW4mPzv6E&noredirect=1.

19. All quotations from Gunnar Grimsson, cofounder of Citizens Foundation, are from an interview with Michael D'Antonio in Feb. 2012.

20. All quotations from Robert Vidar Bjarnason, cofounder of Citizens Foundation, are from an interview with Michael D'Antonio in Feb. 2012.

21. All quotations from Snorri Valsoon, manager at Hotel Holt, are from an interview with Michael D'Antonio in Feb. 2012.

22. All quotations from Sandra Hrafnildur, employee at Woolcano, are from an interview with Michael D'Antonio in Feb. 2012.

Chapter 3

1. All quotations from Rachel Weisel, brigadier general in the Israeli Defense Force (IDF), are from an interview with John Gerzema and Michael D'Antonio in Mar. 2012.

2. Orna Barbivai, major general in the Israeli Defense Force (IDF), personal interview with John Gerzema and Michael D'Antonio, Mar. 2012.

3. IDF. "Ethics." http://dover.idf.il/IDF/English/about/doctrine/ethics.htm.

4. All quotations from Yadin Kaufmann, founder of Veritas Venture Partners, are from an interview with John Gerzema and Michael D'Antonio in Mar. 2012.

5. All quotations from Ron Huldai, mayor of the city of Tel Aviv, are from an interview with John Gerzema and Michael D'Antonio in Mar. 2012.

6. All quotations from Daphni Leef, political activist, are from an interview with John Gerzema and Michael D'Antonio in Mar. 2012.

7. All quotations from Shai Reshef, founder of University of the People, are from an interview with John Gerzema and Michael D'Antonio in Mar. 2012.

8. All quotations from Ilana Dayan, host of *Uvda*, are from an interview with John Gerzema and Michael D'Antonio in Mar. 2012.

9. All quotations from Efrat Duvdevani, director general of the Office of the President, are from an interview with John Gerzema and Michael D'Antonio in Mar. 2012.

10. All quotations from Shimon Peres, president of Israel, are from an interview with John Gerzema and Michael D'Antonio in Mar. 2012.

Chapter 4

1. Vervaeck, A., and Daniell, J. "Japan—366 Days After the Quake." Mar. 10, 2012. http://earthquake-report.com/2012/03/10/japan-366-days-after-the-quake-19000-lives-lost-1-2-million-buildings-damaged-574-billion/.

2. All quotations from Kohei Fukuzaki, founder of Roomdonor.jp, are from an interview with John Gerzema and Michael D'Antonio in Nov. 2011.

3. All quotations from Nagato Kimura, of the Kinoya-Ishinomaki Suisan Company, are from an interview with John Gerzema and Michael D'Antonio in Nov. 2011.

4. All quotations from Kaori Hayashi, professor at University of Tokyo, are from an interview with John Gerzema and Michael D'Antonio in Nov. 2011.

5. All quotations from Yasuhiro Toudou, founder of U2Plus, are from an interview with John Gerzema and Michael D'Antonio in Nov. 2011.

6. Roan, S. "Japanese Restraint Is Steeped in a Culture of Tested Resilience." *Los Angeles Times.* Mar. 21, 2011. http://articles.latimes.com/2011/mar/21/health/la-he-japanese-quake-culture-20110321.

7. Quotations from Maco Yoshioka, founder and codirector of Madre Bonita, are from an interview with John Gerzema and Michael D'Antonio in Nov. 2011.

8. All quotations from Chisato Kitazawa, co-director of Madre Bonita, are from an interview with John Gerzema and Michael D'Antonio in Nov. 2011.

9. All quotations from Yosh Kanematsu, founder of *Greenz*, are from an interview with John Gerzema and Michael D'Antonio in Nov. 2011.

10. All quotations from Eriko Yamaguchi, founder of Motherhouse, are from an interview with John Gerzema and Michael D'Antonio in Nov. 2011.

Chapter 5

1. Garde, F.I. "Bridging Development—The Medellin Experience." Tholons, Feb. 2011. http://www.tholons.com/nl_pdf/Tholons_Medellin _Whitepaper2011.pdf.

2. Beck, E. "Project Medellin, Columbia." Oct. 2009. http://changeobserver .designobserver.com/.

3. All quotations from Catalina Cock Duque, head of Mi Sangre, are from an interview with John Gerzema and Michael D'Antonio in Apr. 2012.

4. Latinobarometro. "The Study." 2011. http://www.latinobarometro.org /latino/latinobarometro.jsp.

5. Grant Thornton. "International Business Report: Optimism (Global)." 2012. http://www.internationalbusinessreport.com/Results/index.asp.

6. All quotations from Gaston Acurio, chef, are from an interview with John Gerzema and Michael D'Antonio in Apr. 2012.

7. Encyclopedia of the Nations. "Peru—Poverty and Wealth." 2010. http:// www.nationsencyclopedia.com/economies/Americas/Peru-POVERTY -AND-WEALTH.html.

8. All quotations from Carmen Zavala are from an interview with John Gerzema and Michael D'Antonio in Apr. 2012.

Chapter 6

1. All quotations from Rose Goslinga, founder of Kilimo Salama, are from an interview with Amy S. Choi in Feb. 2012.

2. Quotations from Lucy Muriuki are from an interview with Amy S. Choi in Feb. 2012.

3. All quotations from Stephanie Hanson, director of policy and outreach at One Acre Fund, are from an interview with Amy S. Choi in Feb. 2012.

4. All quotations from Guy Vanmeenan, from Catholic Relief Services, are from an interview with Amy S. Choi in Feb. 2012.

5. All quotations from Farouk Jiwa, cofounder and director of Honey Care Africa, are from an interview with Amy S. Choi in Feb. 2012.

6. Quotations from Erik Hersman, founder of Ushahidi, are from an interview with Amy S. Choi in Feb. 2012.

7. Quotations from Robert Collymore, CEO of Safaricom, are from an interview with Amy S. Choi in Feb. 2012.

8. All quotations from Joel Jackson, founder of Mobius, are from an interview with Amy S. Choi in Feb. 2012.

9. Polgreen, L. "U.S., Too, Wants to Bolster Investment in a Continent's Economic Promise." *New York Times*, Aug. 8, 2012. http://www.nytimes.com/2012/08/09/world/africa/us-seeks-to-step-up-africa-investment.html?pagewanted=all&_r=0.

10. "The Hopeful Continent: Africa Rising." *Economist*, Dec. 2011. http://www.economist.com/node/21541015.

Chapter 7

1. All quotations from Manjula Pradeep, lawyer and human rights activist, are from an interview with Garrett Fonda and Amy S. Choi in Mar. 2012.

2. Khilnani, S. "Programmed to Survive." *OutlookIndia*, Feb. 6, 2012. http://www.outlookindia.com/article.aspx?279695.

3. Bajaj, V. "Tata's Nano, the Car That Few Want to Buy." *New York Times*, Dec. 9, 2010. http://www.nytimes.com/2010/12/10/business/global/10tata.html.

4. "Ratan Tata Admits to Making Mistakes with Nano." *Kaumudi Online*, Jan. 6, 2012. http://kaumudiglobal.com/innerpage1.php?newsid=14624.

5. United Nations Office on Drugs and Crime. *Women and Drug Abuse: The Problem in India.* 2003. http://www.unodc.org/pdf/india/publications/women_Book-6-5-03/09_statusofwomeninindia.pdf.

6. All quotations from Mariette Fourmeaux du Sartel are from an interview with Garrett Fonda and Amy S. Choi in Mar. 2012.

7. All quotations from Viren Joshi, founder of Manav Sadhna, are from an interview with Garrett Fonda and Amy S. Choi in Mar. 2012.

8. All quotations from Anand Shah, founder of Sarvajal, are from an interview with Garrett Fonda and Amy S. Choi in Mar. 2012.

9. Prahalad, C. K. *The Fortune at the Bottom of the Pyramid: Eradicating Poverty Through Profits.* Philadelphia: Wharton School Publishing, 2004.

10. All quotations from Rajendra Joshi, founder of Saath, are from an interview with Garrett Fonda and Amy S. Choi in Mar. 2012.

Chapter 8

1. All quotations from PT Black are from an interview with Amy S. Choi in Apr. 2012.

2. All quotations from Calvin Chin are from an interview with Amy S. Choi in Apr. 2012.

3. Chen, S. "February Featured People: Mihela Hladin." *Xindanwei*, Feb. 16, 2012. http://xindanwei.com/lang/en/2012/02/february-featured-people-mihela-hladin/.

4. All quotations from Flora Lan are from an interview with Amy S. Choi in Apr. 2012.

5. Koon, S. "Steve Koon." 2009. http://www.avantageventures.com/jp/node/239.

6. "About Our Magazine." *Tea Leaf Nation*. http://www.tealeafnation.com/about-us-2/.

7. Xuecun, M. "Translation: One Author's Plea for a Gentler China." (A. Cappella, L. Carter, and M. Li, trans.) *Tea Leaf Nation*, July 30, 2012. http://tealeafnation.com/2012/07/translation-one-authors-plea-for-a-gentler-china/.

8. Wertime, D. "Chinese Netizens Say Time to 'Clean Up' Foreign 'Trash.'" *Tea Leaf Nation*, May 15, 2012. http://www.tealeafnation.com/2012/05/chinese-netizens-say-time-to-clean-up-foreign-trash/.

9. All quotations from David Wertime, cofounder of Tea Leaf Nation, are from an interview with Amy S. Choi in Apr. 2012.

10. All quotations from Bessie Lee are from an interview with Amy S. Choi in Apr. 2012.

11. All quotations from Guanshen Gao are from an interview with Amy S. Choi in Apr. 2012.

12. Loader Wilkinson, T. "Chinese Philanthropy Slides Nearly a Fifth in 2011." *Wealth Briefing*, May 9, 2012.

13. "Sun Culture Foundation." http://www.sunculturefoundation.com/en/index.php.

14. Ibid.

Chapter 9

1. All quotations from Maria Ziv, marketing director at VisitSweden, are from an interview with John Gerzema and Amy S. Choi in Feb. 2012.

2. Curators of Sweden. "Hanna Frange." 2012. http://curatorsofsweden.com/curator/hanna-fange/.

3. Worstall, T. "The Amazing Thing About American Inequality: How Equal the Country Is." *Forbes*, Sept. 22, 2012. http://www.forbes.com/sites/timworstall/2012/09/22/the-amazing-thing-about-american-inequality-how-equal-the-country-is/.

4. All quotations from Lotta Rajalin, cofounder of Egalia, are from an interview with John Gerzema and Amy S. Choi in Feb. 2012.

5. All quotations from Måns Adler, cofounder of Bambuser, are from an interview with John Gerzema and Amy S. Choi in Feb. 2012.
6. All quotations from Jonas Vig, cofounder of Bambuser, are from an interview with John Gerzema and Amy S. Choi in Feb. 2012.
7. All quotations from Ijad Madisch, founder of ResearchGate, are from an interview with John Gerzema and Amy S. Choi in Feb. 202.
8. All quotations from Tim Kunde, founder of Friendsurance, are from an interview with John Gerzema and Amy S. Choi in Feb. 2012.
9. All quotations from David Koehler, Berliner Seilfabrik, are from an interview with John Gerzema and Amy S. Choi in Feb. 2012.
10. All quotations from Leo Riski, Finnish official at the Felleshus, are from an interview with John Gerzema and Amy S. Choi in Feb. 2011.
11. All quotations from Maria Damanaki, commissioner of the EU Maritime Commission, are from an interview with John Gerzema and Amy S. Choi in Feb. 2012.

Chapter 10

1. All quotations from Siok Sian Pek-Dorji are from an interview with Garrett Fonda and Amy S. Choi in Mar. 2012.
2. All quotations from Tshering Tobgay, People's Democratic Party, are from an interview with Garrett Fonda and Amy S. Choi in Mar. 2012.
3. All quotations from Karma Wangdi, Center for Bhutan Studies, are from an interview with Garrett Fonda and Amy S. Choi in Mar. 2012.
4. Sachs, J. *World Happiness Report*. New York: Columbia University, 2012.
5. All quotations from Karma Tshiteem, secretary of the Gross National Happiness Commission, are from an interview with Garrett Fonda and Amy S. Choi in Mar. 2011.
6. All quotations from Kama Wangdi, founder of the Voluntary Artists' Studio, Thimphu, are from an interview with Garrett Fonda and Amy S. Choi in Mar. 2012.
7. Choden, T., and Kusago, T. *Gross National Happiness and Material Welfare in Bhutan and Japan*. Bhutan: Center for Bhutan Studies, 2007.

Conclusion

1. All quotations from Marc Spencer, head of Juma Ventures, are from an interview with Michael D'Antonio in June 2012.
2. Roberts Enterprise Development Fund of San Francisco. "About REDF." http://www.redf.org/about-redf.

3. Quotations from Joanna Sodillo are from an interview with Michael D'Antonio in June 2012.
4. James Luo, interview with Michael D'Antonio in June 2012.
5. All quotations from Carla Javits, founder of REDF, are from an interview with Michael D'Antonio in June 2012.

Acknowledgments

We are in enormous debt to some wonderful people on our team, without whom this book would not be possible. Amy S. Choi is a brilliant journalist who traveled with us to many places around the world. In addition to her reporting, Amy's insights and ideas helped shape the content of this book. So too did terrific leadership from Will Johnson and Garrett Fonda, who wore many hats from reporting to marketing to managing this highly complicated project. We also thank Julia Feldmeier, who served as a terrific editor and adviser.

Bringing the triple threat of analytics, femininity, and millennial know-how were Jessica Li and Jennifer Jorgensen, who guided the global quantitative surveys. Together, they teased out amazing insights from mounds of data. We also thank Stephen Lenzen for his thinking and design on the research, as well as Michele Jee, who fielded thirteen countries under tight deadlines and made it look easy and effortless, although we know that was not the case.

We are grateful to some remarkable leaders, who inspired this book and lent their support and encouragement in one way or another. They include Denise Morrison, CEO of Campbell's; Ursula Burns, CEO of Xerox; and Karen Quintos, CMO of Dell, who invited us to speak at Dell's Women's Empowerment Network (DWEN) event in Delhi. Janet Walkow and Christine Jacobs, cofounders of the organization Leading Women, not only granted

283

interviews but lent us their support as well. Scott Siff, who is John's partner at the office, brought both great ideas and constant encouragement, as did Young & Rubicam's CEO, David Sable. Tyler Fonda lent his smarts to our conclusions, and Mike Lundgren, a TEDx organizer, was an early proponent of our ideas. And many thanks go to Geoff Halber and Kyle Blue at Everything Type Company, whose graphic design magic transformed our heady data into visually digestible charts.

We also had friends help us from all over the world. In Japan, we thank Natsuko Yamamoto, our translator (and a proud Yale graduate), who gave us a lot of great ideas while moving us rapidly along the JR Line. We also thank Kaoruko Ishibushi from NHK World, who trailed us with a film crew, as well as Ai Nakajima, our publisher in Japan, who traveled with us to many interviews and lent her keen perspective. Masanori Togawa was a valued contributor and friend from Dentsu Young & Rubicam Tokyo. We thank the entire management of DY&R for their support.

In London, we're grateful to Katie Mowat for granting us an interview and connecting us with Granny Holly, and to Gustavo Montes de Oca at Hackney City Farms, who introduced us to some wonderful interview subjects in addition to his views. In Tel-Aviv, we were so fortunate to have Reut Schechter and Shlomi Avnon help us gain access to many interviews, as well as offer their valuable perspectives on Israeli culture.

In Shanghai, Normandy Madden at Thoughtful Media is not only an old friend but also a valued networker who gave us introductions for many of our interviews there; consultant Neil Liang ensured that we never got lost. In Colombia, Sarah Berghorst, previously a director at Ashoka Entrepreneur Program Latin America and now a consultant at Bain & Company, and filmmaker Marc de Beaufort helped shape our trip. Traveling through India and Bhutan would have been far more challenging if not for the efforts of Sunetra Lala at the United Nations in New Delhi, and Christine Rock and Karma Tenzin at the Uma Paro Hotel. We are thankful to Zahra Ismail of the Institute for Peace & Justice in San Diego (and its resident Kenya expert) and Sara Fajardo at Catholic Relief Services in Nairobi for their invaluable advice in Kenya, as well as to Chris Harrison and Neil Drewitt.

Making this book would not be possible without the insights from our editor Genoveva Llosa and her fantastic team at Jossey-Bass, including senior editorial assistant John Maas. We also thank Chip Kidd for the Athena cover design and Mark Fortier and Norbert Beatty for their public relations expertise. We thank our agents and advisers James Levine and Kerry Sparks at Levine Greenberg, as well as Ashima Dayal at Davis and Gilbert for legal guidance. Pat Przbyski and Farrah Landry brought keen financial counsel, and Caroline Pinto developed marketing strategies before returning to school in North Carolina. Tom Neilssen and Freya Joy at BrightSight Group act as John's speaker's bureau and constant partners, advisers, and supporters (www.brightsightgroup/johngerzema). We thank Maria Callaro for organizing travel far and wide. Thanks to all.

Most of all, we thank the goddesses of wisdom in our lives: John's wife and daughter, Mary and Nina, and Michael's wife, Toni, and daughters, Amy and Elizabeth, all of whom nodded approvingly at the idea of this book without ever asking why it took us so long to reach such obvious insights.

About the Authors

John Gerzema is a bestselling author and an internationally known social theorist on consumerism and its impact on growth, innovation, and strategy. As a consultant to corporate leaders, he is a pioneer in the use of data to identify social change and help companies anticipate and adapt to new customer interests and demands.

Gerzema's first book, *The Brand Bubble*, predicted changes in consumer attitudes that preceded the financial crisis and was number three on Amazon's best business books of 2008 and *Strategy + Business*'s best marketing books of 2009. Gerzema's analysis of consumer behavior has been widely cited in such publications as the *Journal of Consumer Psychology* and Kotler and Keller's *Marketing Management*. His next book, *Spend Shift*, with Pulitzer Prize winner Michael D'Antonio, explored consumerism after the Great Recession and was a *Wall Street Journal* bestseller, a *Washington Post* bestseller, one of *Fast Company*'s Best Business Books of 2010, and Book of the Week from the *Week* magazine. It also won gold at the Axiom Business Book Awards.

Gerzema's extensive research and writing has garnered praise from the *Wall Street Journal*, NPR, *Huffington Post*, *Forbes*, *Financial Times*, *Harvard Business Review*, *USA Today*, and CBS *Sunday Morning News*. *Fast Company* has noted his insights as "the future of commerce," and CNBC credits his understanding of new marketplace trends as "a new revolution." The *Boston Globe* says that Gerzema "breaks trends down to a very relatable, human scale while providing a heavy dose of education." *U.S. News & World Report* describes his thinking as backed by "heavy duty consumer research." Gerzema is a highly sought after analyst on culture, trends, and innovation; his columns "Trend Watcher" (*Inc.*) and "On Marketing" (PSFK) are widely read. He's been published in management journals around the world, and his article "The Trouble with Brands" was named one of the fifty classic management articles by the editors of *Strategy + Business*. Described as a "marketing guru" by Google, a "consumer expert" by the *New York Times*, a "marketing whiz" by TED, and a "brilliant presenter" by the *Economist*, Gerzema lectures at the Columbia and MIT/Sloan Schools of Business and is an in-demand public speaker. His TED talk has been viewed by over a quarter of a million people.

Gerzema cofounded Account Planning at Fallon Worldwide before overseeing strategy for the Young & Rubicam Companies as global chief insights officer. As executive chairman of BAV Consulting, he guides a global management consultancy with expertise in corporate, brand, and marketing strategy and innovation. He also oversees BrandAsset® Valuator, the world's largest consumer survey with data on over seventeen thousand consumers quarterly and fifty thousand brands in fifty countries.

Gerzema has a bachelor of science degree in marketing from the Ohio State University and a master's in journalism/integrated marketing from the Medill School of Journalism at Northwestern University. He is a board adviser for both Wanderfly and University of the People.

• • •

Michael D'Antonio is the author of more than a dozen books on topics ranging from business to science and sports. *Hershey*, his biography of the chocolate king, was named one of *BusinessWeek*'s best books of the year, and his book *The State Boys Rebellion* received similar honors from both the *Chicago Tribune* and the *Christian Science Monitor*. While at *Newsday*, D'Antonio won the prestigious Alicia Patterson fellowship for journalists and was a member of a team of reporters who won the Pulitzer Prize. His original story for the film *Crown Heights* earned him the 2004 Humanitas Prize. His work has appeared in the *New York Times Magazine*, *Esquire*, *Discover*, the *Los Angeles Times Magazine*, and many other publications. D'Antonio's most recent book, *A Full Cup*, on Sir Thomas Lipton's extraordinary life and his quest for the America's Cup, has been favorably reviewed by the *Wall Street Journal* and NPR.

Index